The Anatomy of Partnership

Contents

CONTENTS

PART THREE

PARTNERSHIP IN PRACTICE

PART FOUR

THE FUTURE OF FEDERATION

APPENDIX

AFRICAN NATIONAL CONGRESS STATEMENT

POSTSCRIPT

Illustrations

It is not to be thought of that the Flood
Of British freedom, which, to the open sea
Of the world's praise, from dark antiquity
Hath flowed, "with pomp of waters, unwithstood",
Roused though it be full often to a mood
Which spurns the check of salutary bands,
That this most famous Stream in bogs and sands
Should perish; and to evil and to good
Be lost for ever. In our halls is hung
Armoury of the invincible Knights of old:
We must be free or die, who speak the tongue
That Shakespeare spake; the faith and morals hold
Which Milton held.—In every thing we are sprung
Of Earth's first blood, have titles manifold.

Wordsworth

Poems dedicated to National Independence and Liberty, No. XVI.

Preface

In writing about Africa today one is inevitably outstripped by events and by the emergence of fresh information. The statement for instance on page 225 of this book that bloodshed and violence have been notably avoided in newly independent African states needs qualification in the light of developments in the Congo. But the extreme paternalism of Belgium's past colonial policy, and the extreme haste with which the Belgian Government launched its ward on an independent career when it showed signs of unruliness make the Congo a very special case. Its troubles are a retrospective criticism of *de-haut-en-bas* paternalism, not of African freedom. The points I make there, that independence does not lead to bloodshed and that Europeans who claim that it does are using casuistry to cover their own interest in white supremacy, still hold good. My other main contentions have been in general confirmed by what has happened, whether at Sharpeville, in Somalia, or in the development of United Federal and Dominion Party policy in Central Africa. The D.P. has split on the day I write into a secessionist Southern Rhodesian party under Mr. Harper and a Federal Dominion Party at Federal level.

Britain's Central African policy remains, at the time of writing, an enigma. It is equally possible to hope that the present Government will have the clear-sightedness and courage to recognize the impossibility of continuing Federation in anything like its present form and to fear that it may attempt to muddle through with a mixture of prevarication, ill-founded optimism and Micawberism without facing the facts emphasized in the last chapter or the need for the kind of action described on page 212.

What stands out with increasing clarity is that the vital issue is Northern Rhodesia. It is accepted, if still tacitly, that Nyasaland cannot in fact be kept in any sort of Federation the Federal Europeans would agree to. The danger is that Britain, having satisfied her conscience by giving Nyasaland independence, may continue to support Federal white supremacy in Northern Rhodesia, consent to yet another constitution there whose liberalism is a mere illusion, and attempt to preserve the *status quo* at Federal government level.

To do so would bring about a great deal more bloodshed and violence than independence has brought to the Congo; fair African representation and a genuinely liberal constitution would guarantee the peaceful progress of Central Africa and vastly enhance British prestige on the whole continent.

Most of the changes that have taken place in the past six months demand no more than a change of phrase. For instance, on page 21 I say that if you travel from the Sudan to the Cape, every yard you cover is under British rule. Developments in Tanganyika make this now only technically true, but the historical truth behind it remains valid. It is pleasant to record that the *Central African Examiner* after a chequered career, first under the influence of the Rhodesian Selection Trust—which with the aid of the *Economist* was a beneficent one—and then under the domination of the United Federal Party, is now reconstituted under a liberal-minded trust and has emerged as an admirably and excitingly progressive periodical in its last few issues. I have added a few additional notes in Postscript to keep abreast either with the times or with my own reading.

My thanks are due to the University of Reading for giving me leave of absence to visit Africa; to Makerere College, the University College of East Africa, for a grant towards the expenses of my study of Central Africa; to the editor of the *Spectator* for permission to use material originally published by him; to the editor of *The Times*, the *Rhodesia Herald* and the *Central African Examiner* for permission to quote from their columns; to Messrs. George Philips and Son and Mr. Alan May of the Reading University School of Art for the map of Africa (which aims only at general orientation and is forced by its scale to omit recent political developments in the French-speaking West). I thank also Guy Clutton-Brock, for the inspiration to write this book; Tommy Fox-Pitt and Colin Leys for much help and time given to the proofs; and Faith Raven for some penetrating comments. I thank Mrs. Sybil Armstrong for most of the typing and Mrs. W. A. Chantler for additional aid: Kenneth Mackenzie, Peter Kuenstler, Jane Symons and the staff of the Africa Bureau, and innumerable other friends for assistance, time and information.

One's chief thanks, in any work on Africa, go to its people.

The Warden's Lodge
St. Patrick's Hall, Reading

T.R.M.C.
7th July 1960

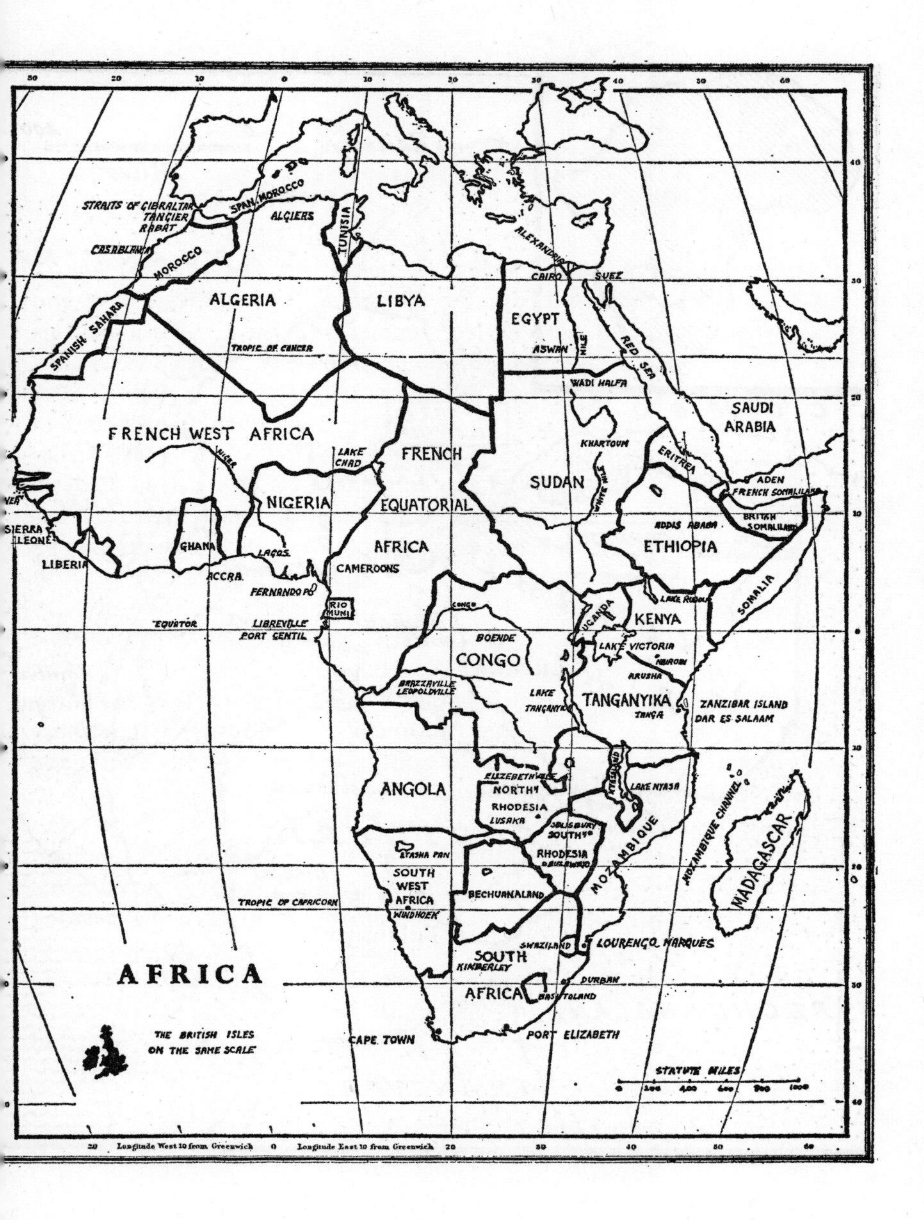
AFRICA
THE BRITISH ISLES ON THE SAME SCALE
STRAITS OF GIBRALTAR
TANGIER
RABAT
CASABLANCA
SPAN. MOROCCO
MOROCCO
ALGIERS
TUNISIA
ALGERIA
LIBYA
SPANISH SAHARA
TROPIC OF CANCER
ALEXANDRIA
CAIRO
SUEZ
EGYPT
ASWAN
NILE
RED SEA
WADI HALFA
SAUDI ARABIA
FRENCH WEST AFRICA
NIGER
LAKE CHAD
FRENCH EQUATORIAL AFRICA
KHARTOUM
SUDAN
WHITE NILE
ERITREA
ADEN
FRENCH SOMALILAND
BRITISH SOMALILAND
ADDIS ABABA
ETHIOPIA
NIGERIA
SIERRA LEONE
GHANA
LAGOS
LIBERIA
ACCRA
CAMEROONS
FERNANDO PO
RIO MUNI
EQUATOR
LIBREVILLE
PORT GENTIL
CONGO
BOENDE
UGANDA
LAKE RUDOLF
KENYA
SOMALIA
LAKE VICTORIA
NAIROBI
ARUSHA
BRAZZAVILLE
LEOPOLDVILLE
LAKE TANGANYIKA
TANGANYIKA
TANGA
ZANZIBAR ISLAND
DAR ES SALAAM
NYASALAND
LAKE NYASA
ANGOLA
ELIZEBETHVILLE
NORTH RHODESIA
LUSAKA
SALISBURY
SOUTH RHODESIA
MOZAMBIQUE
MOZAMBIQUE CHANNEL
MADAGASCAR
ETASHA PAN
SOUTH WEST AFRICA
WINDHOEK
BECHUANALAND
TROPIC OF CAPRICORN
SWAZILAND
LOURENÇO MARQUES
SOUTH AFRICA
KIMBERLEY
DURBAN
BASUTOLAND
CAPE TOWN
PORT ELIZABETH
STATUTE MILES
Longitude West 10 from Greenwich
Longitude East 10 from Greenwich

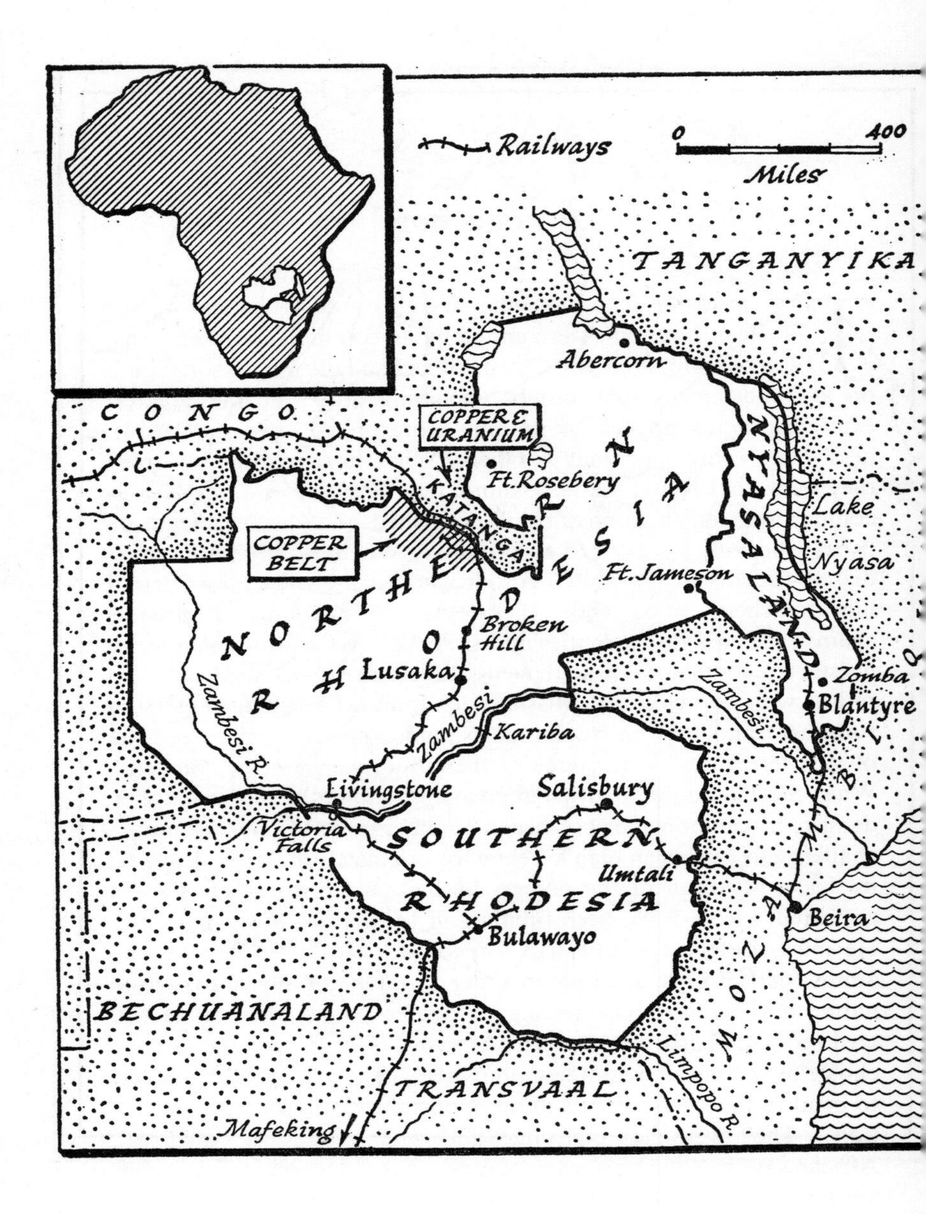

Railways
0
400
Miles
TANGANYIKA
CONGO
COPPER & URANIUM
Abercorn
Ft. Rosebery
KATANGA
COPPER BELT
NORTHERN RHODESIA
Ft. Jameson
Broken Hill
Lusaka
NYASALAND
Lake Nyasa
Zomba
Blantyre
Zambesi
Zambesi
Kariba
Zambesi R.
Livingstone
Victoria Falls
Salisbury
SOUTHERN RHODESIA
Umtali
Beira
Bulawayo
BECHUANALAND
TRANSVAAL
Limpopo R.
Mafeking

Introduction

The various Europeans who travelled to Africa during the nineteenth century were united by no common purpose. Some went to win souls for Christ, others sought for personal gain or aggrandizement and others, including some of the greatest explorers, were impelled by nothing more precise than inquisitiveness. They went to see what was there. Whyever they went, wherever they went, they found the same thing: huge areas of wild, mysterious country sparsely inhabited by ill-nourished and inscrutable black tribes whom they described as primitive. Whether they were immediately friendly to the white man, or whether they began by offering him treachery or violence, they were all inherently defenceless against his superior capacities and skill. Where the white man went, he started some sort of settlement; he either stayed or decided to return with companions. Missionaries founded permanent mission stations: traders set up trading posts, and explorers took possession of vast territories in the name of their European mother countries. When they had done so, often at great cost and in the face of extreme danger, a common purpose began to emerge. Africa represented a challenge to European man's feeling for organization. He must repeat in this new continent the process he had so laboriously but, as it appeared, successfully, been fulfilling in Europe for many centuries. He must use the tools he had forged and slowly tempered to an almost perfect edge at home in order to tame and develop African nature and to introduce among its peoples some form of decent, civilized, social organization. The Africans, being defenceless, had no choice but to put up with these uninvited guests and, sooner or later, to bend to their will. They had no opportunity of rejecting "civilization". They were not consulted and when, today, a "civilized" African says to you in his own country: "Yes, I know you Europeans are here to stay. We have got to accept your presence. And I admit you have brought us great benefits as well as great disasters, you have robbed us with one hand and fed us with the other. But don't forget we never asked you to come and meddle with us. And it is possible we might have got on much better if we'd been left alone to evolve on our own lines over the slow course of ages than we have done in the forcing house of an alien culture"—when he says this there is no answer except that it didn't turn out that way.

Africans generally did not find the ways of European civilization easy to accept. It was rooted in conceptions of private property, struggle and achievement, rigid government and a written rule of law. It was brusque, forceful and always in a hurry. It was founded on authority, not on consent. They showed little inclination to practise its rules or its techniques. The Europeans, with a few imposing exceptions such as Livingstone, failed to perceive that they were confronted by another culture, another way of life founded upon tribal communism and government by consultation and compromise; a culture which preferred the warm security of tribal subsistence, in spite of its hardships and brutalities, to the rigours of advance and self-improvement; and which had, above all, no understanding of or use for hard cash. They saw African life as a social vacuum which must be filled and African reluctance to change it as evidence of a primitive mentality. If Africans could not see and willingly accept what was good for them, they must be forced, like fractious children, to take it from their betters. So where the white man settled he imposed forms of government and social organization which he believed to be as much in the interests of the African population as they were in his own. And he stayed. He has found it hard to accept the results of the changes he has imposed. He cannot easily understand that, in three generations, Africans have learnt what he had to teach and are clamouring to practise it for themselves. He wishes for the good old days when all Africans were "primitive" and all Europeans were masters, and too often persuades himself that they still exist. In fact they are as dead as the dinosaur. Many Africans are far more "westernized" than many Europeans who live alongside them. The white man has been left behind by the historical and social processes he set in action.

Since the various settlements were founded in such different ways, and from such different motives, there was no homogeneity in the forms of government they produced, nor in their ultimate aims nor in their attitudes to the African population. Colonies existed in a haphazard and empirical way before there was such a thing as colonial policy. The existence of colonies evoked colonial policies; and the colonial policies of most European nations have always been a jump or two behind what was actually going on in Africa. This is why colonial powers have so often been overtaken by events and in the last resort forced by the subject people to do at short notice things they had not properly thought out in advance. This has happened to the British in the Sudan, Ghana and Nigeria, and is happening to them in Kenya. It has happened to the French, in different ways, in the whole of West Africa and in Algeria. It has happened to the Belgians in the Congo. There has never been a master plan for African development. Colonial policy has been a matter of hand-to-mouth improvisation.

This may be in many ways a good thing. Rigidly preconceived plans are seldom successful. And it does not mean that there have not been certain guiding principles which have been on the whole faithfully observed; the British conception of indirect rule, and European trusteeship for the "paramountcy" of African interests, for instance, or the French vision of equal citizenship for metropolitan and African Frenchmen; or the Belgian policy of paternalist insulation. But it does mean that, wherever a group of resident Europeans acquires landed rights, and economic interests in the development of the country, these principles will only be applied by the colonial power in so far as suits the immediate wishes of these settlers. The word "settler" has acquired a pejorative significance, though there is nothing fundamentally wrong with settling in another country, because the power and privilege possessed by skilled Europeans firmly entrenched with the blessing of the colonial power in a land of unskilled, uneducated Africans has always proved an irresistible temptation to quick enrichment and neglect of African rights. Where there are numerous settlers, their wishes have always taken precedence over the policies or principles of the European colonial power. This is evident in Algeria or Southern Rhodesia. It is apparent in the difference between Kenya and Uganda. The "natural" rights of the African populations must in theory be identical, but Uganda is being developed as "a primarily African country" as a matter of course and Kenya is having to struggle against white supremacy. It is noticeable in the settled areas even of Ruanda-Urundi. No metropolitan government will ever seriously defy settlers of its own race and colour but will trim its principles to suit their demands as long as it can. This does not mean it will completely abandon its principles. Britain has compromised in Kenya for forty years. But in European-settled countries, the only force capable of asserting the paramountcy of African interests (which, for Britain at least, used to be an axiomatic principle in non-settled ones, and is synonymous simply with the will and the welfare of the vast majority of the inhabitants) is the protests of the Africans themselves. And unfortunately these are generally so long bottled up and so strongly resisted that they have to take a more or less violent form before they are effective.

Since the exploration and settlement of Africa took place in a manner so capricious and fortuitous, we find no logical scheme in the political and social pattern distributed over the continent. In the Union of South Africa European supremacy and African subjection have been axiomatic for centuries. Yet at the same time as South Africa, with all its apparatus of racial discrimination and oppression, was thought to be being absorbed into the structure of the British Empire at the end of the Boer War, the Imperial Government was lavishing tender attention upon the rights of the indigenous inhabitants of Uganda and establishing the Protectorate as "a primarily African country with adequate safeguards for minorities". When the British South Africa Company abandoned its rule over Southern Rhodesia in 1923, the Imperial Government handed full powers to the local settlers to rule over a million Africans in their own European interests because the settlers were there. But when it took over Northern Rhodesia in 1924, it declared it a Protectorate, to be developed as an African country on the basis of paramountcy of African interests, because there were so few settlers that it was possible to do so. In Nyasaland we found, till a few years ago, the epitome of slow-footed paternalism at its most benevolent, while in Kenya European pretensions were enough to spark off the sinister and destructive explosion of Mau Mau. There is no consistency in the distribution of the political and social systems which Europe has tried to impose upon Africa.

Nevertheless the River Zambezi is the most significant division in Africa. To the north of it every black territory in the continent is formally dedicated to the paramountcy of African interests and, like Tanganyika and Kenya, is moving irresistibly towards a system of government that will place the major part of political power in the hands of the majority of the population. South of the Zambezi lie the hopeless lands where white oligarchies perpetuate the rule of force and fear over black populations five or ten times their size by the doctrines of *apartheid* and *baaskap*, discrimination and domination. Southern Rhodesia, just south of the Zambezi, is the most northerly outpost of the South African ethos and outlook; Northern Rhodesia the southern limit of British trusteeship and African paramountcy. When Britain established the Central African Federation in 1953 she sought to combine these two systems into a single political structure, stretching a new doctrine of partnership across the Zambezi, and calling in Nyasaland, with a history and tradition in many ways different from the other two, to cling to its northern end. Whether the attempt can succeed, whether it is possible to associate the two doctrines of colonial overlordship and paternal protection, is open to question. But this is what Federation is trying to do, and so far it has not succeeded.

Southern Rhodesia, with its large European population and its tradition of European self-government, inevitably became the senior partner in Federation. Southern Rhodesia's attitude to Africans, their development, advance and political future, is radically different from that of Britain and the Colonial Office. It has had, so far, the decisive influence on the Federal Government's policy, despite the rather half-hearted checks and balances by which the Federation's constitution sought to avoid this. The nature and quality of Southern Rhodesia's culture is therefore of the utmost importance to the future of the Federation and, since Britain has committed herself to Federation, to the future of Britain's influence and standing in the whole continent. This book is an attempt to examine the Federal structure and the influence exercised on it by Southern Rhodesian culture; and to study the effect of the Southern Rhodesian tradition upon the lives of Africans and upon the relations between Africans and Europeans.

PART ONE

The Approach to Partnership

CHAPTER I

The Formation of Southern Rhodesia

If you travel from the southern frontier of the Sudan to the Cape of Good Hope, a journey of nearly three thousand miles, you will not spend a single minute in a country which has chosen its own government. Every yard of ground you traverse is, in one way or another, under foreign occupation. Everywhere, that occupation enjoys the sanction of the British Crown and is in some more or less intimate relation to the British Government which you, as a British elector, have helped to choose. North of the Zambezi every country you visit is controlled by the Colonial Office from Whitehall, by a Colonial Secretary responsible to the Westminster Parliament. South of the river the power of Britain is non-existent or nugatory, and her relations to the local legislatures are founded on the more or less reluctant acceptance of the Commonwealth as a symbol. If you travel leisurely you will be fascinated by the variations on the colonial theme that you meet on the way, the contradictions between theory and practice that litter the roadside, the wisps of colonial history that cling, like early morning strips of mist, to the hillsides surrounding you. As you go south, you will meet in hotels and rest-houses or at lonely petrol pumps in the bush, an increasing number of European travellers from south of the river who astonish by their strange ways of speech and thought. If you have lived in Uganda or Tanganyika, you will for the first time hear Africans habitually described as Kaffirs, Munts, niggers or just blacks. The unfamiliar terms fall flatly on your ears like uncouth obscenities. You will marvel, and perhaps giggle, at such remarks as: "Dar es Salaam? Used to be a fine place. But I never go there now. Not enough colour bar for me any longer", or "So you come from Uganda. What are the Kaffirs like up there now? Getting a bit uppish, aren't they?" You will experience the paradox of Northern Rhodesia, a country pledged to the paramountcy of African interests and governed by your own Colonial Secretary, in which, apparently with his consent, and at least under his nose, the introduction of a system called interracial partnership is causing the eclipse of African paramountcy and an increased domination of white settlers. But on the whole you will be aware that the dominant influence in the history of these countries north of the river has been the British Colonial Office's classic conception of the paramountcy[1] of African interests and of the Europeans' trusteeship for them. That is to say, all these countries are destined, in a future however distant and remote, to be governed by the democratically expressed will of all their populations, to be self-governing, predominantly black African countries, if possible within the British Commonwealth.

In Southern Rhodesia you enter for the first time the orbit of South African history.[2] It is a longer history than any we have met so far and a more disagreeable one, the history above all of the gold and diamonds of Kimberley and Johannesburg, and of the uncivilized international riff-raff that came out in search of them, of vast fortunes pouring into irresponsible hands and of high finance flourishing among the whisky cases and ox wagons of shabby frontier settlements. Business and business interests directed the course of events and seem to have been successful in getting whatever they wanted alike from the chiefs of African tribes and from the puzzled representatives of British Governments who could never decide what their aims were in South and Central Africa. They met determined opposition only from the Boers who, when they could not be bamboozled were either reduced by the Queen's obedient soldiers or left, like the Transvaal Republic, as defiant pockets of discontent in the rear of the British expansion northward. The folly of all this became clear in 1899 and South Africa is still expiating it today. The avarice of ruthless men set both the pace and the tone, and over the whole

[1] We shall meet this word often again. Its meaning is clear, but it is well elucidated by a remark in the Report of the Joint Select Committee on Closer Union in East Africa, 1931. "Paramountcy", it says, "means no more than that the interests of the overwhelming majority of the indigenous population should not be subordinated to those of a minority belonging to another race, however important in itself."

[2] Lord Hailey writes: "There is thus a characteristic difference between the position of the Union [with regard to African political rights] and that of the present British dependencies in Africa. In Southern Rhodesia, for example, which presents the nearest analogy to the Union, the process of constitutional development is likely to be increasingly influenced by a Federal Legislature in which Africans are represented." (*African Survey*, p. 152.) We shall shortly inquire how far this development is taking place, and how effective the representation of Africans is. Lord Hailey's *African Survey* will be frequently quoted, and will be referred to simply as *Hailey*. All references are to the revised edition, Oxford University Press, 1959.

process brooded the unscrupulous romanticism of an emotionally retarded solipsist—Cecil John Rhodes.

Rhodes was in a very real sense the maker of Southern Rhodesia. He bequeathed his spirit and ideals to it and they live there to this day. It is important to understand him, because Rhodesian society has produced few dominating personalities, creative thinkers or considerable intellects over the past half century. There has been no unusual degree of mental or spiritual ferment and Rhodes' attitudes still do much to condition public opinion. "Matabele" Thompson, one of his closest associates and collaborators, the man who lived for months at Lobengula's court when the Matabele king was still a proud, independent and dangerous monarch, and who actually induced him to sign the concession that made him Rhodes's vassal and his country his possession, writes in his autobiography:[1] "... as a fact, Rhodes never had a friend in the rich or inner meaning of the word. His friendship was often calculated in terms of pounds, shillings and pence. . . . His human sentiment at all times was subordinate to his vast ambition." It is worth adding that African friendship at that time had no value in pounds, shillings and pence, and Rhodes's attitude to Africans was pragmatic. He was no crude Kaffir hater, and showed a deep understanding of Africans when it was necessary to his purpose, as at the famous indaaba with Lobengula's successors, as well as great personal courage. But it crossed his mind no more than those of his contemporaries that Africans could ever demand or deserve the same human or political rights as Europeans, or that both South Africa and Rhodesia would find ultimate stability or disintegration, success or failure, in precise proportion to their ability to solve the problem of integrating African and European society.

Rhodes was a permanent adolescent. His need for power was compulsive and neurotic. He never understood this need because, like all daemonic characters, he was seeking for self-escape without self-confrontation. He absorbed himself in gaining and wielding power and yet more power, exploring and controlling ever increasing tracts of African bush, in order to escape from the unexplored and ungoverned deserts of his own heart. The ideal of a British Empire from the Cape to Cairo was an empty and materialistic dream but he invested it with self-centred glamour like a schoolboy dreaming of

[1] *Matabele Thompson. An autobiography.* Edited N. Rouillard. Faber and Faber. 1936.

his First Eleven colours. He despised money except as a means to power, but amassed an enormous fortune and outdid in successful predatoriness even his most grasping competitors. He clung to a form of religion, without significantly practising its rites or its precepts, for the sake of security. His morbid fear of death, his vanity, his curious old-maidishness,[1] his contempt for companionable good living and his increasing reliance upon alcohol, his horror of "idlers", his ignorance of the liberal arts, the confused intensity of his feelings towards the University of Oxford, even his squeaky, high-pitched voice, are all characteristic of the man who has never grown up, who combines the gifts and skills of an adult with the inner instability of an adolescent. This is nowhere clearer than in his attitude to people. He was capable of highly emotional friendships with men and of the self-abnegating loyalty he showed to Jameson after the Raid; but people to Rhodes were a means to an end not individuals to be respected in their own right.

Matabele Thompson tells us: "One of his sayings when working with white labour was: 'Throw blood to the hounds; they have a right to some of the profit.' . . . He always respected the honest man, hated the scoundrel, loathed the fool; but in turn he used each to his own advantage. All who worked with him knew that he would not brook opposition."[2] Studying Rhodes' career today, one is struck most by the superficiality of his genius. He was a master tactician without the faintest grasp of strategy or principle; he had Napoleon's opportunist ambition without Napoleon's logical notion of synthesizing what he had won, and this half-baked daemon has left a dire heritage in South and Central Africa. His portentous statue with the detail of his moustache, his collar and tie, and coat and trousers faithfully delineated, stands today at one end of Salisbury's main boulevard, facing a sitting statue of Alfred Beit at the other end, brooding over the town as his spirit is said to brood over the whole country from his tomb in the Matopos Hills. This statue is known to Salisbury's black population simply as "the Munt"—the Shona word for a man. They do not know, or care, who it represents. It is a metal man, a convenient landmark. But Munt is the word normally used by white Rhodesians, condescendingly, humorously, a little contemptuously, to describe black men in general—a friendlier

[1] "I remember Alfred Beit once making a rather broad jest. Rhodes's jaws clenched like a vice and Beit never did it again, intimate friend though he was." Matabele Thompson, op cit., p. 221.

[2] Ibid., p. 215.

equivalent of Kaffir. ("The Munts are a lazy crowd." "I respect the Munts in their way.") There is a delicious irony in hearing the subject race describing the Founder's memorial by an innocent word of their own which has acquired an unpleasant association through the conquerors' use of it. Rhodes, a beatified figure, is still invoked to gloss over political or moral arguments that might otherwise appear questionable; and, with an odd redolence of public schools and Oxford colleges, there is an annual bank holiday in the first week of July called Rhodes and Founders Day.

History is very much alive in Southern Rhodesia and one feels its breath like a current of chilly air soon after crossing the Zambezi. Southern Rhodesia is a land of tradition. People will talk to you about "We Rhodesians" or "the Rhodesian way of life". The majority of the 250,000 Europeans expect to end their days there; a good many were born there or even had fathers who were born there. European life can still be raw, crude or graceless but, where it is, these very qualities have acquired a certain patina. Nothing has become so covered by the veneer of tradition as the doctrine of white supremacy.

Europeans on the copperbelt in Northern Rhodesia are paid between seventeen and twenty times as much as Africans in the same industries and are continually demanding more. They are probably the most privileged group of industrial workers in the world. But they barely attempt or expect to convince by their half-hearted protestations that the black man cannot be initiated into the same skills as they use. White exclusiveness is based frankly on cupidity. The black man is to remain in a second class so that his competition may not endanger the flashy but expensive standard of white living.

In Southern Rhodesia by contrast racial discrimination and segregation enjoy a traditional, almost philosophic, respect. We are in the ambiguous atmosphere of British–South African economic racialism before the Afrikaners enforced discrimination as a sanctified Revelation. These attitudes were prescribed by Rhodes and Founders, and a few discreet veils must be drawn aside before we come upon the real basis of the colour bar. The Boers who hunted the Bushmen across the veldt as wild game, the Kimberley miners who introduced the "compound" system, and Mr. Rhodes who dreamed of an unending African empire for Britain, had one thing in common despite all their disagreements: their success depended on cheap black labour. They had to diddle the native to get his work and the resources of the country he lived in and they knew it. They had to believe that the African was inferior—intrinsically inferior—to justify their actions. The tradition survives unimpaired among their descendants today.[1]

Rhodes did not mean the country named after him to be the end of his imperial progress. He envisaged it as no more than a stepping-stone to the Nile and a source of mineral wealth to finance his projects. It was believed on quite inadequate evidence that Matabeleland and Mashonaland contained gold and diamonds in even larger quantities than Kimberley or the Rand and Rhodes sent his representatives to negotiate with Lobengula, King of the Matabele, for concessions over the mineral deposits, in the hope of starting new mines and of gaining possession of the countries themselves. His emissaries disavowed any territorial ambitions and, as Matabele Thompson tells us, compared the country to a cow: "The cow, O King, will remain yours. We will take only the milk"; but this was disingenuous. He bought the concession from Lobengula for a thousand rifles and ten thousand cartridges (which were illegally imported in small consignments "so as not to attract attention") and a gunboat on the Zambezi which was never delivered.

Ironically the gold and diamonds were not there in anything like the expected quantity. Deposits in Southern Rhodesia are relatively unimportant. And after Jameson upset Rhodes' apple cart, his influence never crossed the Zambezi. The stepping-stone to the Nile became the tomb of his ambition (Rhodes was proud nevertheless to be the only conqueror to have a country named after him. "They don't change the names of countries, do they?" he asked anxiously in his last years) and the chartered company formed to exploit its minerals found itself in control of a predominantly agricultural country. Nothing in the foundation of Rhodesia turned out quite as was intended.

Lobengula was dispossessed, robbed of his unexpectedly dry cow in spite of the undertakings he had been given, and Matabeleland and Mashonaland were made into a single country, which became

[1] Of course Rhodes' doctrine was "equal rights for every civilized man south of the Zambezi"; but when he enunciated it, he was not thinking of Africans. He meant that the franchise should, in British territories, be shared by British and Boers. It was only towards the end of his life, when much of his European support had abandoned him, that he began to think Africans might ever be regarded as civilized.

the possession of the British South Africa Company under charter from Queen Victoria. The Colonial Office was allowed some say in "native policy" but the African inhabitants were placed under control of the Company's officials. They were allowed to retain their own tribal institutions if they behaved themselves, deprived of very large tracts of their ancestral land for the benefit of incoming white settlers, and shorn of their liberty—of which, it is perfectly true, they had made no particularly good use in European terms. They had lived for millennia after the static, unchanging manner of Africans, growing enough for subsistence by shifting cultivation and stock-holding, dying like flies in bad years and scrapping from time to time with their neighbours. They had not invented the wheel, nor developed any form of writing; they worshipped their ancestors and the forces of nature. They had neither architecture nor the artillery which can destroy it, neither Western Christianity nor the atom bomb.

What Rousseau called "the savage" is not noble. But his short life is neither so nasty nor so brutish as it appears to European immigrants, and he himself is nothing like so savage as they generally think. He has developed a high degree of adaptation to his environment and his communal life provides a close network of responsibilities and warm human relationships, based on the family and the clan, so that every man's needs are fulfilled equally, according to what is available, and no man is solitary in this world. The white men seldom got far enough inside African life to recognize the strength and stability of its institutions or its power as a system of human relationships. Nor did they recognize the personal dignity, the quick adaptability and the unlimited latent ability, both intellectual and practical, that lay behind these uncouth exteriors—uncouth and apparently barbarous, as any people are whose standard of living has never risen above bare subsistence. When the white man took over the Africans and set them to work for him, he destroyed their institutions less by deliberate disruption than by putting the white man's need invariably first and overriding the traditional wisdom of the chiefs whenever it was inconvenient to white interests. The day of second class citizenship in a white man's world, of literal helotry in their own ancestral countries, had begun for the Mashona and Matabele, and continues to this day.

Matabele Thompson, Rhodes' representative at Lobengula's court when the King was still King, met one of Lobengula's senior chiefs years later on a railway station. The King was dead; the Matabele reduced to insignificance; the chief a man without power. "O Tomoson," he said, "O Tomoson, how have you treated us after all your promises, which we believed?" Ruefully, in his autobiography, Thompson tells us: "I had no answer."

From 1890 to 1923 Southern Rhodesia was governed by the British South Africa Company. Its white population in 1923 was about 34,000. Today it is 219,000. The pioneers stayed, settled and farmed and were joined over the years by increasing numbers of new immigrants as the tobacco farming industry developed. They were mostly English, but a fair sprinkling of continental Europeans came too and a number of Afrikaner Dutchmen from the south.[1] A measure of representative government was first introduced under the Company in 1898, and was extended in 1914.[2] It followed the old Cape franchise law which gave the vote to all citizens with property or an income of a certain value, regardless of race or colour. This did not express the slightest positive intention to enfranchise Africans, either in Cape Colony or in Southern Rhodesia. The need for excluding them had never entered anyone's head, because, in those days, it did not seem conceivable that Africans could possibly attain to the minimum qualification for a vote. It was assumed that both colonies would be governed by a white electorate, parliament and cabinet, and this was what happened. But as Africans worked their way up, towards higher wages, the repeal of the Cape franchise, the establishment of white parliamentary representatives for Africans and the exclusion of black and coloured people from politics in South Africa as well as the various electoral manœuvrings in Southern Rhodesia and the Federation described in Chapters V and XVIII were considered necessary to support white supremacy.

In 1923, after a referendum among the white population only, Southern Rhodesia decided by 8,774 votes against 5,989 to end the chartered company's rule and set itself up as a self-governing colony with a constitution given by Order in Council from His Majesty in

[1] The Afrikaner population of S. Rhodesia is now officially put at 13 per cent. S. Patterson, *The Last Trek*, Routledge, 1957, suggests 20 per cent. They have their own schools, church and newspaper, and a strong tribal consciousness. South African immigration still goes on but under stringent control. There is a feeling that Afrikaners might form a dangerous fifth column if there were serious racial disagreements in Rhodesia and South Africa and the Nationalists tried to annex the country.

[2] Nominated officials held a majority in the legislature till 1914; after this elected representatives did.

Westminster. About a million Africans, who were given no part in the referendum, had no alternative but to accept their masters' decision. A virtually autonomous independent country, possessing in practice all the rights, but not the prestige, of a British Dominion, was created overnight.[1] The lengthy, deliberate devolution of power from a Governor responsible to the paternal Colonial Office to a locally elected legislature, which is not yet completed after sixty years of British rule in the Uganda Protectorate or the Crown Colony of Kenya, was by-passed altogether. The Governor of Southern Rhodesia retains the theoretical right, as representative of the Sovereign, to veto any legislation, more especially if it discriminates between the races, and to submit it to the Westminster Parliament, but this right has not been used once in thirty-six years.[2] But he has no power to initiate; he does not govern. The local legislature has, under the titular authority of the Crown, the same autonomy to legislate and govern in the Colony as the United Kingdom Parliament has in the British Isles. Southern Rhodesia is in an altogether different position from a Crown Colony or a Protectorate, and an immeasurably stronger one. The Governor of Kenya or Uganda is appointed by the Colonial Office and enjoys something like the powers of an American President. He really *governs* the country on lines laid down by London. Representative local legislatures are slowly being built up and the Governor is already handing his powers over to them but the Colonial Office attempts to ensure that this transfer takes place *pari passu* with the development or full representation of all races, communities and interests in the country. Meanwhile the British Government, through a Governor whom it appoints, retains supreme legislative and executive authority. There can be no Prime Minister of Kenya to challenge the Governor's rule until the Governor decides to appoint one and delegate his powers to him. And this will not happen until

[1] Southern Rhodesia "has so much the aspect of a Dominion that it is treated as lying within the sphere of interests dealt with by the Commonwealth Relations Office". *Hailey*, p. 275.

[2] Constitutionally it incontrovertibly exists and the fear that it might be used probably helped to introduce some slight modification into Sir Edgar Whitehead's repressive measures in March 1959. Britain has too few levers in this part of the world and this one should not be forgotten; though the appointment in July 1959 of a Southern Rhodesian, Mr. H. V. Gibbs (now Sir Humphrey Gibbs), to succeed Vice-Admiral Sir Peveril Barton Reiby Wallop William-Powlett makes it less likely than ever that a difference of opinion between Governor and legislature will arise. Sir Edgar Whitehead is now demanding the formal abolition of Britain's powers.

the British Government is satisfied that a Prime Minister can be elected to govern with the consent of the majority of the inhabitants.

Kenya or Uganda are largely administered by civil servants ("officials") from Britain—men without a stake in the country. The local inhabitants, black or white, do not possess full control of their destinies. The ultimate fountain of power is Westminster, not Nairobi or Kampala. The settlers of Kenya have been demanding full self-government for thirty years and grousing about the inequity and inefficiency of "government by officials" as opposed to white self-government. The reason they have not been given it is mainly the sense of responsibility of successive British governments for the African inhabitants of the country and a belief that they were likely to care better for their interests than the settlers. The same considerations applied much less in Southern Rhodesia because the British Government was less directly involved in the early settlement of that country. The Company, not the Colonial Office, was responsible for its administration though Britain claimed certain rights over policy on and administration of native affairs. The Company was in fact the Governor and, given a divided responsibiiytl for the government of Africans, there was no one to act, as many of the early governors of Kenya did, as Britain's conscience towards the African population or as a restraining influence on the settlers. Thus, when the settlers in 1923 asked for full self-government, London did not consider that the same objections applied as in Kenya. It was a question of replacing one largely independent administration by another, not of abdicating any responsibilities wholly exercised by London. The electorate consisted almost entirely of white settlers, because they alone fulfilled the property qualifications (though a few Africans who attained them had also the right to vote). It was given the right to elect its own supreme parliament, to appoint a government headed by a prime minister and responsible only to the electorate. It established its own civil service and did not draw upon colonial servants from Britain. Unlike Kenya, it became a self-governing country and the British Governor, who replaced the Chartered Company, was a symbol of the Crown, a constitutional monarch without legislative or executive powers. As a result, an enormously larger African population was subjected to the complete control of a white minority, with no guarantees for its rights except the discretion of the European government, and no parliamentary representation except the exiguous opportunities offered by the common roll as a few more

Africans earned the financial qualifications for the franchise. The settlers governed the Africans as they wished and Britain always followed a policy of non-interference.

This was the situation up to Federation in 1953. At no time in its history was the government of Southern Rhodesia subject to any real restraint or control from London. The country has been insulated from the political and ethical results of two world wars though they have served to stimulate its economy. It has been cut off from the social revolution that has transformed Britain. It contained no institution for the higher education of any race until 1956 and has avoided contact with the liberal and progressive thought of Europe for half a century. It is the supreme illustration of the truth that people with white skins who stay long in Africa too often cease to be Europeans in any spiritual or intellectual sense. A façade composed of all the material appurtenances of the twentieth century conceals antediluvian attitudes and beliefs, which appear fragrantly picturesque or pathetically parochial and complacent, according to your viewpoint. The British Labour Party, for instance, appears as a gang of extreme and dangerous revolutionaries; the whole idea of Socialism is dismissed with the emotional abhorrence it evoked among the British middle classes in the nineteenth century. The word "Empire" means what it meant to Mr. Rhodes and the conception of Commonwealth has barely penetrated the general public.

All this history is very well known, but one needs to be reminded of it to understand the change of atmosphere that strikes one south of the Zambezi. It helps to explain how illiberality and emotional thick-headedness have become hallowed national attitudes in Southern Rhodesia. We have swum into a backwater of the main stream of social evolution where a small shoal of fish has been growing in isolation.

The country remained on the whole poor, beset by the problems of poor land, erosion, water shortage. It attempted to maintain a high European standard of living (though there was considerable European unemployment at times), from a wasteful and not particularly well developed or competent agriculture, served by a growing African population that was underpaid, underfed and consequently lackadaisical. The Government was perpetually in mild financial straits. The need to set up other industries and free the country from its total dependence on agriculture and fluctuating world tobacco prices was recognized but the capital required for this as well as for general development was not adequately available. (The pre-Federation main roads of Southern Rhodesia—two strips of tarmac like broad railway lines, a car's width apart, set in the dust and gravel bush tracks—are a relic of this era. They were built with what little capital could be found, largely to provide work for unemployed Europeans.)

There was always talk of joining South Africa, and tapping the assets of Kimberley and the Rand in return for a diminution of national independence; but the growth of Afrikaner nationalism, inherently anti-British and potentially republican, repelled the majority of the European population which is still devoted to an Edwardian way of life and imbued with a vague, Kiplingesque loyalty to the British flag and Crown. These symbols were no less powerful because no one was quite sure what values lay behind them; and the changes in their real meaning for Britain and the Commonwealth between 1920 and 1950 were not registered. From the end of the First World War till the early 1950s Southern Rhodesia faced difficult economic problems. The Government was impotently aware of them. And the bluff bonhomous antediluvian Europeans whose helpless dependence upon an economically impossible standard of living was the cause of the trouble, took refuge in the present security of hospitable sundowners and agreeable horse shows from a precarious future they were not equipped to understand.

CHAPTER II

Southern Rhodesia and the Northern Protectorates

It was never seriously considered that salvation might come from association with the British territories to the north. Northern Rhodesia was a British Protectorate governed by the Colonial Office. The chiefs, and other representatives of the African people, had agreed to this status when the private rule of the British South Africa Company ended as lately as 1924. They assumed that African interests would be treated as paramount by the Protecting Power, and had too much confidence to seek the detailed statutory confirmation of this which subsequent events show they would have been wise to demand. Excepting the Barotse, they probably had at this stage no clear conception of the political future they desired for the country and none of African independence; but their self-consciousness was to expand fairly quickly. Northern Rhodesia had a minute permanent European population of farmers and traders. It was governed by civil servants from London. The influence of the fifteen thousand or so European settlers over the Government grew steadily during the 'thirties, not from any set purpose in Whitehall but because the colonial policies of pre-war British governments were as changeable and ill-defined as their European ones. The Europeans of Northern Rhodesia were the strongest proponents of association with Southern Rhodesia—the amalgamation of the two countries was the commonest suggestion at this time—because they felt it offered them "emancipation" from the Colonial Office. The result was weak administration in Lusaka, with no firm sense of direction, and a readiness to comply with the only articulate and well-organized pressure group, the settlers.

Official policy was *the paramountcy of African interests.* A more enthusiastic application of this principle than prevailed in the 'thirties would have meant at very least increases in African wages, a general development of the economy in favour of the advance of the African population and some improvement in the standing of

Africans *vis-à-vis* resident Europeans. It should, if logically enough interpreted, have meant that control of the country would ultimately pass from the hands of London and the European settlers into those of its African inhabitants. Though the tide was temporarily flowing in the opposite direction, as long as paramountcy of African interests remained in name Britain's formal policy, Southern Rhodesia could never tell when a new British Government, or an energetic Colonial Secretary, might commit Northern Rhodesia to a Native policy that contrasted inconveniently and uncomfortably with its own. Southern Rhodesia always desired the elimination of the Colonial Office from Northern Rhodesia and the "emancipation" of the northern settlers, but rather in order to remove a possible danger than because closer association promised very positive benefits.

Northern Rhodesia is a vast country and consists mainly of great expanses of flat infertile bush sparsely inhabited by Africans living at subsistence level. There is good farming land in places and here the Europeans had settled. There were known to be rich deposits of copper and their exploitation had developed to a considerable extent by the end of the 1930s. But no one could foresee within what political framework it would continue, nor what its effects on the political situation in Central Africa would be.

Nyasaland lay to the north-east. It had no common frontier with Southern Rhodesia, being separated from it by the tongue that Portuguese East Africa thrusts up the Zambezi, but a long one with Northern Rhodesia. It had been opened up by Livingstone and other Church of Scotland missionaries in the second half of the nineteenth century. Their chief concern had been to convert and educate the group of tribes they found living along the length of Lake Nyasa. Livingstone observed that parts of the country were suitable for European farming and, with his belief in both settlement and commerce as agents of Christian advance, advocated both for Nyasaland. But no one was more careful of the rights of African peoples. The chiefs and people of the area which had come to be known as Nyasaland trusted the missionaries; consequently they trusted the British and in 1891 entered voluntarily into treaties with Queen Victoria, which placed them under her government and protection. Some European individuals and companies had acquired land in Nyasaland by this time and the Protectorate confirmed their claims if they could show that a recognized chief had agreed to them on reasonable terms. But chiefs and people thought they had a clear understanding that Nyasaland would be developed as an African country and that African interests would be paramount. Over the next fifty years a very small number of Europeans were allowed to acquire land—not more than a few hundred—and a minute white farming community developed. Most of the alienated land was held by a few large companies. By the late 1930s the resident European population, excluding migratory civil servants, numbered about 4,000 to between two and three million Africans. It was taken for granted that Britain was still the trustee of African interests. This, presumably, would mean the ultimate development of African representative institutions and in the course of time of some form of African government. British policy in Nyasaland lacked all dynamic force and was never able to emerge from the stage of paternal authoritarianism which arose with the acceptance of the Protectorate. But it was committed in theory to building a self-governing, self-determining African state. No one has ever questioned that Nyasaland is a black man's country.

Nyasaland had no important mineral wealth and few economic resources. It was overpopulated; there was barely enough land to sustain the existing African community by the traditional methods of subsistence agriculture. Its one staple export was the labour of its young males, nearly all of whom spent (and still do) the most vigorous years of their lives working in the mines of Johannesburg or, as servants, in the farms and urban areas of Southern Rhodesia, earning the cash that evades them at home. Its shape made it expensive and awkward to administer—six hundred miles long, often less than twenty and never more than fifty miles wide, a rough mountainous strip of beautiful but impoverished scenery along the lake.

The majority of Southern Rhodesians had never looked with favour on the idea of closer association with either of these territories, except on terms that Britain could not easily have accepted. Their main reason, whether expressed or not, was dislike of the racial policies of the Protectorates and suspicion of the Colonial Office. The paramountcy of African interests was unacceptable to a country committed to European supremacy; the idea of self-governing African countries was unwelcome.[1] Most Southern Rhodesians genuinely

[1] Cf. *Hailey*, p. 276. "The discussion which arose from the White Papers [on East Africa] of 1923 and 1930 and the reference made to the paramountcy of Native interests caused much anxiety among the European population of Northern Rhodesia and Nyasaland and stimulated a movement in favour of amalgamation with Southern Rhodesia as likely to provide the only means by

did not believe—and still do not—that it will be within the capacity of African communities to govern themselves anything like as soon as it will be possible for men to land on Mars. It seems to them unfair to expect it of people who are "so far behind us". The British Colonial policy of trusteeship which has developed empirically and almost unconsciously over the years, of leading Africans on to control their own affairs and handing power to them when they are considered able to exercise it, appears as unrealistic, sentimental and dangerous to Southern Rhodesians as it does condescending, paternalist and dilatory to Africans.

A Central African Council, which had been under consideration before in 1939, was set up at the end of the war. It consisted of the Governors of the three territories and four members from each of them. Its opportunities were limited by the differences between the territories both constitutionally and as regards Native policy as well as by the fact that it had only advisory powers. As Lord Hailey says: "The Council succeeded in arranging for the extension of a number of Southern Rhodesian services to cover the northern territories, but its activities were hampered by the fact that it had no machinery for eliciting the public support necessary to ensure that its recommendations would be carried into effect."[1]

What changed the whole outlook was the tremendous expansion of the Northern Rhodesian copperbelt during the 1939 war. It became one of the richest and most highly developed mining areas in the world. It achieved perhaps the highest standard of living, for white men, ever found anywhere. The European population increased fourfold in four years by immigration and, being indispensable to the new mining economy, increased its hold over the Government. Northern Rhodesia was moving in fact towards becoming a settler dominated country like Southern Rhodesia, whatever the Colonial

which Northern Rhodesia could hope to achieve the status of responsible government. . . . They were told that the British Government, while considering that amalgamation was not possible now, did not wish to reject the idea in principle. . . . In 1936 amalgamation had the support of all the Southern Rhodesian political parties and of the majority of elected members in Northern Rhodesia; a conference held at Victoria Falls agreed on the terms of amalgamation to be submitted to the Government of the United Kingdom. They were told that there had not been such a change in conditions as to justify reconsideration of the decision of 1931. In 1937, . . . a Royal Commission expressed the belief that the three Territories would in the course of things become more and more closely interdependent. . . . Amalgamation was regarded as the ultimate objective, but there were for the moment differences, particularly in Native policy, which stood in the way."

[1] *Hailey*, p. 277.

Office continued to say about the theory of African paramountcy. And the revenues from the booming copperbelt promised all the capital which Southern Rhodesia so urgently needed to establish a new prosperity based equally on European agriculture and European industry and commerce. As the copperbelt developed, and impoverished Northern Rhodesia became a country of immense wealth, closer association with it became progressively more desirable to Southern Rhodesia. The poor relation had come unexpectedly into a fortune and Southern Rhodesia badly needed some of it.

For partly different reasons, closer association became increasingly desirable also to the Colonial Office at the end of the war. Planners and policy makers realized that the Afrikaner Nationalists were going to rule South Africa for a long time to come—at least for many decades—and they were concerned above all to contain any possible northward extension of Afrikaner power or influence. For this purpose, the first necessity was a viable, prosperous Southern Rhodesia which could not in any circumstances be tempted by gain, or driven by poverty and a feeling of isolation, to join the Union The second was a stable and developing political and constitutional situation in Northern Rhodesia. Nearly 40 per cent of Northern Rhodesia's white population was Afrikaner, and 20 per cent of Southern Rhodesia's. The Nationalists in Pretoria regarded these Afrikaners as Hitler had regarded the Auslandsdeutsche. The Governor-General of South Africa, addressing Southern Rhodesian Afrikaners in 1953, said: "Your loyalty to the country where you are now settled does not detract from the maintenance of the spiritual possessions which are your own. It does not mean that ties of blood and tradition have necessarily been broken." The Afrikaners in both countries mostly agree with him, though there are some who have come north to escape the rigours of Nationalist rule. They mixed little with the English. Most of them felt a strong sentimental allegiance to their native country. The possibility of decisive Afrikaner infiltration into the Rhodesias, or even of direct annexation, could not be excluded if these countries were weak. Interracial tensions were building up on the copperbelt, where economic development had outstripped social progress, and a new, deeply resentful spirit was arising among the African labour force. Civil disturbance and interracial rioting, such as could arise in an uncertain constitutional situation under a weak colonial government, might invite Nationalist intervention "to restore order". And if the idea of

African paramountcy and the development of black self-government was unsympathetic to Southern Rhodesia, it was anathema to South Africa. She might put up with it in Ghana or Nigeria, but would take any measures open to her to scotch it nearer home.

Farther north, Tanganyika, Kenya and Uganda were all on the verge of great changes likely to involve periods of political weakness or confusion. If Nationalist influence got a foothold north of the Limpopo, then north of the Zambezi, there was no knowing where it might stop nor what harm it might do to Britain's plans for colonial liberation and African development in the whole continent. The will to extend *apartheid* and *baaskap* was not lacking; they could be expected to penetrate any undefended points of weakness.

The design to federate Northern and Southern Rhodesia which the Colonial Office recommended, and the Labour Government of 1945 accepted in principle, was intended in the first place to contain South Africa and erect an inexpugnable barrier of British liberalism across the southern half of the continent. It would assure Southern Rhodesia's prosperity and independence. A wise constitution would guarantee the political stability of Northern Rhodesia. It would spread the riches of the copperbelt evenly over the whole of British Central Africa. It would strengthen the forces of liberalism, inter-racialism and African emancipation.

It was Britain who wanted to include Nyasaland in the new Federation. This seemed the most promising future for the country, and Britain, faced with the need of post-war retrenchment, would not be sorry to be rid of the labour and expense of running it. It bordered Northern Rhodesia and belonged more obviously with it than anywhere else. If Northern Rhodesia belonged with Southern Rhodesia, then surely all three countries belonged together. By federating them Britain could simultaneously contain South Africa, guarantee the peace and prosperity of the whole area and diminish her own commitments. It was a tidy, neat and apparently foolproof solution to several awkward problems.

It was in these terms that the Labour Government first discussed Federation with Sir Godfrey Huggins (then Prime Minister of Southern Rhodesia, now Lord Malvern). He made it clear that he and his supporters would prefer Federation with Northern Rhodesia alone but would accept Nyasaland as well to oblige Britain, or, put more bluntly, would not refuse it if this were Britain's price for the copperbelt. It is important to remember this in view of subsequent events. And it is only fair to be clear that Southern Rhodesia had no "imperialistic" designs on Nyasaland. She saw it would be an embarrassment and had no desire to federate with it; but as Britain wanted to be rid of it, she felt it could be handled.

If the Colonial Office and the Government in London had considered this deeply, they might have realized that Southern Rhodesia and Britain were approaching the idea of Federation in quite different spirit and for quite different reasons. They were not thinking in the same language, whatever they were saying. Britain intended Federation to be an association between equals for the benefit of all, which would break down racial barriers and bring black and white into cooperation. Southern Rhodesia wanted to perpetuate its own European way of life, which is essentially a South African one based on white supremacy and racial segregation, and to expand the self-governing colony into a great white Dominion. It needed the riches of the copperbelt to realize its ambition, and felt pretty sure that it could assimilate Northern Rhodesia because of its large, increasing and powerful white population. It might take time to whittle away Britain's protecting powers and her obsession with African paramountcy; but there was a good chance of turning Northern Rhodesia into a settler country. The vast prize made the attempt worth while. It would be out of the question to do the same to Nyasaland. The European population was too small, the Africans a good deal more united and self-conscious than in Northern Rhodesia; the tradition of benevolent British paternalism was more deeply rooted and had worked better. Nyasaland had nothing to offer a white-dominated Federal Dominion but three million independent-minded Africans.

It is impossible to resist the conclusion that the men in the Colonial Office and the British Government who planned Federation were inadequately informed about the Southern Rhodesian conception of it; and inadequately informed about the condition of race relations and the racial attitudes of the Europeans in the colony. This is not incredible. Southern Rhodesia had never been under the Colonial Office; it had been self-governing, with its own civil service and administration. Britain had few sources of intelligence there. White Rhodesians have always professed, and honestly believe they are honouring, liberal principles which nothing whatever is done to carry out. They are genuinely unaware of the discrimination and oppression which most of their laws, customs and institutions involve and are, in consequence, ingenuously persuasive in convincing outsiders that they do not. Lord Malvern is notorious for his racy charm and can make it irresistible, when he wants, to the most hostile critics of his native policy. It is very hard for visiting V.I.P.s or touring cabinet ministers to find out for themselves how Africans really live and what they really think. You must get down to the grass roots to do this and their hosts do not allow them to, nor have they the time. Finally, Southern Rhodesia desperately needed the copperbelt money and was prepared to accept Nyasaland in the Federation, to find out as it went along the meaning of the doctrine of partnership between the races, and generally to make a good many promises whose significance it did not, perhaps, fully understand, in order to get it. It would not be surprising if the Colonial Secretary's advisers were persuaded that Southern Rhodesia was racially a good deal more liberal than was really the case during the negotiations leading up to Federation.

None of this was understood in London between 1945 and 1953. Those in power reached the mistaken conclusion that the differences between Southern Rhodesia and the Protectorate with regard to African emancipation were mere differences of method and timing and not differences of basic practice or objective. A team of civil servants, reporting to the Government on their study of a survey[1] previously made of the subject, said "the most striking conclusion we draw from our examination of the survey is the degree of similarity between policy and practice of the three governments (Northern and Southern Rhodesia and Nyasaland) rather than the degree of difference".[2] Not only is the conclusion false but the survey, in so far as it says anything, incontestably says the opposite. It was decided that Federation was necessary, that it could work, and that nothing must be allowed to stop it. It soon became apparent that the whole African populations of Northern Rhodesia and Nyasaland were opposed to it and that Africans throughout the world regarded it as a pretext for extending white supremacy.

It is generally alleged that the Africans of Northern Rhodesia, represented by the African Representative Council, agreed to Federation on a basis of partnership between the races. Most of its members deny anything of the sort. A conference was held at the Victoria Falls between Mr. James Griffiths and Mr. Patrick Gordon-Walker and delegations from all three territories in 1951 to discuss

[1] Cmd. 8235. 1951.
[2] Cmd. 8233. 1951.

Federation. In connection with this, a meeting of the Northern Rhodesian African Representative Council was called at Lusaka. It rejected Northern Rhodesian participation in Federation as it was then presented to it. After the formal sessions were over, a British official raised the question of Federation and partnership again with its members and, of the fifty odd councillors present, all except five left immediately, packed their bags and went away. They could not agree to the suggestions and their sense of politeness forbade a further direct refusal. The five who remained agreed to the formula that they would consider Federation if partnership was defined acceptably and progressively put into action, and on this slender basis the official reported to the Victoria Falls conference that the chiefs were in favour of Federation. But any African agreement to Federation and to partnership was of a very tentative and uncertain nature and was not at all widely representative.

Partnership with Europeans did not at first sight, or at a longer look, seem to African representatives to be a step up for Africans. It seemed, as it was, a dilution of the paramountcy of African interests—a step down for Africans and up for Europeans. For twenty years the Government had been telling them that this was their country, not the Europeans', and one day they would rule it for themselves. Now they were being asked to share it with Europeans as permanent partners, which could only mean it was to be as much the Europeans' as their own. The African view was put a great deal more cogently to the African Representative Council of Northern Rhodesia by Mr. D. Siwale, B.E.M., the representative for Isoka, than it was ever put to the Victoria Falls conference or the Colonial Secretary. "Mr. President," he said,[1] "I beg to move that this Council strongly disapproves of the proposals . . . on closer association of the two Rhodesias and Nyasaland and considers that the contents therein are detrimental to African interests. . . . I think in about 1930, a memorandum was issued by the Colonial Office on colonial policy, and Native policy. The instruction said wherever the interests of the African conflict with those of immigrant communities, the interests of the African must be paramount. This brought bitter and unfriendly feeling among the European settlers, and so amalgamation was proposed, just to free themselves from the native policy of the Colonial Office. If you want to be quite certain about this I will quote what was said by Mr. Welensky on 12th

[1] Proceedings of the A.R.C., 12th September 1951.

January 1950: 'I am a bitter opponent of the Colonial Office. It is my intention to break its stranglehold on our country.' The same gentleman, Mr. Welensky, said—you can find this in the *Rhodesia Herald*, reported on 18th February 1949—'Our best chance of breaking with the Colonial Office lies in Federation.' That is why the Africans always distrust the European community in this country. . . . We all know very well that the aim of the British policy in Africa was clear and unequivocal, namely ultimate self-government, but . . . it did not seem to be true in Northern Rhodesia. The aim of policy was not self-government in the sense of majority rule, but in the extremely ambiguous term of partnership of the white and black community. I have used this word 'ambiguous' because partnership is only used on lips and in papers and is not in practice. . . . Instead we are looked on as inferiors, and what the European is striving for is European supremacy. . . . In a Federal parliament we find inadequate and poor representation on the Africans' part. We, all of us, remember that we demanded an increase of African representation in the Legislative Council recently, and our request was denied by the Government of Northern Rhodesia. (Hear! Hear!) They say that we are not fit to sit in the Legislative Council and we cannot express ourselves fully in English. . . . That also puzzles an African because we are told to work as partners. . . . We are quite determined in rejecting federal government because we are well aware of the attitude of most Europeans towards the African people in this country. There is no doubt about this. It is shown in Post Offices, banks and the shops where the African is not served as a human being. . . . Gentlemen, I think you will all agree with me that every African in this territory respects our Europeans more than he respects his own chief. . . . I think most of the elderly people here will agree with me that in our day we trusted our officials very well indeed because they did what they could for the indigenous people. Now an African sees a great difference and assumes that the officials are getting tired of their responsibilities and therefore want to hand over the poor Africans to a government which will not do justice to Africans. I say that if any union comes at all it will have to be imposed by brute force and I can assure you, sir, that this territory of Northern Rhodesia will not be at peace."

No attempt at all was made to consult the Africans of Nyasaland about Federation, though it was discussed without enthusiasm by the African Protectorate Council, because it was known they would not agree. They made their opposition perfectly clear by all the limited means of expression they possessed. There were continual protests and some demonstrations against the proposed Federation from the time it was first discussed. A number of Africans were killed by police in anti-Federation riots in the early 1950s and the authorities' efforts to pretend that a contented, carefree people had been stirred up by the Rev. Michael Scott convinced nobody. (A faithful and detailed account of this affair will be found on pp. 628–32 of John Gunther's *Inside Africa.*) It is well known that four hundred thousand Nyasalanders subscribed a penny or two each to send a delegation of chiefs to London in 1952 to protest against Federation to the Queen and to present a memorandum to the Colonial Secretary; and that the Queen, on ministerial advice, refused to receive them, the Secretary of State rejected their document and returned it to them. All over the country Africans explained to the authorities that they did not want to be associated with Southern Rhodesia because most of them had worked there at some time and they knew that Africans were not well treated. They did not believe that they could preserve the sense of independence and human dignity which they enjoyed under the paternal rule of the Colonial Office if Nyasaland were to any extent controlled from Salisbury. It is useless to argue that these simple people had no idea how a Federation worked and that their fears were groundless. A good many of the chiefs and political leaders had a very clear conception, and those Africans who had not knew something much more important. They knew better than the British or Nyasaland Governments how Southern Rhodesia worked and they were determined to have nothing to do with it. Federation was imposed on Nyasaland without the consent and against the will of the people in the face of an almost universal popular emotion of a kind no government can afford to ignore.

In its original desire under Mr. Griffiths to show fairness, the Colonial Office instructed District Commissioners that they were to *explain* the scheme to their people in the years before Federation but not to advocate it. This was a part of Labour's policy, but was not rescinded by the Conservatives. This made no difference in fact, since Africans had shown as long ago as 1938, in evidence to the Bledisloe Commission, that they were opposed to any closer association with Southern Rhodesia. When it became the policy of the Conservative Government of 1951 to impose Federation regardless of African objections D.C.s found they were simply stating that father says you are to take your nasty medicine, it will do you good in the end and it's no good arguing or asking why. But when the D.C., who by tradition in Nyasaland was accessible to the people and open to every form of consultation, was found to be saying, about the most important decision ever taken for the country, "I cannot advocate this. I can only explain what London says," the conclusion drawn by Africans was that he did not really believe in it himself (which as a matter of fact was very often the case), and suspicion of Federation grew in consequence. Apologists of Federation maintain that, but for this error, the whole Nyasaland attitude to Federation might have been radically different; that the people would have accepted it if it had been properly put across—"sold to them" is the expression sometimes used. This is not true, for there was nothing to sell; there was no answer to the Nyasalanders' objections; and nothing could have induced them to consent to Federation. The important result of the prohibition of advice and discussion by D.C.s was that it put the Government out of touch with the people. The D.C.s really ceased to know what they were thinking on the subject, and were unable to give London one last warning of the dangerous intensity of popular feeling. This was the origin of the rift between Government and people which appeared as an unbridgeable abyss in 1959 and forms the subject of much of the Devlin Report.

The Federal plan was conceived under a Labour Government, with first Mr. Creech Jones, and later Mr. James Griffiths, as Colonial Secretaries. The Labour Government fell in 1951, when the spade-work was done and the crucial decision whether Federation should take place or not was imminent. Mr. Griffiths states today[1] that "we as a Labour Government regarded a decision on this matter, which inevitably affected the whole future destiny of these peoples [of Northern Rhodesia and Nyasaland] as one which they themselves should take. Neither we nor officials in the Colonial Service had any right to take this highly important decision for them. As democratic Socialists we believe in the right of all individuals to determine their own future." He goes on to say that after investigating the situation on the spot he and Mr. Patrick Gordon-Walker, the Secretary of State for Commonwealth Relations, "were left with no doubt that African opinion was overwhelmingly hostile to the Federal scheme." He implies, though he does not say outright, that Labour would have accordingly dropped, or drastically altered, the proposals. And in

[1] Letter to *The Times* on 24th September 1959.

fact it is likely that Labour, had it remained in power, would have expressed significant second thoughts about Federation, even though it was already fairly deeply committed to Lord Malvern and representatives of the European communities in the north by this time, and even though its advisers in the Colonial Office urged it to proceed. Nevertheless, Mr. Griffiths's reliance on the doctrine of individual self-determination suggests that even today Labour has not fully grasped the difficulty of applying this formula to countries where individuals are divided sharply into conflicting groups—a powerful articulate minority with political rights and a weak inarticulate majority without them. Self-determination for either group inevitably leads to a result the other cannot accept. No amount of self-determination can bridge the gap between the two. The Protecting Power must do this by taking responsibility simultaneously for extending African rights and safeguarding existing minorities. Once the European appetite for Federation had been stimulated by the British Government's advanced development of Federal plans it was going to be very hard to induce Europeans to bow to African self-determination and watch the meal vanish uneaten. The mistake Labour made, on the advice of its civil servants, was to go so far with the Federal scheme and to give it so much publicity before ascertaining clearly the attitude Africans were likely to adopt.

The Conservative Government of 1951 inherited the scheme from its predecessor and, Mr. Griffiths goes on in his letter to *The Times*, "immediately declared that it would press on with Federation. It instructed colonial officials to persuade Africans to support the Federal scheme. As a result these officials found themselves becoming increasingly unpopular with African opinion in their districts. The consequence has been to discredit the British administration throughout Nyasaland and Northern Rhodesia. . . . The Conservative Government next called a conference in London. When it became clear that African representatives would boycott the conference, my colleagues and I appealed to the Conservative Government not to proceed and warned them of the consequences of acting further against the wishes of Africans." Labour did oppose the Federal bill's passage through the House, but was in a vulnerable position as author of the plan. Shifts of emphasis in the conception of Federation took place. Economic progress and business development came to the fore and interracial equality and the welfare and development of all the inhabitants became perhaps less important. The final draft of the Federal Constitution gave the settlers more independence of Britain at once, and the promise of very much more in the near future, than Mr. Creech Jones had ever envisaged, and left open a number of loopholes for encroachment on African rights that Labour might have sealed. But the Conservatives do not seem to have realized, any more than their Labour predecessors, how close to *apartheid*, and how opposed to the Protectorate doctrine of the paramountcy of African interests the Southern Rhodesian mentality was, nor how powerfully the attitude of the Federation's senior partner would influence the reactions of both African and European in Northern Rhodesia and Nyasaland. The European minorities would see Federation as a means of putting the clock back to white supremacy and would turn away from any readiness to co-operate on equal terms with Africans, and ultimately live under a black government. The African majorities would offer sullen resistance to Federation and would lose all confidence in a Britain which, they felt, had betrayed them to Southern Rhodesia.

For it was an illusion to suppose that Southern Rhodesia could form the cornerstone of a bastion of British liberalism or become the senior partner in a Federation devoted to interracial partnership and equality. Its "Native policy" is, and always has been, much closer to Pretoria than to Westminster. Its white ruling class is, and always has been, opposed to liberal views on racial questions and to any conception of racial equality. It is a country founded on discrimination and rooted in segregation. If this had been understood in Westminster and Whitehall, the Federation as it now exists would probably never have come into being. It is because it is founded on an illusion that it has engendered little but trouble, injustice and discontent in its first six years and is likely to endure worse unless radical adjustments are made. And it was this illusion that condemned the beneficent intentions of its Labour founders to frustration from the outset.

The basic fallacy is to suppose that the Southern or Northern Rhodesian settlers' practice of white supremacy and racial discrimination can in any circumstances be compatible with Britain's responsibility for the paramountcy of African interests in the northern territories and that these two completely opposed attitudes to interracial relations and African advancement can coexist as parts of a single political system, such as the Federation. One or the other must prevail in the Federal Government. If it is the conception of

African paramountcy and white trusteeship, this calls for a complete change of heart in settler attitudes to Africans, and would involve a social revolution. There is no indication that the Europeans are prepared for this. If white supremacy prevails, Britain's responsibilities to the Protectorates cannot be fulfilled since you cannot have European supremacy and the paramountcy of African interests in the same country at the same time.

Events have placed the emphasis on Nyasaland, but it is in Northern Rhodesia that it should really lie. Nyasaland would have been omitted from the Federation if Sir Godfrey Huggins had had his way. But Northern Rhodesia had to be a member because Southern Rhodesia wanted to share in its wealth. The essence of Federation as seen from Salisbury was to harness the resources of the copperbelt to the expansion of a predominantly European economy. This, in the long run, could only mean the amalgamation of the two countries and the extension of the social pattern of Southern Rhodesia to Northern Rhodesia. It was unthinkable that Southern Rhodesia, with its firm belief in white supremacy, could ever allow the basis of its economy to come under the control of a black government. The success of the Federation as envisaged by Southern Rhodesia depended, and still depends, upon the "emancipation" of Northern Rhodesia from Colonial Office rule and the extinction of the paramountcy of African interests for which the Colonial Office is supposed to stand; that is to say, upon Britain's abdication of her responsibilities and abandonment of her promises to the chiefs and people. It would be relatively easy even today to remove Nyasaland alone from the Federation. The only real reason the Federal Government has resisted secession so hotly is that it would set an example the Africans of Northern Rhodesia would be anxious to follow. If Britain is to honour her solemn undertakings to the chiefs and people of Northern Rhodesia, this must mean the dismemberment of Federation or the most radical changes in its whole structure. The future of the African population of Northern Rhodesia is the key to the future of British Central Africa. And the extent to which the Native policy and outlook of Southern Rhodesia is allowed to dominate Northern Rhodesia through the agency of the Federal Government will decide the future of British influence in the whole continent.

When Federation was imposed, Britain had a perfectly clear duty to protect the African inhabitants of Northern Rhodesia and

Nyasaland from Southern Rhodesian, or any other, white domination, and to guarantee the paramountcy of African interests. She has this duty today and it is based on the constitutions which founded the Protectorates. She attempted, as we shall see, to incorporate these undertakings in the Federal Constitution. Africans believed that, whatever was promised or written, the actual effect of Federation would be to cancel all the safeguards they possessed and expose them to white domination on the Southern Rhodesian pattern. In spite of the attempts of the Federal Constitution to avoid it, this is so far what has happened. Nyasaland is held within Federation at the point of the Sten gun, although it has clearly expressed its desire to leave at any price. Northern Rhodesia is ruled by a predominantly white Federal Party Government, elected mostly by Europeans, and the Colonial Office undertakings enshrined in the Federal Constitution are withering away. None of this is what Britain intended in 1953. What, then, did the Federal Constitution mean to achieve and by what means did it hope to achieve it? Could it have attained its objective? And what has the influence of Southern Rhodesia been?

PART TWO

Federation in Action

D

CHAPTER III

The Federal Constitution[1] and Race Relations

Federation, as we have seen, was proposed by the British Government at the end of the war as a solution to various political and administrative problems, espoused by Southern Rhodesia as a means of gaining access to the wealth of the copperbelt and resisted by about seven million voiceless Africans by the very limited means available to them. After some years of discussion and consideration in the restricted circles in Britain that take account of such matters, this child of a Labour administration was adopted by the Conservatives and formally accepted by the Westminster Parliament. Some formidably authoritative voices were raised against it. The Government was well warned. Miss Margery Perham, in a letter published in *The Times* on 9th June 1953, the day before the final parliamentary debate, wrote:

"A recent visit [to Africa] has confirmed my fears that by the form of Central African Federation and the way in which it has been handled we risk losing the greatest asset we have on the continent—the confidence of Africans. Some eleventh hour pledges and concessions on tomorrow's debate might at least lessen this risk.

First, with regard to the imperial connection, the Government have made the almost unbelievable assertion that the erection of a strong Federal Legislature over the Territorial Governments in no way impairs their protectorate status. They must prove this by word and act, since it is only by making the utmost use of the powers left to her that Britain can keep the promises the Government are now making to the British electorate and to Africans. . . . I believe that British authority and influence in the high democratic spirit reaffirmed at the Coronation were never more needed in Central Africa or more desired by Africans. There are especially three ways in which the Government should pledge their exercise.

[1] For a clear and illuminating analysis of this instrument see Faith Raven, *The Constitution and Race Relations in Central Africa*. Africa Bureau. 1958.

(1) There should be no impairment of the position of the Colonial Office, the expulsion of which is stated as a chief aim by the European leaders—a point which the Government have not answered—or of the Colonial Service. The liberal purposes of the Imperial Government can be exercised in province and district only through a trained and impartial administration. Upon this subject the hurried report of the Civil Service Commission was highly equivocal.

(2) The British civil liberties must be carefully safeguarded to allow Africans to organize themselves politically in order to make full use of the limited representation allowed them. Admittedly this is a difficult matter among the tensions of a racially mixed society. But nothing could be more fatal than, by a severe treatment of fancied sedition, to foster real sedition and drive the strong leaders Africans must try to throw up, or their European friends and advisers, into courses which lead to deportation or gaol. This comment has no relation to current cases,[1] about which I have insufficient evidence, but is based on unhappy experience elsewhere and the imperative need to foster constitutional African leadership.

(3) With regard to the promised economic development, which seems, mistakenly I believe, to have led many of the otherwise unconvinced to accept Federation, the Government should be asked to show that they have the power and the policy that will enable them to shelter the peoples of the Protectorates from such truly horrifying schemes as Mr. Welensky has proclaimed. The pressure of such rapid and extensive development on a scanty population already strained to the utmost and based on the present destructive system of migrant labour, could so undermine the natural morale and economy of African society that all the revenues produced will be needed to buttress it artificially by expensive social service including additional police force and prisons.

Secondly, if the Africans are to be given an increasing share in the legislative and executive branches of the Constitution, there must be active measures to train them.

One of the greatest causes of African bitterness is the belief that

[1] This reference is to the deportation of the Rev. Michael Scott from Nyasaland in particular.

tardy and inadequate help is given to raise them from the ignorance and inexperience which is so frequently emphasized. Even if the problems—and they are many—which beset the proposed interracial university are solved quickly, it will take at least five or six years before the first fully qualified Africans pass out of it. Nothing could do more to overcome that deep suspicion of the white man's intentions which blight co-operation in Central Africa than the announcement by the Government of a generous and immediate provision of scholarships and grants to expedite the training of Africans for political leadership, for the Civil Service and for industry.

May we also hope that in this debate some of the oft-repeated clichés will not be used again? It is no defamation of 'our kith and kin' in the Rhodesias to believe that no small local minority should be given such wide powers over a subordinate race and class without Britain retaining the fullest possible rights to influence and revise. As for rejecting either 'white or black domination' it may be asked whether power can be indefinitely suspended between the two.

The Bill legislates for white domination now, but unless the experience of history and of all British policy and principles are to be reversed, there must one day be black domination in the sense that power must pass to the immense African majority.

Whether it passes peacefully, without destroying the influence of the European minority and the great contribution they and their nation have made to Africa, may depend on the deliberations of Parliament tomorrow and the spirit in which this hazardous Constitution is instituted."

The Church of Scotland, whose deep and sympathetic contact with Nyasaland dates back to Livingstone, spoke the plain truth in words that are equally prophetic. From Edinburgh, its Foreign Mission Committee sent a grave and sober expression of its expert opinion to all participants in the London Conference on Federation of April 1952—to the Secretaries of State for Commonwealth Relations and for the Colonies and to the delegations from the three Central African governments. Quoting a resolution it had passed on 15th April 1952, it said:

". . . The Foreign Mission Committee, convinced that the decisions of Her Majesty's Government about the proposed Federation in Central Africa between Southern Rhodesia, Northern Rhodesia and

Nyasaland, will be regarded both in this country and in Africa as the acid test of the sincerity of its Commonwealth policy; and having grave doubts about the trends of the present negotiations, records its opinion that there should be no Federation in Central Africa without full consultation with, and the agreement of, the Africans in those territories.

The Foreign Mission Committee further records its conviction that a new approach should be made by the sending of a Royal Commission to Central Africa to discuss with residents of all races the steps which can be taken to ensure the undoubted advantages of closer association, without any fear of halting the political, economic and social advance of Africans in the territories."

It went on to draw attention to the Church of Scotland's seventy-five years of close connection with the development of Nyasaland and Northern Rhodesia and said that the Foreign Mission Committee recognized the great difficulty of the social and political issues under consideration but "felt itself under an obligation to emphasize as the primary consideration the achievement of good relationships based on human freedom and justice between the different races among whom the Church is working".

The Church of Scotland Mission Council of Nyasaland, meeting at Blantyre in September 1952, went into the matter in more detail. Its resolution is so pregnant and so tragic to read after 1959 that it is necessary to quote it at length. (The Minister of State referred to was Mr. Hopkinson, at that time Minister of State for Commonwealth Relations.)

"(1) The Council regards it as a first principle that the achievement of racial harmony outweighs the economic advantages that might be gained from Federation.

(2) The Council is concerned that the Minister of State on his visit to Nyasaland expressed the opinion that the African opposition to Federation is not as solid as this Council has represented in statements that reached him from Edinburgh. Since his visit members of Council have verified the facts and see no reason to modify in any way their former statements. It is a complete misapprehension to suppose that the opposition is confined to a politically minded minority. As missionaries, Council is surprised at the knowledge of the issues involved in Federation shown by ordinary Africans. Their opposition is not to details of the scheme, but to the whole principle, and it is for this reason that they refuse to discuss details.

(3) The opposition is now assuming the nature of a mass movement and the African is becoming more and more involved emotionally. His sense of insecurity and fear—an emotion that readily changes into aggression—is shown in the resolution of the African National Congress calling for a day of National Prayer.

(4) The Council is also concerned at the impression which the Minister of State has formed with regard to intimidation. The Council is not satisfied with the evidence given. . . . Both African members of Legislative Council have denied that they have been intimidated or that they ever wished or intended to support Federation in any circumstances. If intimidation exists, why has not the appropriate police action been taken?

(5) Reports of pressure and bribery from the other side were current long before those of intimidation by anti-federationists.

(6) Unless the charges of intimidation can be proved by court action, they should not be used for the purpose of influencing public opinion, since whatever effect this might have on British public opinion, Council knows the danger of suggesting to Africans such political tactics.

(7) The Council believes that the Minister of State has been misled by unrepresentative evidence and it urges that an impartial and independent investigation be made . . . into (*a*) the extent and the nature of the opposition to Federation and (*b*) the evidence of intimidation or corruption on either side.

(8) Discussions on Federation have increased racial antagonism so that there is no chance of attaining that measure of racial partnership which is necessary to make the Federation workable. The Council pleads that a decision on Federation be delayed meantime, and that steps be taken to prove the sincerity of Europeans' desire for partnership. The Council urges that this be proved in the following ways:

(*a*) In order to prove that there will be no barriers to Africans who have reached a high cultural level, an early statement be made by the Government of Southern Rhodesia that the proposed Central African University shall be interracial socially and academically.

(*b*) That the pass-laws in Southern Rhodesia and the Copper Belt be modified to exempt many more Africans.

(*c*) That a statement be made with regard to the stages by which the franchise will be extended to more Africans.

(*d*) That industrial legislation in Southern Rhodesia and Trade

Union Colour Bar Rules in the Copper Belt restricting the acquisition of skill be withdrawn.

(*e*) That African membership in the Legislative Council of Northern Rhodesia and Nyasaland be increased to equal that of the European unofficial members.

(*f*) That a scheme of training be inaugurated to prepare Africans in Northern Rhodesia and Nyasaland to occupy official posts now held by Europeans.

(9) Once the African is assured on these points, which Council regards as prerequisites of any scheme of Federation, Council believes he will be ready and willing to discuss the matter."

It is strange that Mr. Oliver Lyttelton and the Central African Governments could remain as impervious as they did to such good advice.

A referendum was held among the enfranchised population of Southern Rhodesia. 25,000 votes were cast in favour of Federation, 15,000 against it. The majority was 63 per cent. Of the 40,000 people who voted, 429 were Africans who were on the electoral roll. No Africans were directly consulted in either of the Northern Protectorates. The Order in Council establishing the Federation of Rhodesia and Nyasaland was signed on 1st August 1953.

The Federation was equipped with an elaborate Constitution designed mainly by civil servants advised by an academic constitutional expert. The aim of the Constitution was to allow each of the three territories, Southern Rhodesia, Northern Rhodesia and Nyasaland, to retain its existing forms of government for internal, domestic, and particularly African, affairs while placing them all under the co-ordinating control of a Federal Government which would co-operate with each of the three territorial governments separately. The Federal Parliament and Government were to be elected directly by voters in all three territories, not through the existing territorial governments. The Federal Parliament would lay down its own uniform requirements for the Federal franchise in all three territories irrespective of the methods of electing or appointing individual territorial governments. Southern Rhodesia was to continue as a self-governing colony under the rule of a European minority electorate and resolve its internal racial inequalities or antagonisms according to the law of its own being without Federal influence. Northern Rhodesia and Nyasaland were to remain under the administration of the Colonial Office for all domestic purposes, and the rate of constitutional advance, the promotion of the African majorities to political influence and the form of representation and government that was to prevail internally, were to be decided by the Colonial Secretary, deriving his authority from the British Parliament. This, it was considered, guaranteed the paramountcy of African interests in the Northern Protectorates while leaving Southern Rhodesia free to follow the path chosen by its permanent settler population.

The subjects of government are divided between two lists, the Exclusive List and the Concurrent List. The Exclusive List contains those matters which are reserved to the Federal Government: external affairs, defence, immigration, customs, currency, railways and trunk roads, posts and telegraphs, major irrigation and construction work, higher education, all *non-African* primary and secondary education, all *non-African* agriculture in Southern Rhodesia.[1]

The Concurrent List contains matters which are to be dealt with by the individual territorial governments and the Federal Government jointly in co-operation, or according to whatever arrangements they work out between themselves. These are: health, inter-territorial migration, broadcasting, industry, electricity and scientific research; and non-African agriculture in Northern Rhodesia.

By implication, all other subjects are reserved to the territorial governments. They are specified only by their omission from the other lists, the residue at the bottom of the barrel. They include those things which are considered to concern the African population—African education below university level, African agriculture, land and land tenure.

We must explore the significance of these divisions before investigating the rest of the constitution. It seems to have been believed that by segregating African affairs from other more general ones, the development of African life and the paramountcy of African interests in the territories where it applied could be secured. But this assumes that African interests will always remain within the limits that now confine them. African land tenure and agriculture will remain a narrow under-capitalized matter of peasant subsistence farming controlled by the territorial government, while *non-African* (i.e.

[1] Non-African agriculture in Nyasaland is under the territorial government but the Federal Government is avowedly anxious to transfer it to the Federal List. Non-African agriculture in Northern Rhodesia is now on the Concurrent List, and is administered by the Federal Government.

European) agriculture under Federal control in the heavily settled territories, may forge ahead to rival the opulent prairies of the Middle West. African education will remain a matter of primary and secondary "bush schools" under local control, perpetually distinct from the facilities available to non-Africans. African life is going to remain at a lower level than that of Europeans and can be placed within a separate compartment. The two will never overlap and Africans should be thankful for paramountcy within their own educational or agricultural systems, running forever alongside but separate from the European. This conception is barely distinguishable from the *apartheid* Dr. Verwoerd is finding it so hard to apply in the Union. It implies the perpetual existence of two different sets of interests—two nations—within the Federation, divided along racial lines.

In fact, the interests overlap everywhere. Kariba, a major construction work, is a Federal project on the Exclusive List. But it has involved the expropriation by force of thousands of Northern Rhodesian tribesmen, and their compulsory removal to other areas. The Northern Rhodesian Government undertook this expropriation at the behest of the Federal Government and it is impossible to argue that, in firing on Africans who threw spears at its policemen, it was consulting the paramountcy of African interests. It was co-operating with the Federal authorities because Kariba is a Federal undertaking. The shores of Lake Kariba are being made into an expensive pleasure resort with hotels and restaurants, offering every form of aquatic recreation compatible with the presence of the crocodile, and it is not easy to believe that the advertisements of development plots on easy terms that are appearing in the London *Times* as I write are aimed at Africans whose interests are paramount.

Immigration is a Federal prerogative. But can it possibly be said that who is, or is not, allowed to enter Nyasaland or Northern Rhodesia does not concern the interests of the African population? The exclusion of Mr. John Stonehouse from the territories was a Federal decision not involving their regional autonomy. But its effect upon Africans at the time of the Emergency, upon the future conduct of visiting Members of Parliament and upon the whole right of Parliament to gain first-hand information about countries under its titular control is incalculable, whatever the rights or wrongs of the Stonehouse case may be. Is it no concern of the African inhabitants of Nyasaland that the Rev. Tom Colvin has been declared a prohibited immigrant? He was a pastor to many devout black Presbyterians, and friend and counsellor to many more, and as far as can be discovered, his offence in the eyes of the Federal Government was that he was too successful in carrying out the avowed Church of Scotland policy of building an independent, interracial church in Nyasaland. It is incontestably an offence against local autonomy that, by a decision from Salisbury, he is not allowed to return. It is equally an offence against Northern Rhodesian autonomy that Mr. A. E. Lewis, chosen by the European Mine Workers Union as their Secretary-General, was declared a prohibited immigrant because of his connection with socialist trade unionism in Britain.

Customs, to choose another subject on the Exclusive List, affects the interests of all members of the community. It is of vital concern to all Africans which are more heavily taxed, cosmetics and cameras or tractors and pressure lamps. The amount of revenue collected, and the goods it is levied from, affect their daily standard of living. The shops of Blantyre or Lusaka are full of luxury goods, imported at low rates of duty for the benefit of a handful of Europeans, and the decision to allow this is taken by the Federal Government. The interests of all are inseparable unless an abiding natural inequality is assumed and the attempt made by the Federal Constitution to divide them is an admission of *apartheid*, all the more significant because unconscious and well meant. It is impossible for the territorial governments, or the Colonial Office, to guarantee the paramountcy of African interests within the very narrow limits of local autonomy allowed by the Federal Constitution and according to so restricted an interpretation of what concerns Africans. It is hard to see how African interests can be protected by this kind of separation of functions or how African advance could be promoted in Federation as it is except by giving Africans much more electoral power over the Federal and territorial governments.

The Constitution does recognize the possibility of interracial tension and the need to protect African rights. The Preamble, which is not in law a binding part of the instrument, contains various expressions of aspiration, which are not legal safeguards. The provision for the African Affairs Board, the limitation of Federal powers in certain fields, the checks on Federal power to amend the Constitution and the demand for a review of the Constitution, though they are not proving very effective, are constitutional safeguards.

The aspirations of the Preamble are not. Nevertheless, they are quoted, if not implemented, as if they were. The Preamble states that "Northern Rhodesia and Nyasaland should continue, under the special protection of Her Majesty, to enjoy separate Governments for so long as their respective peoples so desire, those Governments remaining responsible (subject to the ultimate authority of Her Majesty's Government in the United Kingdom) for, in particular, the control of land in those territories, and for the local and territorial political advancement of the peoples thereof".

But the powers of the northern territorial governments are so much eroded by the distribution of functions contained in the Constitution itself that this is virtually meaningless. It is obvious nonsense to pretend that the inhabitants of Nyasaland or Northern Rhodesia want to live under the territorial governments they now have. The need for repression in both countries has been caused by their protesting that they do not. It is equally obvious nonsense to claim that Africans have chosen these governments or have any control over them. Compare the constitutional provisions with the Federal Prime Minister's statements, and compare his statements with Mr. Siwale's speech quoted on pages 41–42.

On 29th January 1959, just before the Emergencies began, Sir Roy Welensky said: "It has got to be recognized, once and for all, that when we talk of maintaining high standards in the Federation and Africa, we mean white standards, which are standards accepted as being normal in the older Western countries of the world. It must be accepted, furthermore, that these standards are worthwhile, and every endeavour must be made to maintain them here. Finally, it must be recognized that, if the Western world wants to be sure of access to the minerals and other wealth of Africa, the stabilizing influence provided by the white man must be preserved." He went on: "The plain facts remain that the unbridled African nationalism of today, which suits the communist book to the last letter, is being opposed by the established white civilization of the continent." A little later, on 10th March, he stated: "I should make it abundantly clear to those people who have in their minds that we, the element that I consider as civilized in this part of the world, are likely to abdicate in ten or fifteen years, that they ought to prepare themselves for a rude shock." In the Federal Assembly on 7th April 1959 he said that the general state of "restlessness" among a section of Africans in the Federation had its origin at the very time of the inception of Federation, when there was strong political opposition in the United Kingdom to the Federation as a whole, and to the inclusion of Nyasaland in particular. Africans were, from the start, encouraged to believe that it was only a temporary experiment, and that if it failed, the Federation could be broken up. Thus they were encouraged to keep up pressure against Federation. "I think therefore it is about time we made it clear that our original willingness and present unchanged willingness to include Nyasaland within the Federation are due to what we hope is a far-sighted approach to the problems of this part of the world. We feel that the evolution of Nyasaland is in the long-term interests of all of us in this part of Africa and I see no reason why Nyasaland should not progress to full self-government within the Federation; accepting the implications of normal political evolution; regulating its own affairs in the territorial sphere and sharing by representation in the House in the regulation of those matters which are reserved for the Federal Government." This willingness to accept Nyasaland in Federation a few weeks after the African population—over 99 per cent of the whole population—had demonstrated its unwillingness to be included in it by the events which led up to the Emergency, and which the Devlin Commission considered received overwhelming popular support, is at least a misplaced generosity. A few weeks earlier, Sir Roy had sent Federal troops into Nyasaland at the request of the Governor and proclaimed that he would use "the most rigorous methods legally at our disposal to maintain law in the territory". As *The Times* pointed out on 26th February, these troops were under the command of the Federal, not the territorial, Government.

The British Government of the day was little more intelligent. Lord Perth said in Lusaka at about the same time: "Federation has got to work. It is in the interest of everybody. There is no alternative plan in the mind of the Colonial Office."

Lord Malvern made the true situation a good deal clearer when he said that the Federation had no intention of letting Nyasaland go to its ruin outside Federation even if it wanted to. "It is a very good thing the balloon went up in Nyasaland. It would have been a lot worse if it had been two or three years hence. . . . If Imperial troops had gone into Nyasaland with no one knowing anything about the African there would have been hundreds shot in ignorance. As it was, half the row turned into a sort of whistling match. With our own men there, they knew the African and the African knew them. . . .

Europeans here are sensible enough not to care two hoots what is said in the House of Commons. The formula for those in control of the Federation must be: for oversea critics as much contempt as you can, and for our own people, keep the public sweet." He accounted for the Nyasaland troubles by saying that "the African loves a scrap". It was a scrap, or a whistling match, in which fifty-one Africans, and no Europeans, were killed. Yet according to the Constitution, the Africans were "enjoying separate government for as long as they desired".

The complexion of the northern governments is conditioned by the relations and agreements existing between the Colonial Secretary, who prescribed their constitution and appoints and instructs their Governors, and the Federal Government, not by what the Africans desire. A certain degree of electoral representation (based on a qualitative franchise) was introduced by the new Northern Rhodesian Constitution of March 1959 and has been promised to Nyasaland sometime after May 1961, but this does not affect the issue. The electoral system is carefully calculated, under a mask of common roll interracialism, to give overwhelming political influence to the European minority and to make the real representation of African views impossible. Only if the African populations had been consulted about the constitutions under which they live could the governments resulting from them be said to represent African wishes. The Colonial Secretary did not consult the African population, but he did consult the Federal Government before deciding the constitutional futures of both territories; and herein lies the weakness of the whole arrangement. Like all written constitutions, the Federal one depends for its success less upon what it says than how it is operated. And it has been operated by the Conservative Government between 1953 and 1959 in a manner to satisfy the Europeans and preserve at least the appearance of good relations between the British and Federal Governments. A Colonial Secretary who is prepared to stand up for African interests is legally in a position to insist upon territorial constitutions in Northern Rhodesia and Nyasaland that respect the rights of the African populations. To do so he would have to risk a major show-down with the Federal Government and the possible disintegration of the Federation, on the lines discussed in the concluding chapter of this book. He would have to place justice and the fulfilment of Britain's pledges before expediency. He would have to face the possibility of a complete breakdown of the

1953 policy as we have analysed it in the previous chapter. He would have to envisage alternative means of attaining Britain's objectives—the containment of South Africa and the economic and political stability of British Central Africa. Neither Mr. Oliver Lyttelton nor Mr. Alan Lennox-Boyd was prepared to contemplate any of this.

There are some crucial ambiguities at the root of the aspiration we are discussing, that the inhabitants of the northern territories shall continue to enjoy the forms of government they desire. First, they have never had an opportunity to express their desires or choose what system, or what government, they wish to live under. Second, who are "the inhabitants" and how are their wishes to be expressed? Mr. Oliver Lyttelton said categorically in the debates on 9th and 24th June that the constitution meant "a majority of all the inhabitants without distinction of race or colour" to decide. It was on this understanding that Parliament accepted the Federal Constitution. But the argument has since been frequently heard in Central Africa, and was implicitly accepted by Parliament in the debates on the Federal Constitution Amendment Bill and the Federal Electoral Law, in the autumn of 1957 and early in 1958 respectively, that it cannot have meant this because there is no machinery for consulting all the inhabitants of these countries and they are too ignorant and illiterate to have any sensible wishes or to know what Federation is all about. If the original undertaking could not be carried out, or if it was considered inexpedient to do so, it was a deception of Parliament to enter into it. This prevarication will look unusually moth-eaten to the African historians who will one day come to write the history of the British in Africa.

Significant changes have been made in the forms of government under which all the inhabitants live. Their constitutional position, their rights and future prospects are unrecognizably different from what they were ten years ago and the enormous majority of Africans has not been consulted in any way. The Colonial Office has taken the liberty of interpreting their wishes and deciding their futures in the manner least inconvenient to itself and most acceptable to the Federal Government. It has been content to maintain the mere machinery of British protection in the northern territories, for the look of the thing, while abdicating the actual control of African development to the Central African Europeans. This aspiration of the Preamble has failed to produce what was expected of it. So, alas, has one of the fundamental and binding constitutional safeguards, the African Affairs Board.

It is constitutionally a Standing Committee of the Federal Assembly, and consists of the three European members for African interests and one of the "special" African members from each territory.[1] Its present members are the Rev. J. Pretorius, and Mr. C. J. Matinga (Nyasaland), Mr. R. Moffat and Mr. J. A. Lewanika (Northern Rhodesia) and Mr. H. Davies and Mr. C. M. Chipunza (Southern Rhodesia). Some of these are Federal Party members elected by a predominantly European vote, so that the Board's sympathies are unlikely to be against the Government in any extreme way; but this is no criticism of its impartiality.

Its job is to act as a watchdog against the introduction of any legislation by the Federal legislature which may be a "differentiating measure". A "differentiating measure" is defined as "a Bill or instrument by which Africans are subjected to any conditions, restrictions or disabilities disadvantageous to them to which Europeans are not also subjected or made liable". Its most important power is to request the Governor-General of the Federation to withhold assent from any bill passed by the Federal Legislature which it considers a differentiating measure. Any such bill will then be "reserved for the signification of Her Majesty's approval" which means in practice for the consideration, and eventual amendment or veto, of the House of Commons. The Board also has the power to report any "subordinate legislation" (such as regulations made by the Federal Government under authority conferred on it by the Legislature) as a differentiating measure to the British Government. The British Government may, in this case, annul any such "subordinate legislation" within twelve months of its receipt of the report from the African Affairs Board.

In effect, therefore, any major or subordinate legislation of the Federal Government or Legislature which the Board reports as differentiating is likely to be debated in the House of Commons and to be dealt with according to the policy of the party which commands a majority in the House.

The African Affairs Board could have been a powerful influence in favour of interracial justice and in defence of African rights if Britain had been ready to back it up. When it decided to act, it was composed of the most moderate, sober individuals, both European

[1] See table on p. 86.

and African, under the chairmanship of Sir John Moffat, a member of Livingstone's family and a man no one has ever accused of being a firebrand. In 1957 it declared the Federal Constitution Amendment Bill to be discriminatory and differentiating, as it unquestionably was. Its purpose was to enlarge the Federal Parliament by twenty-four seats. By allotting an increased number of seats to Africans, as racial representatives specifically, it put up a smoke-screen of liberalism. Behind this it increased the ratio of European representatives to the total number of the population, which was its real aim. It was the groundwork for the new Federal Electoral Law, which was introduced shortly afterwards and was also discriminatory and differentiating. The Conservative Government in Britain took the side of the Federal Government against the African Affairs Board and asked Parliament to reject its protest, which it did, as a matter of party discipline. Neither the Colonial Secretary nor the Under-Secretary for Commonwealth Relations appeared to show the remotest interest in whether the measures complained of were really discriminatory and differentiating. They refused to depart one inch from the party line of the Federal Government's controversial and vulnerable White Paper rebutting the Board's report; and by making the matter a party issue, and uncritically backing the Federal Government, deprived Britain of her role of impartial referee. African confidence not only in the African Affairs Board but in the integrity of the British Parliament and nation, and in the validity of all British promises to the Northern Protectorates, was destroyed. The African Affairs Board was reduced to a constitutional cipher, a mere unnecessary letter and, realizing that no one had the slightest intention of listening to it however good its grounds and well-reasoned its arguments, has not said another word from that day to this. The Federal Government went triumphantly on its short-sighted way.

Certain powers, regarding especially Federal acquisition of African land and the amendment of the Constitution, are reserved for the decision of the United Kingdom. The British Government has been no more than the compliant tool of the Federal when such questions have arisen. The Constitution provides for a review of itself and its working by delegations from the British, Federal and Territorial Governments, to take place between 1960 and 1962. This review will be held in the Autumn of 1960, after the Monckton Commission has reported, and Britain's attitude to it has yet to be made plain. Though it is possible to feel more hope for the future in January 1960

CHAPTER IV

The General Constitutional Machinery

The rest of the Federal Constitution need not detain us long. It attempts to define the relation between three quite differently constituted locally autonomous states under the overriding authority of a Federal Parliament elected by voters in all three. The Federal capital is Salisbury, which is also the capital and seat of government of Southern Rhodesia. The Federal head of state is the Governor-General (at present Lord Dalhousie) who is a constitutional figure-head representing the Crown as the Governor-General of Canada or Australia does. He accepts the advice of Federal Ministers and he has no power to govern or initiate legislation. He gives the Royal Assent to Federal legislation and may withhold it, but only within the strict limits laid down by the Constitution concerning differentiation against Africans and the specific subjects we have mentioned. He would do so only on the advice of British Ministers, by whom, with the concurrence of the Federal Government, he is appointed. It should never be forgotten that the Constitution reserves to the British Parliament the right to veto such types of Federal legislation, even though no government will use it that is not prepared for a major row with the Federal Government.

Each territory has its own governor, representing the Crown there independently of the Governor-General of the Federation. The Governor of Southern Rhodesia is another constitutional figure-head, advised by the elected ministers of Southern Rhodesia, and responsible for giving the Royal Assent to bills of the Southern Rhodesian Parliament. He has the right to withhold it in certain circumstances and refer them to the British Parliament but, as we have noted, this right has not once been used in thirty-six years. The governorship of Southern Rhodesia is an honorific position and must be one of the least exacting in the world.

The Governor of Nyasaland is a full-blown colonial governor. He not only represents the Crown. He is head of the executive, his own

Prime Minister. He controls a majority in the Legislative Council.[1] This does not mean that he can govern without regard to it but that in the last resort he can always carry it with him. He is, under the authority of the Colonial Secretary, the active head of the Government—as far as his own local autonomy goes. He could not under any circumstances touch any function reserved to the Federal Government.

The Governor of Northern Rhodesia used to have similar powers, but they have been very considerably diluted, first by an amendment to the Constitution introduced in 1953 and later by the new Constitution brought in by Mr. Alan Lennox-Boyd in 1959. It is now possible for the governor to be outvoted on the executive by the unofficial members, who are independent of him and, though this would be an unlikely event, decisive power has passed into the hands of any political party which gains a clear majority in the representative election introduced by the 1959 Constitution. Since it is a system which represents mainly Europeans, under the franchise described on pages 83–85, this is at present the United Federal Party. This significant qualification of the principle of allowing the inhabitants to enjoy separate governments (for it is straining truth to describe the territorial U.F.P. in this way) "under the special protection of Her Majesty, for so long as they desire" has been achieved by detailed constitutional provisions without any open attack on Colonial Office rule.

Thus, the constitutional situation is different in each territory. The authority of the Federal Government is the same over all. This produces such an intricate network of power relationships and such a complex series of constitutional problems that on the whole the simplest thing turns out to be for everyone to do as little as possible except the Federal Government whose authority is open to no sort of question. It also provides the necessity of four governors, four parliaments and cabinets, four separate constitutions, four different but, between the Federation and the territories, overlapping franchises, four distinct civil services, two prime ministers with the promise of more to come and, consequently, an enormous amount of palaver and expense. All this is essential if the Federation is to attain,

[1] For the method of its appointment, see pp. 82–3. There is no direct election to the Legislature. African members are appointed by the Governor on the recommendation of African local councils; non-Africans directly elected by non-Africans. The number of seats for each racial group—and therefore its proportionate influence—is laid down by the Constitution.

even on paper, the balance of forces and interests it must have. But for a country of eight million inhabitants it is a pretty good crop of brass and problems and one wonders, all the more since it has not so far fulfilled its intentions in practice, whether the complication of the scheme alone might not have given a warning of the fallaciousness of the whole conception.

Each territory has its own civil service for dealing with internal affairs. Southern Rhodesia's is organized and recruited by the local government; the other two are composed of British colonial servants but arrangements exist for their progressive transfer to the Federal civil service, and this is likely further to undermine territorial autonomy, such as it is. The Federation organizes and recruits a civil service of its own which operates in the Federal offices in Salisbury and, as far as Federal Government functions are concerned, in the three territories also. Thus, for instance, the customs and immigration officers in Northern Rhodesia and Nyasaland are Federal officials. They are generally Southern Rhodesians or young Britishers who have been indoctrinated with the Salisbury ethos. And one is asked to believe that the manner in which they deal with young Nyasaland Africans travelling to and from their work in Johannesburg, the attitude they adopt to them at frontier posts, is not a local African interest and does not affect the Africans' sense of human dignity as citizens of an allegedly free Protectorate. It is not that they ill-treat them but that they treat them according to the ways of the self-governing colony of Southern Rhodesia and not of the Nyasaland Protectorate.

Medical and health services, which are on the Concurrent List but have been "federalized", are controlled by Federal civil servants. Policy decisions tend to be taken in distant Salisbury by officials who have little knowledge of local conditions in the territories, and may well be out of sympathy with their racial policies. This leads to a great deal of confusion and frustration and the doctors on the spot will tell you that they find it a great deal easier to get what Salisbury thinks good for them than what they really need. Even those more intimately concerned with the internal administration of African life within the territories suffer from the sense of serving two masters. It is hard to be certain which of the multifarious matters a District Commissioner has to pass on to higher authority will be decided by the local government, by people aware of local needs and customs and in touch with British Protectorate policy, and which will go up to Federal level. Nor can the D.C. any longer be sure when a civil servant from Salisbury may turn up in his district with a Federal policy or scheme unrelated to what he and his government are trying to achieve. Exasperation among D.C.s, especially in Nyasaland, is very noticeable and one of them described the situation aptly when he said: "We've been told Federation has got to work. We're not allowed even to think about whether it can."

Finance and taxation are centralized in the hands of the Federal Government. All major taxation, affecting Europeans principally (such as personal income-tax, company profits tax, and export duties), is levied by the Federal Exchequer. The Federal Government is required by the Constitution to repay, after deducting the cost of collection, fixed proportions of the whole revenue to the territorial governments, namely, 13 per cent to Southern Rhodesia, 17 per cent to Northern Rhodesia and 6 per cent to Nyasaland. Any territorial legislature may impose additional taxation on the income or profits of its own subjects (known as a territorial surcharge). This will be collected by the Federal Government and paid to the territorial after the costs of collection have been deducted. African poll tax or hut tax is collected by the territorial governments.[1] Loans required from the external money market by either Federal or territorial governments must be negotiated through the Federal Loan Council on which all are represented.

The major part of the Federal revenue comes from the companies' profits tax and the largest part of this has till lately been paid by the Northern Rhodesian copper mines.[2] The 6 per cent of the Federal revenue paid to Nyasaland, with its minute number of personal income-tax payers, and its few commercial and industrial undertakings, certainly represents a very considerable subvention. Nyasaland gets back several million pounds more than it contributes. This is the basis of the Federalist argument that Nyasaland must remain in Federation for its own good, that Federation has conferred enormous economic benefits on Nyasaland, which it must not be allowed to give up even if it wants to, and that Nyasaland could not survive without Federation. As against this, it must be remembered that the Nyasaland Government has lost to the Federal substantial sources of revenue such as customs and excise; that Nyasaland, before Federation, was

[1] There are 120 Africans paying income tax, because they alone come in the income-tax bracket according to the latest available Federal Income Tax Annual Returns.

[2] For the position last year, see p. 217.

able to balance its own budget; and that neither the productive capacity of the Nyasaland economy nor the general standard of living has increased significantly if at all since Federation. No important new industries have been established there, though they are greatly needed. The main development has been concentrated in Southern Rhodesia. The 6 per cent of the Federal revenue has been treated more as a grant in aid for the improvement of existing services than as a development fund to transform or expand the economy and much of it has not been used productively. The extent of the real benefit of Federation to Nyasaland is an extremely debatable economic point.[1] There are grounds for believing that it is positively disadvantageous. It is certainly not indispensable.

The belief that Nyasaland cannot survive without Federation has been sedulously fostered by those who, for reasons unconnected with Nyasaland's welfare, want to keep the Federation intact. Sir Roy Welensky said in the Federal Parliament on 7th April 1959: "For the sake of its own people, Nyasaland should not be called upon to stand on its own feet. It could not do so now and there is no indication of it being able to do so for many years to come. Left to itself it would degenerate into what has been termed by economists a rural slum, and it has been well put in the United Kingdom that Nyasaland is not essential to the Federation but that the Federation is to Nyasaland." This kind of argument has led a lot of people in Britain who are opposed to compulsion as a general principle to believe that Nyasaland is a tragic exception, a country which must be forced to accept for the sake of economic survival a political system which is revolting to it. If it were true, Nyasaland would be unique in political and economic history.

There is no such thing as a country which can only stand on its own feet economically in one particular set of circumstances. Every community depends upon a balance between political and economic factors and it is best if this balance is decided by the majority of the community, not by an arbitrary external force. Britain could improve her general standard of living by becoming the newest state in the U.S.A. The reasons for which she does not apply for membership are the same as Nyasaland's reasons for rejecting Federation.

An independent Nyasaland survived with only a very modest amount of British assistance for sixty years before Federation. It

[1] For illuminating discussions see Guy Clutton-Brock, *Dawn in Nyasaland*, Hodder and Stoughton, 1959, pp. 162–74.

balanced its budget in the year or two immediately preceding Federation. That is, it received no subsidy from the British Treasury and required none. It participated in the Colonial Development and Welfare Fund in the same way as almost every other dependent territory. It could survive quite as well in the future. It could expand its economy if outside capital were made available to do the two things Federation has not done: establish a reasonable amount of industry in a few centres and found a system of co-operative farming and land development for its peasant population. There are possibilities of closer association with Tanganyika (and with Northern Rhodesia, if it became an African country) which offer more stability and prosperity than Federation in the present circumstances possibly can. Under Federation, Nyasaland has been starved of development capital, which has gone primarily to Southern Rhodesia. Virtually no industry has been started and the organization of peasant agriculture has not been tackled, though the territorial authorities have done what they can to develop the land, against the handicaps of lack of means and of imaginative planning.

The African standard of living has not risen significantly and the young men still go to seek their fortunes in Southern Rhodesia or South Africa, and are encouraged by officially sponsored schemes to do so. Southern Rhodesia's ability to absorb Nyasaland labour is diminishing but so far little has been done to provide alternative work. The Federation has shown no inclination to help Nyasaland to become a self-supporting country in which its people can live prosperously at home. It continues to regard it as a source of migrant labour, and a land of impoverished peasants, instead of providing opportunities for industrial and agricultural development. Considering the world capital available for under-developed countries, and the relative smallness of Nyasaland's total requirements, there is a strong case for believing that Nyasaland could be better, not worse, off as an independent country in control of its own economy than it is in the leading strings of Federation. For Sir Roy's solicitude to be convincing, he should provide the necessary capital rather than weep crocodile tears over Nyasaland's poverty. The reason "there is no indication of its being able to stand on its own feet for many years to come" is that the Federation has done nothing to help it. Six per cent of the Federal budget makes Nyasaland a stationary pensioner, not a developing country. And political frustration paralyses the efforts of its inhabitants.

Even if Nyasaland gained much more than it does from Federation, the crucial fact would remain that under the existing constitutional arrangements the money available is spent according to European wisdom, not according to the wishes or, very often, the needs of the African population. Such development as takes place proceeds according to European conception of what is good for the Africans, and this, in their eyes, vitiates its benefits. Suspicion of the two governments, which has been consolidated by the events of 1959, is an immovable obstacle to confidence and co-operation. It will continue to be one at least until Africans can see some very much more solid advantages than they have so far received.

Propaganda from Central Africa about the benefits of Federation to Africans needs to be read with caution. Sir Gilbert Rennie's answer to the Church of Scotland's criticisms of the position in Nyasaland, published under the rather juvenile title *Why not be fair?* is little more than an extended statement that Europeans know much better than Africans what Africans really want. A somewhat one-sided pamphlet issued by the Southern Rhodesian Government and called *The Progress of Africans in Southern Rhodesia* does little to explain why none of the discriminatory restrictions on Africans discussed later in this book can be removed. And none of this propaganda takes account of the fact that the enormous majority of Africans in all three territories do not agree that they have received any benefits from Federation and earnestly desire its end.

A final twist of cumbrous complexity is that the Constitution divides British responsibility for Central Africa between two government departments and ministries in Whitehall. Federal and Southern Rhodesian affairs are handled by the Commonwealth Relations Office which during most of the Federation's history has been under Lord Home and Mr. Cuthbert Alport; the two northern territories are under the Colonial Office, which has been in the hands of Mr. Alan Lennox-Boyd. As might have been foreseen, this has not contributed to making British policy precise or clear cut. The Commonwealth Relations Office has little specialized expert knowledge of Africa and its problems may well not appear in their true light to ministers and officials accustomed to dealing with, say, Canada or New Zealand and their quite different racial minorities and constitutional situations. The Colonial Office might be expected to be more adept at the art of governing subject territories than of negotiating with a near-sovereign government. The division of responsibility, both in the House of Commons and in Africa, has made it doubly hard for Britain to keep any real control of events and has provided a camouflage of confusion for the steady entrenchment of European supremacy.

The Federal Constitution looks strong enough on paper. It has proved weak in practice because its definition of the relation between the territorial and Federal governments is too imprecise to mean anything in the absence of a real spirit of compromise and of a genuine readiness on the part of the Europeans to respect the paramountcy of African rights in the Northern Protectorates. It is not surprising that this has been found wanting since not the paramountcy but the subordination of their rights is the doctrine of the powerful European population of the Federation's senior member, Southern Rhodesia. It is questionable whether any written constitution could have made it possible for two such radically opposed racial policies to coexist and flourish under a single Federal umbrella.

It should never be forgotten that Parliament is still theoretically supreme in Central Africa. It could even take such drastic steps as revoking the Federal Order in Council and dissolving Federation, or suspending the Federal Constitution and replacing it by another. It has a perfect right to veto any Federal or Southern Rhodesian legislation that is harmful to African interests. It could insist upon the introduction of really liberal constitutions in the northern territories. But it has never for a moment considered doing any of these things. By following the Federal Government's lead throughout, it has chosen to throw away the power and influence Britain possesses and to abdicate our responsibilities to the local European populations. That these populations are hostile to African constitutional advance is conceded by even so sober an authority as *The Times*. In a leading article on the Northern Rhodesian Constitution it wrote, on 20th September 1958: "Introducing two African ministers in Northern Rhodesia is . . . a landmark in Central African history. It is bound to be unpopular among most Europeans. . . . If Northern Rhodesia or Nyasaland is to be kept anything like in line with other territories, British or French, on the African continent, they must have African representation at policy making level. . . . [The Colonial Secretary] has increased the number of African ministers from one to two and thereby provoked a hostile reaction among Europeans. . . . A critical point is being reached not only for Northern Rhodesia but for the whole Federation. Fundamental issues . . . are at stake."

Such teeth as the Constitution possessed have been drawn, or filed down, by a British Government which has consistently interpreted it in the European interest. Far from standing up for British rights and responsibilities, Mr. Lennox-Boyd assured Sir Roy Welensky, the Federal Prime Minister, in the 1957 Convention they agreed upon, that Parliament would refrain from using the right affirmed in Article 29 of the Constitution to "make laws for the Federation of the Territories" except at the Federal Government's request.[1] Broadly interpreted this meant a good deal more than it says and Sir Roy was not mistaken in taking it as a blank cheque in his favour.

The African Affairs Board was overruled on his electoral policy and reduced to impotence. And the Government's conception of African rights and interests in the northern territories has been so narrow as to deny them any real protection. Northern Rhodesia and Nyasaland have not been brought into line with other territories, British or French, on the African continent. They are steadily being forced to keep step with Southern Rhodesia. What the Federal Constitution teaches us is that there is no longer such a thing as "Native policy" in a vacuum, distinct from the policies affecting other members of the community. This is the basic fallacy that undermines it. African interests are the interests of the whole society and society must be conceived as an integrated whole united by rights and obligations common to all. Africans, whether "educated and Westernized" or still "ignorant and illiterate", have realized this and will not put up with anything less. To conceive of African interests as merely a matter of land tenure, native law and custom and segregated education amid the rapid development of European industry and commerce in a powerful Federal state is to relegate them to neglect. The fundamental principle of the Preamble, that the northern territories are to retain their present separate governments subject to the ultimate responsibility of Britain, has failed because the separate governments have so little to govern about and Britain has not discharged her responsibilities.

Let Lord Hailey sum up the position: "The Constitution as finally enacted makes it clear that the two Protectorates are to retain the right to enjoy separate governments for as long as their respective

[1] Such "conventions" have been made between Britain and various Dominions. But none of these has had the same problems, or involved Britain's obligations to subject races, as the Federation does.

peoples desire, their governments remaining responsible (subject to the ultimate authority of the Government of the United Kingdom) for the control of land in their territories and for the local and territorial political advancement of their peoples."[1] He goes on:[2] "It remains to be seen how far it will serve the purpose originally aimed at. The structure of the Federation is essentially a compromise. . . . Southern Rhodesia has gained the financial advantage which Federation seemed to open to it. . . . On the other hand the formal association now established with the two Protectorates seems likely to constrain the European community of Southern Rhodesia to make larger (or at all events earlier) concessions to African claims than would otherwise have been the case."

This might have happened if Britain had resolutely maintained the Protectorates as strongholds of liberalism. The contradiction was that, since Africans in both of them abhorred the idea of Federation with Southern Rhodesia, they had to be forced into it against their will. And this involved the sacrifice at the outset of those liberal principles which the Protectorates were supposed subsequently to exemplify. Lacking their stimulus, the European communities of Southern Rhodesia have not made either larger, or earlier, concessions to African claims. They could see no reason why they should. One hears a lot, for example, about liberal advances in Southern Rhodesia since Federation. It all boils down to very little. Parliament, we are told, has passed the Industrial Conciliation Act, which for the first time in history accords African workers the legal standing of "employees" and provides for interracial trade unions. But its real effect is to give European workers special voting rights within these unions so as to ensure European control of them.[3] An amendment has been made to the Land Apportionment Act to permit

[1] *Hailey*, p. 279.

[2] Ibid., p. 281.

[3] Compare the two following quotations from the Salisbury *Sunday Mail*:

"January 1 was a remarkable day for the workers of Southern Rhodesia. The coming into force of the Industrial Conciliation Act marks a new epoch in the Colony's trade unionism. . . . Under the Act only one union can be officially registered to represent workers in a particular job in Government-aided conciliatory negotiations. That union must be multi-racial—and there is no way of squirming out of it. The Act does not allow a European minority to control a union by manipulation of voting powers." (*Sunday Mail*, 3rd January 1960.)

"Trade unionists and S.R. Government labour officials have discovered a loophole in the Industrial Conciliation Act which is political dynamite . . . it has been found that the Act actually allows European minorities to control multiracial unions with majorities of African members by manipulation of voting powers." (*Sunday Mail*, 10th January 1960.)

the establishment of hotels prepared to receive black and white under the same roof, but only two have as yet been started. Separate entrances and counters for the two races in Post Offices have been abolished. The Federal and territorial governments are making all they can of this pitiful record in the hope of convincing the outside world that these are significant advances and of distracting attention from the abuses that remain. Mr. Jasper Savanhu, Federal Under-Secretary for Home Affairs with special responsibility for Race Relations, claimed in London on 8th September 1959 that Federation was giving people a lead towards abolishing the colour bar. "Under Federation, the colour bar is no longer as serious as it used to be. Hotels in Southern Rhodesia can now apply for multi-racial licences and the separate entrances in Post Offices for African and European members of the community have been abolished. No hotels however have yet applied for multi-racial licences since the Act was passed and this only shows that the Government can only do a limited amount unless it is genuinely supported in its measures."

Yet when the Act allowing interracial hotels was debated in the Southern Rhodesian Parliament in February 1959, discriminatory legislation was described, by speakers from the powerful Dominion Party opposition, as the thing "upon which the whole racial structure of this country has been built", as "the cornerstone of our society" and "the Magna Charta of the European". And in August of the same year, an opposition motion was presented to Parliament which read that "in no circumstances should this House agree to any arrangement with the British Government whereby Southern Rhodesia, under Federation, was subjected potentially or actually to the political domination of the African electorate of Northern Rhodesia and Nyasaland". It was replaced by a Government Party motion which read that "this House will not be able to agree to any arrangement with the British Government, under Federation, which failed to remove the existing restrictions on the Southern Rhodesian Parliament in the territorial sphere and failed to ensure that government remained in the hands of civilized people in the Federal sphere". Both say the same thing—that Southern Rhodesia is determined to restrict the political influence of Africans in the northern territories. The latter says it, though more obliquely, considerably more strongly since it claims, in defiance of the Federal Constitution, a greater territorial autonomy for Southern Rhodesia than is allowed the Protectorates. Lord Hailey's hope has not been

CHAPTER V

The Franchise

I am reluctant to lead the reader deeper than necessary into the horrible complexities of the Federal and Northern Rhodesian franchises. But the means of choosing the government is important to the working of the Constitution. I shall try as far as possible to describe the general principles and leave out the details. The intention evident behind all the franchise arrangements in force in Central Africa can be described in two ways, which both mean the same thing in the end. One can say that it is to keep decisive political power in European hands for as long as may be, if possible for ever; or that it is to withhold political power from Africans until they are able to use it properly. Probably a third description is more accurate. The objective of the Central African franchises is to keep the decisive vote away from Africans so long as they cannot be relied upon to use it in the way Europeans would like them to. This could be a benevolent or a repressive intention according to what Europeans *would* like them to do. But Europeans would like Africans to vote for the continuation of European privilege and this makes the chances of the easy development of a liberal interracial democracy a little remote under the existing Constitution. Whether a liberal interracial democracy is the best political pattern for these countries is a different question; but it was the declared aim of the British Parliament when it imposed Federation.

THE TERRITORIAL FRANCHISE

(*i*) *Southern Rhodesia*

The theories underlying the Southern Rhodesian franchise, and the difficulties of changing it, are discussed in Chapter XVIII. Here we need describe only the machinery of the electoral law introduced by Mr. Todd's Rhodesia Party Government (it soon afterwards became the territorial branch of the Federal Party) in 1957.

The Assembly has thirty seats, representing single member constituencies. There is no special representation for Africans or any other race and there are no nominated members. All Members are elected by a common roll divided into two parts, the ordinary and the special. The qualification for the ordinary roll is literacy (i.e. the ability to fill in the voter's application form in English, which a voter may be required to do in the presence of the returning officer) plus either

(*a*) £720 per annum or property worth £1,500

or

(*b*) £480 per annum or property worth £1,000 plus complete primary education

or

(*c*) £300 per annum or property worth £500 plus four years' completed secondary education.

The qualification for the special roll is literacy plus either

(*a*) £240 a year

or

(*b*) £120 plus two years' completed secondary education.

The minimum age for the vote is 21, as it is in the Federal and Northern Rhodesia franchise. A voter must be a Southern Rhodesian or Federal citizen. The alternative vote, which aims at obtaining a clear majority by making use of the second choices of those whose first choice was a lost cause, is employed in Southern Rhodesia but nowhere else in the Federation.

The law lays down that a vote cast by a special voter has exactly the same value as one cast by an ordinary voter but as soon as "the total number of registered special voters is equal to twenty per centum of registered ordinary voters", no further enrolment of special voters may take place.

This means exactly what it says. When the number of people of all races who have *registered* for a vote, not cast it, on grounds of £240 a year or ten years at school is 20 per cent of all those who register for a vote on any other qualification, £240 a year or ten years' schooling ceases to be a qualification for a vote. The roll is closed *for good*, to this qualification. Only *new legislation* could open it again. Two men may have the same qualification: one gets the vote, the other is debarred from it on statistical grounds. The election candidate is virtually assured that not more than one-sixth of his constituents will be African. He need not consider the African portion of the electorate at all, except in one or two very unusual constituencies, and, though a minute proportion of Africans is entitled to cast a vote (the number is about 16,900 in all, special and ordinary, out of 2,800,000, as against 75,500 Europeans among 219,000), it confers no effective representation whatever.

Mr. Todd would probably have liked a much wider franchise, but he knew the electorate would not accept it. He had an amazing amount of trouble in getting even this through, and it was one of the things that caused his ultimate fall. He was forced to speak with brutal frankness about his franchise law to persuade the European public to accept it. "The truth," he said, "is that we are raising the qualifications in every way." He went on to point out that the bill was designed to limit the number who actually voted on the low qualification "to a fraction and would eventually close that door permanently after which literacy must be combined with £60 a month. Money qualification will, in the future, be checked against the value of the pound."[1] He went on: "The new law will be a fulfilment of our promise made at the last election to legislate before the next election to ensure that the present inadequate franchise law is replaced by one which will guarantee that civilization will remain secure in Southern Rhodesia."[2]

Mr. Todd has subsequently resigned and come out publicly for a much truer conception of interracialism. That a man as honest and humane as he is (he would probably be a Bow Group Conservative in Britain) should have been forced as Prime Minister to sponsor such a masterpiece of mendacious reaction as the Southern Rhodesian franchise emphasizes the important moral that it matters very little who is Prime Minister of Southern Rhodesia. The white electorate rules. These retrograde proposals caused a storm of protest among the European electorate, in Parliament, and in Todd's own party because "they went too far".

Mr. Todd and his few liberal friends hoped that, though the representation given to Africans was clearly nugatory and risible, the psychological effect of enabling some fifteen thousand of them to vote would be good; that it would be taken as evidence of European goodwill. This attitude underestimated the political maturity

[1] Most Africans were encouraged by this to believe that when they approach any qualification in any large number, it will be raised.

[2] Mr. Garfield Todd, reported in *Rhodesia Herald*, 16th July 1957.

of the African population. They saw that they were being offered a toy, not a means of political expression, and they had no desire to play with it.[1] The fact that only a few thousand Africans, out of the 15,000 or so who may qualify for it, have registered for the special vote is quoted by Rhodesian Europeans as evidence of the political apathy of the black population. "We have proved they don't even want the vote." This demonstrates the gap in understanding between the two races. Africans recognized that there was nothing progressive about the franchise; their failure to register is a gesture of intelligent pride against an imposture that insults the intelligence and a refusal to assist their European rulers in making a liberal advertisement out of a retrogressive system. The Government would like to be able to say "Fifteen thousand Africans voted in our last election" without explaining why their votes had no influence. To deny it this opportunity by abstaining is about the only means of political expression Africans can find.

The objection to any form of qualified franchise, and to the Southern Rhodesian one in particular, is that the governing class is in a position to make up the electorate to suit its taste by the qualifications it lays down. The policies of the Ministry of Native Affairs and the Department of Native Education control to a great extent the limits of African educational and economic attainment. The existing franchise qualifications were fixed after close consultation with both these departments and on a basis of their statistical forecast of the rate of African progress, with a view to ensuring an overwhelming electoral minority for Africans.

(*ii*) *Nyasaland*

The Nyasaland Executive Council is appointed by the Governor. The Legislative Council consists of twelve civil servants *ex officio*, six representatives of the non-African community (European and Asian) elected on a non-African roll by constituencies, and some African members. Up to 1959 five African members were recommended to the Governor for appointment by a system of indirect election from what are, roughly, African district councils. They did, to a certain

[1] The illusory nature of the franchise was increased by the revised delimitation of constituencies which had the effect of breaking up what few large blocks of African voters there might have been. Africans who had begun to register for the vote, on the advice of their leaders to use what civic rights they possessed, stopped when they realized this. The subject is too complex for description here. See C. T. Leys, *European Politics in Southern Rhodesia*, O.U.P., 1959, pp. 231–34.

extent, represent the African popular will. All were Congressmen. Most of them have been to jail and have been deprived of their seats by the Governor since 1959. There were five African legislators to eighteen others in a population of 3 million Africans and about 10,000 other races. The Colonial Secretary has announced that this system with a few insignificant alterations described below will continue until at least May 1961 as a result of the 1959 Emergency, although a new and more liberal territorial constitution has long been promised to Nyasaland.[1] The fact that it was overdue was one of the causes of the 1959 rioting.

After the 1959 Emergency, the Governor decided to appoint two more African members to the Council[2] and two Africans to the executive and to replace the dismissed Congress members by his own nominees. The system of government by appointment works well enough at a certain stage of the development of a colonial territory, so long as the Governor is pursuing the best interests of his subjects, so long as they consent to his general policies and have complete confidence in him and his master, the Colonial Secretary. These conditions have not obtained in Nyasaland since Federation was imposed. The 1959 Emergency arose because Africans had lost confidence in British rule. The prospects of good or stable government under this system are poor. The attempt to restore confidence by appointing one or two more Africans to the Legislative or Executive Councils is unlikely to succeed. It creates an impression of liberal advance in the world Press but is meaningless at home. There is nothing liberal about it and it does not increase African representation. For the Governor will obviously appoint Africans who support his, and the Colonial Office's, policy. If the majority of Africans are against this policy, the Governor's nominees cannot represent African wishes and the colour of their skin is irrelevant. It is nothing but racialism to suppose that any Africans chosen by the Governor will do to represent Africans. They do not enjoy African confidence and might as well be European.

Nyasaland participates in the Federal franchise under the arrangements described presently.

(*iii*) *Northern Rhodesia*

Northern Rhodesia was ruled by Governors appointed in the same

[1] It now appears possible that Mr. Lennox-Boyd's successor may act sooner.
[2] One of them has since resigned as a result of demonstrations of his unpopularity in his home village.

way as Nyasaland until 1958 when a new Constitution was introduced by the Colonial Secretary. Voting for the Legislative Council and territorial government took place for the first time early in 1959. The franchise follows the general lines of the Federal franchise and suffers from the same defects. It contains certain refinements of complexity, such as two members who must be European but are elected mainly by Africans, and two Africans elected mainly by Europeans, to cater for the uneven distribution of population in the country and the great concentration of both races on the copperbelt and along the line of rail which serves it, but these do not affect the issue. The significant difference between the Northern Rhodesian and Federal Assemblies is that the former is still a compromise between rule by governor's appointment and rule by an electorate, the latter is almost wholly elective. The compromise is more ostensible than real in that there are only six nominated officials, and two other Governor's nominees, to twenty-two elected members in a House of thirty. But it is still true that the largest *single* bloc in the Northern Rhodesian Legislature, and the Executive Council, is nominated by the Governor.[1] Two of the elected members must be African and two must be European under the Constitution. All other seats are open to any race. This attempt to reduce the racial element in politics would be laudable if it were accompanied by an extension of the franchise. Its result without this, in the territorial election of 1959, was to return nine Africans (*including* two not elected but nominated by the Governor) to an African population of nearly 3 million, and thirteen Europeans to a European population of 80,000.

The Executive Council of ministers consists of four civil servants, and six unofficial members, of whom two must be Africans. All are appointed by the Governor, but he is obliged to choose the unofficial non-African ministers from the party which wins the majority of elected seats. The result of this first election under the new Constitution has been to give predominant power to the territorial branch of the Federal Government Party, Sir Roy Welensky's United Federal Party, which certainly is not supported by the majority of Africans. Most Africans look to the National Inde-

[1]As we have seen, they can be outvoted by unanimity among the unofficials, if the Africans go along with the Europeans. This can easily happen, since most African members are elected by a mainly European vote and represent the Federal Party, which enjoys the support of most Europeans and few Africans.

pendence Party, the successor to the Zambia National Congress, which was proscribed by the Governor shortly before the election.

THE FEDERAL FRANCHISE

The basis of the Federal, as well as the Northern and Southern Rhodesian, franchises is the common roll principle. They are at great pains to avoid anything that looks like racial discrimination or communal representation. All citizens of all races, colours, communities and creeds who qualify for a vote are on the same electoral roll, all ordinary seats may be contested and held by candidates of any race. Ministerial appointments are open to all races. There are forty-four ordinary seats in the Federal Parliament, which are technically open to all races, and fifteen special ones for the representation of Africans.

The composition of the assembly and the distribution of seats between the territories is set out in a table on the following page.

There are forty-seven European Members in the present House and twelve Africans. This is the minimum number of Africans demanded by the Constitution. None of the forty-four ordinary seats, which alone are open to members of any race, is held by an African; all are occupied by Europeans.

The United Federal Party has forty-four Members in Parliament out of fifty-nine. Thirty-seven are European, seven are African special members, nearly all of whom are elected by a predominantly European electorate. The Dominion Party has eight Members including one African. There is one Independent. The four Africans returned by the African Councils and the two Europeans nominated by the Governor do not represent any party.

The special seats are intended to counterbalance an admitted tendency of the system to under-represent Africans in present conditions. But this is thought of as a temporary expedient and the Federal Electoral Law assumes that Africans will become increasingly able to compete with Europeans on equal terms so that special representation can be progressively abolished. Whether this assumption is justified by the results of Federation so far is questionable. Anyhow, the theoretical foundation of the franchise is undiscriminatory representation by single members elected by a common, interracial roll of all those entitled to vote. It is sound democratic theory, made in England and imported, perhaps even smuggled in, in the

	Territory	Seats
A. *Ordinary Seats* (Elected by the Ordinary, predominantly European, roll)	Southern Rhodesia	24
	Northern Rhodesia	14
	Nyasaland	6
Registered Voters		44
European 85,968		
Africans 1,697		
Other races 3,979		
B. *Special Seats* (Elected by the Ordinary (mainly European) and Special, predominantly African, roll jointly)	Southern Rhodesia	4 (who must b African)
Registered Special Voters		1 (who must b a Europea representin African interests)
European 169		
African 4,877		
Other races 61		5
Registered Voters (Ordinary and Special)	Northern Rhodesia	2 (who must b African)
European 86,137	Nyasaland	2 (who must b African)
African 6,574		
Other races 4,040		
C. African Members elected indirectly by African Local Councils	Northern Rhodesia	2 (who must b African)
	Nyasaland	2 (who must b African)
D. European Members appointed by the Governor of the territory to represent African interests	Northern Rhodesia	1 (who must b European)
	Nyasaland	1 (who must b European)
		59 in all

COMPOSITION OF THE FEDERAL PARLIAMENT

1953 Constitution, to parts of the world that had never given much thought to the parliamentary representation of non-Europeans.

The principle of the common roll encountered another principle firmly held by the European population—that political power must remain in the hands of civilized people. This sounds common sense until one begins trying to define civilized people. Most Europeans in Central Africa believe quite honestly that most Africans are not civilized people and will remain for a long time their inferiors; democratic theory, to work at all, must postulate a reasonable degree of equality between all citizens and a fairly free access for most of them to the common roll. In democratic theory, if over 90 per cent of the population is African, predominant political power will belong to Africans. But, if Africans are really uncivilized, in such a way that their influence would endanger the common weal, means must be found of excluding them from the common roll. The Federal franchise has been obliged, by the conflicting theories on which it is founded, to operate the common roll in such a way as to keep most Africans off it; that is to say, to use a principle which aims at comprehensive, inclusive representation for the purpose of excluding most of the population from political rights. The belief that to put political power into the hands of the African majority would endanger not only the privileges of a European minority but the true well-being of all is incompatible with the beliefs which sustain common roll democracy. In its practical application, therefore, little remains except the name. There is so much distortion and evasion, prevarication and qualification that it would be hard to recognize the system as a common roll if it were not labelled. And it is so full of ambiguities and pretences that it is hard to describe in normal terminology.

For instance, everyone knows that in practice the Federal M.P. for, say, Salisbury or Broken Hill or any other "ordinary constituency", will, under the existing constitution, be a European, elected by Europeans, for at least a generation to come. But the Constitution does not stipulate that this must be the case, and few will admit what everyone knows. It is argued—and by none so hotly as by the Federal Government and by the Member for Broken Hill, the Federal Prime Minister—that there is no reason at all why he should not be an African. This is perfectly true—except that the way the Constitution is applied renders it impossible. It is considered most unfair to describe the forty-four ordinary seats as European seats, because they are not specifically reserved for Europeans. Their occupants just turn out to be Europeans, in the same way as the Members for Bournemouth or Kensington turn out to be Conservatives, but with the difference that the majority of inhabitants, as opposed to electors, in ordinary constituencies would probably choose to be represented by Africans if they were enfranchised. In order to avoid the repetition of such phrases as "seats which in practice are likely to be filled by Europeans", I shall describe seats or Members certain to be European as "European seats or Members". But it must be clear that there are no seats in the Federal Parliament reserved for European occupants as racial representatives though there are fifteen for representatives of Africans.

The Federal franchise modifies—or should one say violates?—the common roll principle by dividing the electorate into two separate classes, ordinary and special voters. The distinction between them is in no sense racial. It is based upon property and education. But it so happens that the lines are drawn in such a way that almost every European in the Federation is an ordinary voter, while very few Africans can be; and that, though only about 1 per cent of Africans qualify even for the special roll, almost all special voters are African. Since the special vote is weak and the ordinary vote powerful, this works out as discriminatory racial representation masquerading as ideal common roll democracy. It gives the substance of power to Europeans and consigns an illusory shadow to Africans.[1] The electoral law achieves this most ingeniously without ever mentioning racial discrimination. It combines the advantages of a liberal advertisement to the outside world with the secure maintenance of European supremacy within the Federation. And its complexity is so great that outside observers cannot detect the illusion without a great deal of laborious study of niggling details. The Federal European can claim with absolute honesty that there are no racial politics in the Federation and no electoral discrimination; the common roll is completely open to all races. He need not admit, and often genuinely does not seem to realize, that he is describing a theory; that in

[1] The number of Africans on the ordinary roll, the only one with real power, is estimated at under 2,000 to about 80,000 Europeans. Reliable figures about enfranchisement are very hard to get as many Africans are reluctant to participate in what they realize is a charade designed to bolster up white supremacy and refrain from either registering or voting. Some do not properly understand that they are entitled to vote. And others, especially in Southern Rhodesia, fear that they may get up against the Native Commissioner by using their rights.

practice the ordinary roll is a European roll and the forty-four Members elected by it are European representatives of a European minority. It is true that lots of Africans—perhaps as many as 60,000—have the chance of registering for and casting some sort of vote in an election. And the total of European voters is only about 85,000. It is just a pity that things are so arranged that the votes of Africans have not the slightest chance of influencing the outcome, that they might as well have been playing skittles as voting. The procedure is sometimes described as "giving Africans practice in using the vote" but this is just what it is not. It is practice in making a meaningless cross on an insignificant piece of paper. And it is training in electoral irresponsibility to give people formal votes which they know cannot possibly affect the issue.

The basic qualification for the ordinary (the more powerful) vote is £720 a year. This applies to all races with no sort of discrimination. The average African income *per caput*, not per breadwinner, for the whole Federation is far below £30 per annum, the average European above £500.[1]

The whole economic structure makes anything like £720 a year out of the reach of more than a tiny portion of the African population until a social and economic revolution has taken place, because economic power is concentrated in European hands. And the franchise is what it is in order to prevent any economic or social revolution in favour of Africans.

Educational attainment is also a qualification for the ordinary vote. Though £720 a year confers the ordinary vote in its own right, provided you can write and read, if you have completed your primary school education you need only earn £480; if you have done four years at a secondary school, £300 a year will make you an ordinary voter.[2] Secondary education is as completely out of the reach of the majority of the Federation's seven million Africans as is £720 a year. The schools for them do not exist. There are two African grammar schools in each territory, taking a few hundred pupils each up to

[1] Federal figures of this sort are hard to compute or come by. C. T. Leys, op. cit., gives £10·7 as the average African man's income in Southern Rhodesia, £487·2 as the European. Considering the African poverty in Nyasaland and large parts of Northern Rhodesia, and European wealth on the copperbelt, the Federal African is probably below £10, the European above £500 by quite a large sum.

[2] Ministers of religion and chiefs get the vote by virtue of their office so long as they are literate.

Sixth Form standard. There are ten or twenty junior secondary schools at most in each territory but they do not equip their pupils to earn £300 a year in large numbers. The opportunities open to African children, and the economic structure of family life, debar the great majority from any secondary education at all. There is nothing approaching universal primary education; and for a large variety of economic, social and personal reasons, a sadly small population of African children who enter primary schools stay in them for long. Even universal primary education would not for a long time turn out many African pupils capable of earning £480 a year in competition with privileged Europeans. There is, however, universal primary education for Europeans, and secondary education for all Europeans with anything approaching adequate ability. Though there are many Europeans who have not this ability, there are very few who do not earn £720 a year in a country where an engine driver (an occupation still virtually reserved to Europeans) earns £1,500 and a shorthand typist little less than £1,000.

But still, if you do not get the ordinary vote, you may still get the special vote. The qualifications for this are £150 a year regardless of education, or two years at a secondary school and £120 a year. Your name will go on a different roll and you will use a different type of voting paper. *And you will only be allowed to vote for the nine racial representatives of Africans.* You will be given no part at all in electing the forty-four ordinary Members of Parliament. You will in fact not be on a common roll at all but on a special devalued, impotent list of African voters whose sole right is to elect a powerless minority of African representatives to sit beside a majority of Europeans. You will have no voice in choosing the forty-four Europeans, but, by the strangest of all the provisions of the electoral law, the European voters will vote for your representatives. The special roll does not vote for ordinary members, *but ordinary electors do vote for special members.* Every ordinary (in practice European) voter has two votes, one for his representative and one for an African; but this does not apply in reverse. Since there are about 80,000 European voters, and, including the highest imaginable estimate of ordinary and special voters, 60,000 Africans, this means that almost every member in the House, whether ordinary constituency representative or special African member, is elected by a European majority.

Almost as odd is the provision of the electoral law that, if ever an ordinary seat is won by an African, one of the special African seats is consequently abolished. This is called the progressive development of racial integration and the withering away of racial representation. It looks more like giving with one hand and taking away with the other. It is very hard to understand why, if one African has the initiative, ability and diplomacy to get himself returned to Parliament as an ordinary member, by a predominantly European electorate, a seat for the special representation of Africans should cease to exist in a House where at present 7 million Africans have fifteen representatives and 300,000 Europeans have forty-four. It is even harder to understand why, if the African ordinary member loses his seat to a European at the next election, the lost special African seat is not restored; but the electoral law prohibits this. A good many Africans genuinely believed, at the last election, that the Federal Party—the Government Party—might put up eight biddable Africans for eight safe ordinary seats and instruct their European supporters in the constituencies to vote for them (eight being the number of African members elected by the two sections of the common roll jointly). At the next election, they could be disowned by the Party on the grounds that a generous experiment in interracialism had failed on account of the poor quality of the Africans, and be replaced by European candidates. The eight special African seats would have been abolished because there had been eight ordinary members who were Africans, and would not be restored when, after their contrived defeat, there were none. It would be an easy way to eliminate African elective representation completely, and quite legally, within five years. This fear exemplifies rather the intense suspicion Africans feel of Europeans than anything that was actually likely to happen. But the electoral law unquestionably permits it.

Such a manœuvre would not have suited the Federal Party's book at all. It is highly important to it to have a number of Africans in Parliament, as an advertisement to world opinion, a badge of liberal interracialism, a symbol of the distinction between the progressive Federation and reactionary South Africa. They are the basis of the Federation's claim upon Britain's approval and support and it is their existence alone which enables the British Government to present to Parliament as progressive such really discriminatory measures as the Constitution Amendment Bill or the electoral law itself. It is as important to the Federal Government's *persona* that Africans should sit in the House as it is to its policy that they should have no real power.

An interesting feature of the system is the extremely small number of electors for most ordinary seats. The average total of registered voters per ordinary constituency works out at about 2,000; the average number of African ordinary voters in each Federal constituency is a few decimal points below 39; of Asians and other races 100. So of the 2,000 voters in each ordinary constituency, 1,861 are Europeans.[1] In the Federal election of November 1958, Sir Roy Welensky, the most powerful individual in the Federation, was elected by 766 votes, and opposed by 490, a majority of 276 in a total poll under 1,300. (There were a few spoilt papers.) In the three ordinary constituencies of Nyasaland where voting took place, the number of votes cast were 309, 317, and 1,129 respectively. But of the 1,129 in the Shire constituency, 804 were spoilt papers. In the other three, no contest took place. U.F.P. members were returned unopposed. The franchise is so restricted that they are virtually Federal Party pocket boroughs. The failure of the Federal franchise to represent popular feeling is demonstrated by the fact that, in the two elective constituencies for African special representation, Federal Party African candidates were returned unopposed. It is impossible in view of the 1959 Emergency and the findings of the Devlin Commission, to believe that many Africans wanted them. But the fact that they would be chosen mainly by European ordinary voters using their second vote on the special roll made it useless for any candidates who really represented Africans even to stand. This contrasts ironically with the fact that all the African representative members of the *territorial* Legislative Council were Congressmen. This is the rather surprising result of what is supposed to be a progressive Constitution and an undiscriminatory franchise in a country where no territorial voting takes place at all and whose political tensions and discontents are apparent to the whole world.

These are the principal provisions of the Federal franchise. They are not part of the Constitution. The Constitution empowers the Federal Parliament to pass its own electoral laws (and for the matter of that to change the Constitution) by a simple two-thirds majority, subject to the theoretical veto of Her Majesty's Government. In this case the electoral law was debated in the House of Commons

[1] These are the figures for April 1959. See No. 3 of *Documents on World Affairs*, United World Education and Research Trust, June 1959.

which accepted it as a fair and justifiable interpretation of the aims of the Constitution despite the protests of the African Affairs Board that it, and the Constitution Amendment Bill which was its groundwork, were differentiating and discriminatory.

CHAPTER VI

Federal Politics

The principal political parties in the Federation are the United Federal Party—the Government Party—led by Sir Roy Welensky; and the Dominion Party under Mr. Winston Field's slightly precarious leadership. They are open to all races and it is greatly to their advantage to have African members and candidates in order to increase their claim to represent the whole population. South African discrimination is based upon emotion and wishes to exclude Africans from all association or fellowship with white men; Federal discrimination is practical and pragmatic. Its aim is to preserve political and economic influence for Europeans and, if this can be done by admitting Africans to formal participation in common institutions, there is not the same abhorrence of a black skin to prohibit it. The declared policy of the Federal Party is to keep political power in the hands of civilized people, but to encourage Africans to develop to a civilized level; that of the Dominion Party is to keep political power in the hands of Europeans and to encourage the development of Africans as a separate community. This is not contradicted by the fact that the Dominion as well as the Federal Party accepts African members. Since the Constitution prescribes African seats, every party wants the ornament of its Africans sitting in them. Candidates for the special African seats in the Federal Parliament may stand in the interests of any party, in the same way as ordinary candidates, and the Dominion Party's conception of the future is probably of a European wing of the party concerned with ordinary seats and an African wing concerned with special. One "special" Federal M.P. is in fact a Dominion Party African, Mr. Samuriwo, returned by the predominantly European vote for African racial representation from one of the most right-wing districts of Southern Rhodesia. This argues no Dominion Party enthusiasm for voting for Africans. If members vote at all for a "special" representative, he must be African, so it is desirable for them to find an African D.P. candidate. (The majority of African representatives are Federal Party members, returned by European Federal Party votes.)

These are the only two parties with any strength in the Federal Parliament. There are one or two independent Members. The Federal Party has a big majority. The Dominion Party is strong in Southern Rhodesia where it came close to defeating the Federal Party in the last territorial election and forms a powerful opposition. It is usual to describe the Dominion Party as right-wing (the Federal Party describes it as "marching boldly into the past") and the Federal Party as the middle-of-the-road party of liberal compromise. We shall consider in Chapter XX whether these descriptions are wholly accurate, and the reader may judge whether liberal compromise characterizes the Federal Party legislation we have considered.

The Dominion Party was built on the ruins of the now extinct Confederate Party founded by Mr. Guillaume van Eeden. The Dominion Party stole its thunder and its members by proclaiming very similar objectives in language as plain to local inhabitants but a good deal less transparent to the outside world. There is less difference than appears between the real aims of the Confederate and the Dominion—or even the Federal—parties; they all aim at European supremacy but some are more successful than others in concealing this from the outside world.

The Central Africa Party, which at present holds no Federal seats but does hold three in the Northern Rhodesian Legislative Council, is the rallying point of European goodwill and its meeting ground with the milder expression of African aspirations. It was born of the collapse of Mr. Garfield Todd, as leader of the old United Rhodesia Party and Prime Minister of Southern Rhodesia, in 1957–58, the defeat of the African Affairs Board by the House of Commons, and the conviction of a small number of independent-minded Europeans in all three territories that Federal Party professions were different from Federal Party objectives. It is founded upon what used to be the Constitution Party (because it called for a consistent interpretation of the Federal Constitution in place of the distortion and evasion of Federal Party interpretations) and the small liberal wing of the United Rhodesia Party.[1] It incorporates as much of the spirit of

[1] This party was obliterated by the growing power of the Federal Party in Southern Rhodesia, which the majority of its members joined. A righteous remnant of Mr. Todd's days of power has come to rest in the C.A.P.

genuine liberalism, tolerance and equality between the races as can possibly be acceptable to Europeans in the Federation for many years to come. (Really radical views, such as have been proposed and practised by Mr. Guy Clutton-Brock or the Rev. Tom Colvin, are not acceptable. Mr. Clutton-Brock was arrested at the time of the Emergency and is tolerated only because he is a Rhodesian citizen and cannot be deported: Mr. Colvin has been declared a prohibited immigrant.) It contains the fairest European minds in the Federation and most of the straight and honest thinkers. It also contains all the tension, confusion of thought and shortness of sight that inevitably afflict the benevolent European during his painful and perilous emergence from the cocoon of paternalist liberalism into the free-flying state of radicalism. It remains to be seen whether it can consolidate its own contradictory tendencies into a platform on which Europeans and Africans can meet in equality, and at the same time gain increased support from both communities. If, as is profoundly to be hoped, it can do this we shall hear more of it. Otherwise it will become yet another crumbling monument to the inability of European liberalism in Africa to advance far and fast enough. Success will demand the most delicate balance; persuasive and diplomatic skill of the highest order, and an inflexible integrity. If it cannot advance to a much more radical position than is possible for it at present, it will forfeit African support;[1] but to do so and simultaneously gain European confidence will not be easy. It has as yet hardly developed a coherent policy in political terms. It would not be unfair to say that it stands for genuinely executing the provisions of the Constitution while the Federal Party stands for paying them lip service.

It is supported by the Capricorn Africa Society, which has decided

[1] Sir John Moffat's speech, on 27th January 1960 in the Legislative Council, as leader of the Northern Rhodesian C.A.P., on his own motion calling for the end of Federation and its replacement by a looser form of association between the three states, was encouraging in this respect. Nobody would deny, he said, that African opposition made Federation in its present form impossible. European leaders, recognizing that Dominion status in 1960 was out of the question, intended to try and get powers just short of it. African opposition was the obstacle, so they would declare that African loyalty to Federation was impossible so long as Africans could "look over their shoulders to Whitehall". But Africans did not mistrust the Federation because they looked to Britain; they looked to Britain because they mistrusted Federation. The suggestion that to sever the link with Britain would bring peace in Northern Rhodesia was untrue. Only Protectorate status had limited the degree of violence there so far. In Nyasaland, Africans "will not consider tinkering with the Federal Constitution or discussing its merits or demerits. The entire people want only one thing—to be quit of it." He called for a radical change in the foundations of the association between the three territories.

not to go into party politics itself. This may be as much hindrance as help. Capricorn has never gained any substantial support from Africans. They suspect it of representing the last hope of white supremacy because, during all the shufflings and tergiversations of its policy, it has never come out for African self-determination; it has said that Africans must have freedom, the vote, social and economic equality and so on, but it has never renounced the principle of the multiple vote by which everyone gets one vote but people who satisfy certain tests get as many as six. This looks dangerously like a variant on the present Federal franchise—a means of giving the illusion of power to the many while reserving its reality to Europeans and "certain selected Africans". It looks to Africans like chicanery and paternalism. Capricorn backs African advancement, interracialism and common citizenship. But it has always left it to European wisdom to decide when and how and has always prevaricated over political rights.

Africans today resent and distrust this attitude more than what they regard as the avowedly oppressive intention of the Federal—or the Dominion—Party to maintain white domination. This at least they can oppose; but Capricorn slips through their fingers. Capricorn's indecisive policies have been vaguely interracial enough to affront many European prejudices without offering Africans solid grounds for hope. The society probably excites much more interest and enjoys much more support at home in Europe than anywhere else. It offers the well intentioned but not very well informed liberal a formula—or is it a mystique dressed up as one?—which seems to solve all racial problems and assures him (or her) that a lot of good people of both races are thinking and doing something constructive together, creating new hope in Africa. But out there it cuts very little ice. For different reasons, it appears wishy-washy both to the dyed-in-the-wool Europeans and the discontented Africans. And it is no good, in Central Africa, appealing to enlightened moderate opinion; there is not enough of it. It has got first to be created and Capricorn has not produced a sufficiently precise and constructive political principle to do this. It falls between two stools. This is what the Central Africa Party must avoid.

The forces of Africanism[1] have not so far succeeded in organizing

[1] This word has been blessed by Lord Hailey in the *African Survey* and I shall use it throughout in preference to "Nationalism". This has always been a misleading name for the spontaneous uncoordinated awakening of African self-consciousness and assertion of African rights that has been taking place in the

themselves centrally for the whole Federation. There were, however, legal African-founded political parties in each territory until the 1959 Emergency and they could have put up a candidate for any Federal or territorial seat. The representative Africanist organizations, the African National Congresses, are at present (January 1960) illegal in Southern Rhodesia and Nyasaland and their most influential leaders are still under indefinite detention.[1] In Northern Rhodesia, the African movement is very deeply divided by questions of policy, principle and personality. Mr. Harry Nkumbula, leader of the African National Congress, actually has a seat in the Legislature. It is alleged that he receives the approval and encouragement of the Government although he preaches African self-government for Northern Rhodesia. He has forfeited much African confidence since he won his seat and he won it by exerting his undoubted personal magnetism over a small body of electors. The Congress Party is a rump and Mr. Nkumbula a spent force. Politically conscious Africans in Northern Rhodesia—and there are a great many of them—look to Kenneth Kaunda and the United National Independence Party, the successor to the Zambia National Congress, for leadership and representation. Kaunda was Secretary-General of Congress under Nkumbula's presidency but felt unable to put up with what he felt to be his leader's increasing weakness and readiness to compromise African interests to please Europeans. He led the majority of Congress into his new organization, but was shortly afterwards rusticated by the Government. He recently served a nine months' prison sentence for failing to get police permission for a political meeting and the pattern of Northern Rhodesian African politics is beginning to crystallize again after his release in 1960.

For all these reasons it is hard to define the place of Africanist movements in the political life of the Federation. But the outlawed Congresses in Southern Rhodesia and Nyasaland, and their permitted successors, unquestionably represent the feelings and aspirations of most Africans there as does the National Independence Party

last few decades among Africans in the whole continent. There is no African nation any more than there is a European or an Asian one. But the process concerns all Africans and Africanism describes it perfectly.

[1] In both countries successors to them have been organized, which are attempting to keep within the narrow limits set by law. In Nyasaland the Malawi Congress Party under Mr. Orton Chirwa who has been succeeded by Dr. Banda since his release; in Southern Rhodesia the National Democratic Party formed by Mr. Michael Mawema. They are in the same relation to Congress as Kaunda's party (National Independence Party) in Northern Rhodesia is to Zambia.

in Northern Rhodesia. There has in the past been very little co-ordination between their policies and activities at Federal level—far too little, their friends would say. There is no form of master congress organization controlling African parties. Each has worked as a separate movement in its own territory. Congress is a generic, not a specific term. Liaison has been limited almost to casual conversations between leaders. There was certainly no concerted action of Africanist movements behind the 1959 Emergency. The only concerted action was that of the governments in suppressing them.

Congress, or its legal successors, and the Northern Rhodesian Independence Party, are no more racial parties than the Federal or the Central African Party. They invite, when allowed by the Government to exist, members of all races to join. Their aim and policy is not racialist; they have never suggested or thought of "kicking out the whites", as many Europeans believe, and setting up African domination. Like all Africans they recognize that Europeans are as necessary to the country as the country is to the Europeans and that Europeans are so used to a privileged standard of living that they cannot do without it. They would consent to Europeans having absolute security of tenure and very considerable economic and social privileges—to their continuing as a kind of aristocracy—if only Europeans would abate their pretension to overriding political power and leadership. Contrary to general belief they are very little concerned about social integration. They are animated not by jealousy but by a sense of justice. They would have no objection to Europeans segregating themselves on an upper shelf if only the normal benefits of society, in terms of public utilities, public facilities and the vote were open equally to all. They have no desire to storm the social seclusion of European clubs. But they do want to be allowed to set up just as good clubs for themselves and not to be restricted to municipally-owned "Kaffir beer" gardens.

The more Europeans persecute and misunderstand them, the more they will force them to extremes. Their policy is to obtain fair and just representation for Africans in the Federation and its component territories. Like the Chartists, or any other movement based on an under-represented majority, they are not prepared to take a blank "no" as a final answer and they will tend increasingly towards impatience and violence as the ways of discussion and negotiation are closed to them.

All political parties in the Federation may be organized either federally or territorially or both. There is no reason why a party should not exist, or even control the Government, in an individual territory and yet have no counterpart at Federal level. The Africanist parties are purely territorial. The major European-controlled parties operate both federally and territorially. The territorial branches are ostensibly entirely independent of the Federal, separate but analogous organizations. The Prime Minister of the Federation, Sir Roy Welensky, has no authority over the Prime Minister of Southern Rhodesia, Sir Edgar Whitehead, though both are Federal Party men. Each is responsible to a different parliament and electorate and in theory could have wholly different policies. This happened in the latter part of Mr. Garfield Todd's prime-ministership of Southern Rhodesia when, as leader of the territorial Federal Party, he took a more liberal line than Sir Roy Welensky. But the result was that when a word from Welensky could have saved him in 1958 it was not spoken and he fell. The tendency at the moment is for the Federal leaders of the European-controlled parties to dominate the territorial organizations. The Northern Rhodesian Federal Party, under Mr. John Roberts, is little more than an outpost of Sir Roy Welensky's command. And as long as Federation in its present form endures, purely territorial parties are not likely to succeed.

CHAPTER VII

The Anatomy of Partnership

I have left Partnership to the end of this description of how the Federation was supposed to work, and how it does. It cannot be defined or implemented like a franchise law or the distribution of powers between Federal and territorial authorities. It has, as Lord Hailey remarks,[1] "a moral rather than a political connotation": it is "rather an aspiration than a policy".[2] Although it is often said to be the basis of Federation, no constitutional lawyer would found an instrument of state on so imprecise a concept. It is not in any real sense integral to the Federal Constitution and it is not an enforceable piece of constitutional machinery. It occurs only in the Preamble and so is not binding in the way that the Provisions are. It is in fact no more than an expression of vague goodwill, thrown in as an afterthought by a civil servant who was passionately devoted to the idea of Federation and anxious to exploit every conceivable apology for it. It is not the new and exciting panacea it is generally supposed to be, having been current as a phrase in Northern Rhodesia for nearly thirty years and in East Africa for almost as long. It has had little perceptible effect during its long history and the fact that such different craft as Kenya and Tanganyika both sail today under the flag of partnership show how variously this aspiration can be interpreted. We shall examine the practice of partnership in our subsequent tour of Southern Rhodesia and are here concerned only with the theory in a Federal framework.

The sole reference to partnership in the Federal Constitution is in the Preamble, which says: "The association of the Colony (of Southern Rhodesia) and the territories in a Federation would conduce to the security, advancement and welfare of all their inhabitants and in particular would foster partnership and co-operation between their inhabitants." Lord Malvern, speaking in the Federal Parliament

[1] *Hailey*, p. 185.
[2] Ibid., p. 193.

in 1954 against a motion to accord equal treatment to all races in all public places, said: "Let us for the sake of Federation, which was for economic advancement, not for the Preamble which was forced upon us, have patience." He spoke the mind of most Europeans in the Federation.

Southern Rhodesia accepted partnership for the sake of economic advance, not from enthusiasm for it as a positive ideal. At best, it saw it as co-operation between two separate racial groups. It has done nothing so far to produce a stable interracial society of the kind that is coming into being in Tanganyika and such utterances as Lord Malvern's, quoted above, show why. The present Federal Prime Minister, Sir Roy Welensky, appears to envisage partnership as at best "not one between the races in bulk, but between the Europeans as a whole and certain selected Africans";[1] at worst as "the partnership between horse and rider",[2] to judge from his evasive and often contradictory remarks on the subject. The Federal Party Congress defined it in 1952 as "the gradual extension of political rights and privileges to those who conform to civilized standards of behaviour and culture". N. Steven-Hubbard[3] describes it as "a sophisticated and Western-centred concept which can never appeal to Africans and is therefore at best only a desperate line of defence against the dangers perceived as a consequence of nationalism". The late C. W. M. Gell[4] posed the fundamental question: "The fact is that the word *partnership* has been deliberately kept ambiguous. Does it mean a perpetual balance between the one-tenth white minority in Southern Rhodesia (or the one-thirty-fifth white minority in the Federation) and the enormous black majority? Or does it envisage a day when black voters will outnumber white voters?"

Any system of partnership which does not carry with it the implication of at least equality of political representation between the groups concerned—not in the remote unforeseeable future, but today, here and now—is the partnership of horse and rider. Southern Rhodesia has set the tone for the interpretation of partnership in the Federation. And in Southern Rhodesia it has so far meant that some Africans are allowed to buy European liquor; they are legally recog-

[1] C. T. Leys, op. cit.

[2] This phrase has been attributed to originators as diverse as Lord Malvern and the Congress movement.

[3] *Africa To-day*, 1955, pp. 256 ff. Quoted by Hailey, p. 186.

[4] *Central African Examiner*, 22nd June 1957.

nized for the first time as employees and allowed to join trade unions;[1] a limited form of home-ownership (but never of the land the houses are built on) is possible in some urban locations; multi-racial hotels, as we know, are allowed by law, though very few have applied for registration as such; and separate counters in Post Offices, for Natives and Europeans, which were first introduced after Federation, have been abolished since the Emergency. But Land Apportionment continues to allocate over forty-eight million acres of the best land to a white tenth of the population and about thirty-nine million of the worse to the black nine-tenths; compulsory segregation of all Africans into municipally-owned locations (where they need the permission of a white official to leave after 9 p.m. or to have friends or relations to stay) persists in all towns; the Native Land Husbandry Act[2] imposes economically impossible conditions on African agriculture; the pass laws require every black man always to carry a piece of paper issued by a white official to identify himself and he is arrested if he is found without it; social contact between black and white in any public place is impossible; the black vote cannot *in practice* count for more than 20 per cent of the white; African life in all its aspects is governed in a watertight compartment by the Native Affairs Department (except for education, but there are two complete secondary schools for 2,800,000 Africans and many more for 219,000 Europeans).[3] As Mr. Todd said lately: "After five years of so-called partnership, an African citizen, clean, well-dressed, educated and ambitious . . . remains a second class citizen unable to enter a cinema or become a fireman on the Government-owned railways."

The conception of "partnership" originated in Northern Rhodesia in the 1920s as a means of enabling a small white group to live in a country where the Colonial Office declared African interests to be paramount; and even in this form, chiefs and people felt it was a dilution of the promised paramountcy of African interests.[4] It cropped up again in Southern Rhodesia after the war when a rival doctrine was needed to the South African Nationalists' *apartheid*—something to disarm criticism of segregation, avoid the odium

[1] But see the reference to the Industrial Conciliation Act on p. 76.

[2] For a full criticism and analysis of this measure by an agricultural officer who tried to administer it, see Ken Brown, *Land in Southern Rhodesia*, Africa Bureau, 1959. Land Apportionment is further discussed on pp. 138–59 of this book.

[3] There are about twenty-five African junior secondary schools. See pp. 164–74.

[4] See pp. 40–42.

Dr. Malan was incurring in the outside world, and attract copperbelt revenues to Salisbury. But now its meaning was reversed—it was a step up for Africans in a society of paramount European interests, susceptible of an infinite variety of interpretation, compatible with the demand that "leadership shall remain in civilized—that is, for the foreseeable future, European—hands". In 1953 partnership had entirely different meanings for the British Government and Colonial Office, and the Rhodesian politicians who accepted it as the cornerstone of Federal racial policy. To Britain it meant a partnership of individuals in a single society, as far as its meaning was thought out at all; to Rhodesia a partnership between separate racial groups of quite unequal size. One can imagine the mental reservations with which Lord Malvern entered into "partnership" with 7 million Africans who, he has told us, are "until they are very much more advanced, all liars".

Since Federation, the Federal Government has adopted the secondary, Southern Rhodesian, interpretation of partnership as its racial policy. It regards *European* interests as paramount and partnership as a device to accommodate a modicum of African development at a very slow pace to this paramountcy. It is the original conception of partnership turned upside-down.

There is more readiness to commend partnership than to define it. Can the Federal spokesmen who invoke it say what they mean in terms of actual social organization? Could Lord Home, when he begged the Lords to suspend criticism and allow time and patience to build partnership, as the only way for the Federation, envisage what he expected to happen? The Federal Government, the *Central African Examiner* and the daily Press repeatedly state that the Federation must hurry up and "implement partnership". But they are never ready to say what this means, except that it does not mean the extension of the franchise, or land reform or economic integration or even social integration between the races.[1] Is it more than a parrot-cry taken from the Federal Constitution and unreflectingly repeated because, as Lord Malvern has said with characteristic saltiness, "it is a very blessed word".

[1] Sir Roy Welensky said at the Federal Party Congress at Lusaka on 17th September 1959: "What now disturbs me is the apparent reluctance on the part of some Europeans to accept the emerged African as a full member of society—and let me add I am not referring to social integration." Only the emerged African is a full member of society, not his poorer fellows. And what is full membership of society without the possibility of social integration?

The very term *partnership* implies *separation*—the continued existence of separate partners—and all healthy societies tend to integration. What reason is there for dividing the Federation into two different partner groups—one of 300,000 Europeans and one of 7 million Africans—unless for some reason they cannot live in one society? If they cannot, can partnership be anything but another name for discrimination? Mr. W. C. de Wet Nel, now Minister of Bantu Development in the Union, whom we shall quote again in this context, told the Tomlinson Commission: "There are only two end-points—total integration and total *apartheid*. There is no middle way."

Partnership between the races, as a phrase, means nothing in practical, social, and political terms. It is the deeds of partnership, the terms on which it is accorded, which give point to this expression of moral aspiration. These terms have never been laid down. No one in the British Government or Civil Service, no one in the Federation, has ever attempted to specify them, for the very good reason that it cannot be done. As soon as one tries to do so with any precision one finds one is defining either racial supremacy, a partnership in which one race is superior to the other, or racial integration, a partnership in which all men have the same social and political rights so that partnership between the races as two different blocs is dissolved in the general partnership of all equal individual members of society without differentiation. This is the only thing that partnership as a political doctrine can possibly mean; it is the only true form of social partnership. But it is precisely the situation that the doctrine of "partnership between the races" keeps at arm's length and the situation which the European Government and population of the Federation can neither envisage nor accept. Their constitutional theory, electoral practice and social custom are all part of an attempt to evade the fact that partnership between individuals, between people, is the only alternative to the domination of one group by another. "Partnership" has been used as a narcotic, sedative word to quiet the objections of British opinion, and the resentment of Federal Africans, against a situation of racial domination by Federal Europeans. But like most sedatives, its effect is diminished by too frequent use and it has by now become clear that partnership has failed Britain's hopes of it and has failed the black inhabitants of Central Africa too, as any so imprecise and illogical a conception was bound to. The outworn slogan must be replaced by a new

CHAPTER VIII

The Failure of the Constitution

If my contention be true that political Federation in Central Africa was a mistake and, because of the difference between race relations in the territories concerned, could not succeed, then no Federal Constitution could have worked. It would be absurd to blame the makers of the existing Constitution for its failure to produce the inter-racial harmony expected of it. It is even more absurd to under-estimate the difficulties of securing joint membership of an equal society for both races in any African country containing a minority of privileged Europeans and a majority of underdeveloped Africans. It is absurd to blame or condemn the settlers for hanging on to their privileges. They could hardly do anything else. But the duty of an Imperial power, and the object of any constitution in such a situation should be to promote the emergence of a single equal society and to coax the settlers into accepting it and the sacrifices and qualification of their privilege it involves with as little pain as possible. The Federal Constitution as a whole, though still more the way in which it has been interpreted by the British and Federal Governments since 1953, may justly be criticized for having failed to do this. It has instead entrenched European privilege even more firmly than before in Central Africa and imported the acute racial tensions of Southern Rhodesia to the northern territories, where conflict might otherwise have been avoided.

Paradoxically, the chief failure of the Constitution, for all its devotion to the inherently separating doctrine of partnership, is that it takes no account of the real differences between Europeans and Africans. Although these are not biological differences but social, cultural, historical, and above all economic ones, they are wide enough to make nonsense of the Constitution's assumption that every African is an embryonic Rhodesian settler who will be given the rights and duties of a member of a settler society when he has satisfied the settler authorities that his re-birth is accomplished. This assumption is at the back of the European insistence on political rights "only for civilized men"; it is at the back of the whole plan for giving Africans the vote when they attain qualifications laid down by Europeans; it is at the back of the conception of partnership as "not between the races in bulk but between Europeans as a whole and certain selected Africans"; it is at the back of Sir Roy Welensky's exhortation to the Federal Party[1] "not to go on treating *an African who is educated and has achieved a standard of culture akin to our own* as an inferior being for all time"—as if those who have not are inferior beings. (This was said at a moment when all the leaders of the Nyasaland African Congress, the Zambia Congress of Northern Rhodesia[2] and the Southern Rhodesian African Congress were in detention because, presumably, they had a different standard of culture from Sir Roy Welensky. His belief that men who have acquired even so much nuisance value, with so little violence, have no culture at all is hard to accept.)

The whole idea of admitting Africans to equality when they have attained the education and culture of the white settlers is rather as if Lord Melbourne had promised to grant all the demands of the Chartists when their followers had arrived at the culture and education possessed by himself and his cabinet. It is a misconception of the social process. Standards, whether of education, culture or political responsibility, do not remain frozen and static while increasing numbers of citizens approximate to them and join the ranks of the elect. The emergence of new classes into power, the granting of their claims because they are irresistible, changes the whole structure of society and the standards of culture, education and responsibility on which it rests. In Britain today we have not got mass participation in Lord Melbourne's world; we have the Welfare State, Trade Unionism, Conservative prosperity and hire purchase. If it be true that we have never had it so good, Lord Melbourne would not recognize the fact.

The Federal Constitution, and Federal practice, assume that standards never change, but citizens slowly graduate to them, because the standards are white and the graduand citizens black—that in some way an African becomes "better" by attaining European standards than by evolving along his own lines as the Congresses have done. This is because they see the differences as between African

[1] Speech at U.F.P. Congress, Lusaka, 19th September 1959. Italics mine.
[2] Now Malawi Congress Party, National Independence Party and National Democratic Party.

ways and European ways and, inherently if unconsciously, believe that European ways are better. In fact they are the differences between rich and poor, between privilege and under-privilege, which must be allowed to modify and transform each other in the process of social evolution, and are not either racial or qualitative at all.

The Constitution, the Federal franchise and the Northern and Southern Rhodesian franchises all give preponderant political power to white minorities on the grounds that these minorities are "civilized" and able to wield it. (In the Northern Rhodesian election of 1959, for instance, 74·9 per cent of the votes were cast by 3·6 per cent of the population.) They justify the under-representation of Africans on the grounds that they are not yet civilized. The theory is that Africans will be brought on to "civilization" by European-administered education and economic advancement until they are fitted to take their place beside the white man in a white man's world. Meanwhile the white man must rule. But what this in effect means is that only those Africans who come on in the way Europeans desire, who will vote for the kind of world he wants and, in the last resort, agree to his senior partnership, count as civilized. The fact that the criteria of "civilization" and of the worthiness to vote are prescribed by European authorities limits the direction in which Africans can advance and is a denial of their freedom and self-determination, not only politically but in the deepest spiritual sense.[1]

The great objection to the Federal Constitution and the whole system of government that depends upon it is that the means by which it professes to give Africans increasing self-determination and political power are the actual means of withholding them. It claims to do one thing and achieves its exact opposite. It gives them, to a limited extent, the right to vote and to sit in Parliament and represents this as progressive and liberal interracialism while withholding the substance of political power. It ensures that African votes cannot swing an election nor African members decide a division, by placing them in an automatic and inescapable minority. Whatever the Constitution professes, its machinery and that of the franchise render it absolutely impossible for voters or members who happen to be African to rival the influence of those who happen to be European, because of the different social and economic positions they occupy.

[1] Whether Africans are in fact uncivilized, whether tests of civilization mean anything and whether civilization as defined in the Federation means anything is a different question and is dealt with on pp. 190–92.

But it is perfectly true to say that there are no constitutional political divisions along racial lines, even though Africans cannot, despite all the theoretical opportunities offered to them, emerge from crushing minority without a social and economic revolution. The very fact that they are allotted a specified number of special African seats indicates that no one expects them to win any more. And enforced and unavoidable minority representation is useless and demoralizing; it is worse than none.

The twelve Africans in the Federal Parliament are stage properties put there by Europeans to advertise an interracialism that is not reflected by the organization of society. No one need listen to them because there cannot be more of them. Their position is undignified and frustrating because they are there by European fiat, the extent of their minority is prescribed by law, and they have been elected by predominantly European votes. It is a mere fiction that African votes, or African members, make any significant difference to what goes on in the country. It is a myth that the Federation and its Constitution offer them endlessly expanding influence. The Federal Government proclaims with bland persuasiveness that there are no racial politics in the Federation: the vote is open to all who can earn £720 a year, quite regardless of race. But it is a system of giving votes, rights and opportunities to "certain selected Africans" who make themselves successful and agreeable in a European-operated system and consigning the remainder to perpetual subordination; of giving Africans theoretical rights and chances while keeping them securely in a position where they cannot use them.

Next—and the importance of this cannot be exaggerated—the qualifications laid down by a European-dominated parliament can always be altered by it before a general election, or at any time if it appears to it that the number of enfranchised Africans is in danger of outstripping the Europeans. Most Africans in the Federation honestly believe that this is what will happen and, whether they are right or not, the fact that such an action would be perfectly possible and altogether legal undermines any confidence in Federal professions of devotion to African advancement. All the decisions are taken by Europeans; Africans must gratefully accept them. They feel they are mere objects moved around like pieces on a draughts board. The success of their own efforts and industriousness can never guarantee them the advancement they are supposed to earn since the standards of achievement are outside their control and can be raised regardless of their will. Whenever the horse shows signs of clearing the jump, the rider can lift the top bar a few notches.

If African suspicions that this will be done appear unworthy, it should be remembered that this is exactly what has happened in Southern Rhodesia. In 1898, when the Cape franchise was first introduced under the British South Africa Company, the qualifications were literacy, judged, as it still is, by ability to fill in an application form for the vote unaided, and an income of £50 a year or occupation of property valued at £75. In 1912 the qualifications were raised to £100 a year or property worth £150. In 1917 it was stated officially that these qualifications would be raised again if there were any danger of their being reached by Africans. The Treasurer (or Company's Minister of Finance) asked[1] "how was the black voter, be he ever so accomplished, going to fulfil the occupation qualification of £150 or the wages qualification of £100 when he received £3 per month? Was not that sufficient protection for years and years to come?" In 1919 the vote was extended to women. They qualified in virtue of their husbands' financial position provided their marriage was not contracted under a system which permitted polygamy. In 1951 qualifications for the vote were raised to an income of £240 per annum, or occupation of property worth £500. As the Tredgold Commission[2] pointed out, the earlier qualifications were found satisfactory during all the economic changes which followed the First World War "and it is a justifiable inference that the increases made in 1951 were not solely related to the changed value of money". They were made to keep Africans off the roll.

A study of official pronouncements and inter-party discussions (those for instance between the United and Liberal parties from 1948–51) leave no doubt whatever that it has been a consistent aim of Southern Rhodesian policy to keep the qualifications well ahead of nearly all Africans' capacities. The record of Southern Rhodesia in this respect was one of the many reasons Africans in the Northern Protectorates had for fearing Federation and believing it would bring them no real advance. They felt that their fears had been fully justified when the Federal Franchise Law of 1957 set the minimum qualifications for an ordinary Federal vote at £720 a year or property worth £1,500, and included a clause providing for raising them at

[1] Proceedings of the Legislative Assembly, 30th April 1917.
[2] Report of the Franchise Commission, Government Printer, Salisbury, 1957, p. 2.

any time in order to keep in step with fluctuations in the value of the currency.

Whatever the intention of the Constitution may have been, its result is to shroud a system of racial politics in a camouflage net of hypocrisy as transparent as the Emperor's new suit of clothes but even more effective in allowing everyone to disregard what everyone knows—that it is a system of racial politics. The Congress movements have committed the solecism of declaring the truth that no one else will admit. The Emperor has no clothes on. The rule of civilized men, the maintenance of European standards, partnership between the races, bringing the African on till he is worthy of the vote are all means of preserving the *status quo*. The *status quo* is European domination. When Africans challenge this conception of civilization the Europeans call their attitude racialism. They cannot see that it is the *status quo* that is racialist. European privilege seems to them to be the natural order in Africa.

When the Federal Prime Minister objected, in September 1958, to the Colonial Secretary's demand that the Northern Rhodesian cabinet of ten ministers (appointed by the Governor from members elected to the Legislative Council) should contain two Africans, his real objection seems to have been to having even two Africans there, as *The Times* correspondent quoted on p. 74 bears out. He defended himself, however, by saying: "The proposal cuts clean across the concept of non-racial politics. . . . It offends against the principle of responsible government and of recognizing a man's merit instead of his colour. It is a flagrant violation of democratic principle." This is a clever argument but it begs the question. An electoral system under which the whole European community has votes and under 1 per cent of the African has any votes at all *is* racial politics and a machine for ensuring white supremacy. Certainly it is mere patchwork to introduce two Africans into a territorial cabinet or twelve to the Federal Parliament (or one to the Federal Government as Sir Roy himself did after the Emergency) and to retain what is in effect a racially restricted franchise. Certainly the only way to abolish racial politics is to extend the vote to all members of the community, regardless of race. But Sir Roy's argument is worse than patchwork. It is hypocrisy to pretend that the present franchise affords even a possible basis for political equality. This can only be achieved by redressing the adverse balance against the black race and it is disingenuous to argue that for Africans to try and remove their disabilities

DR. BANDA AMONG HIS PEOPLE

Lord Home welcomed by Sir Roy Welensky

and disadvantages is racialism. It is a way of ending racialism which Sir Roy, to judge from his statements about the Emergencies, is reluctant to allow.

The claim that the Federation offers equal political, professional or social opportunity to all regardless of race and without discrimination does not bear scrutiny. Political power, parliamentary seats, ministerial positions, jobs from the highest to the lowest in the Civil Service, are open to all without distinction of race. Certain tests, admittedly, must be passed by all who wish to attain them; but the tests are open to all equally and they are the same tests for all. Africans have merely to pass these tests and the preponderance of political power, the highest posts in the state and the administration can be theirs. Racial discrimination has no place in the egalitarian generosity of the partnership state. Merit alone is rewarded.

In fact, the integrated, interracial civil service is as disingenuous a piece of advertisement as the integrated, interracial parliament and cabinet. There are twelve Africans in a House of fifty-three and one under-secretary in a cabinet of twelve. There are over 17,000 non-Europeans[1] in the Federal Civil Service and this sounds imposing. Closer examination of the figures alters their appearance. In Grade I, the equivalent of the administrative grade in Britain, there are 12,428 Europeans and 53 non-Europeans. In Grades II, III and IV, there are 17,065 non-Europeans and no Europeans. Of these, 11,000 are in Grade IV which consists of messengers, orderlies, cleaners, and the like. The other 6,000 are clerks and technicians. Apart from the difficulty for an African to acquire the necessary qualifications, promotion is in the hands of Europeans and will stay in their hands under the existing political and constitutional arrangements. Federal Europeans do not like the idea of being administered by other races and it will be a long time before any significant number of them get top positions. One or two Africans will be promoted and this will be given a lot of publicity, but one should not be over-impressed by it. The Government and the Public Service Commission can easily take care that they are too few to have any real influence and can always be overridden. Promotion and advancement will not be according to merit but according to the proportion of Africans to Europeans in public life that the Government considers expedient. This is the principle behind the whole system and the Constitution

[1] The number of Africans as distinct from Asians is not known.

makes it quite admissible. It is to be a European state and a European civil service with the participation of "certain selected Africans".

The trouble is that you cannot grow undiscriminatory fruit in the soil of discrimination nor found an interracial building on racialist foundations. The whole of Rhodesian society—the *status quo*—is based on discrimination and any system will be operated in a discriminatory way by it. The white man starts so far ahead of the black that he will carry off all the prizes and keep the black man out of the running. The partnership and political power offered to Africans in the present and their prospects of gaining them in the future are ineffective and illusory. African participation in politics is organized minority representation, organized impotence. The standards Africans are expected to reach are far beyond their grasp and can always be raised if they approach them. The only education available to them is segregated African education, in a separate compartment from European education, with a very narrow outlet indeed to higher secondary and university study. To a very great extent it is training for subordination, designed to keep the great majority of Africans at primary school level.

The present system of tests and qualifications for participation in public and political life could only work fairly if existing discriminations between Africans as a group and Europeans as a group were removed—if they started to prove their merit from an equal footing. At present it is like a Derby in which two or three runners have had oats, exercise and first class training and the rest have been half-trained on dry high-veld grass for the whole winter. The result is not in doubt. Simply to introduce an interracial constitution was not enough. To make it successful it was necessary at the same time to take the most energetic measures to remove the actual discriminations between the races that hamstring the African group. This is not being done. Most of the advances the Government claim credit for have been changes of social colour bar, a relatively unimportant affair from the practical point of view, and not changes in discrimination at all. Interracial hotels, equal treatment in Post Offices, permission to use railway dining-cars and so on, have no effect at all on an African's ability to acquire a vote. Universal free elementary education, a dozen more grammar schools, greatly improved access to universities, many more trade schools and apprenticeship schemes, equal pay and equal access, on merit, to all jobs in the railways and mines, an economic minimum wage for Africans (say

£4 a week instead of about the same a month), the abolition of land apportionment, the provision of European-style medical and welfare services, and of pension and insurance schemes, for Africans, an intense effort to raise the productivity of African peasant agriculture by capitalization, co-operation, training and advice—all this and much like it is what is needed to precipitate the social revolution without which the Federal Constitution must remain a mere pretence of interracialism and equality of opportunity covering up the same old discrimination as ever. The argument that the Federation cannot afford the money for this kind of thing is unconvincing. There are many sources of capital for countries with a real will to attack under-development. Social investment of this kind pays a beneficial high return to the community as a whole and would be far more profitable to it, though not to the European minority, than expensive schemes like Kariba.

The Government's professions of "implementing partnership" could only be taken seriously if it were making this kind of effort and devoting the major part of its revenue to overcoming African poverty, ignorance, under-privilege and sickness—to helping these people up to the European standard of living instead of waiting for them to achieve the European standard of culture and civilization. It is not doing this. Much is made of what is being done for African development. But considering the size of the problem—the prerequisite for "partnership" is radically to alter the living standard of 7 million people—the smallness of the effort is remarkable. Six per cent of the total Federal revenue goes from the Federal budget to Nyasaland; a few secondary or trade schools are going up here and there; some aid is being given to African agriculture; the University College of Rhodesia and Nyasaland[1] at Salisbury has African students. But all this is nothing like enough. African development is

[1] The College is a case in point. The Government is continually quoting it as an earnest of its good faith, because the College exists and takes African students on a footing of equality with Europeans. As far as it goes this is exemplary. But the surprising thing is that no higher education for Africans in any of the territories existed till 1955 and that it will now be years before more than forty or fifty can receive it at any one time. The output of twenty or so African graduates a year will not transform African society and the number of places occupied is very small for a population of 7 million. By no fault of the College authorities, the openings it offers are so limited that it can play little part in changing the condition of the African community as a whole. It is like the nine African Members in the House—an interracial ornament that cannot possibly affect the balance of power between the races. Thousands of Europeans will continue to send their children to universities in Britain or the Union and the European lead will be maintained.

subsidiary all along the line to European advance. Until the Government makes the African social revolution its main objective, by concentrating state aid and planning on intensive techniques for dealing with under-development, and gives this a stronger claim on its efforts than the capitalization of European enterprise and the introduction of fresh European immigrants, it will not even be on the way to creating conditions in which the Constitution can justify its liberal pretensions. In one of the richest countries in the world, where European industry, commerce and enterprise are progressing at a fantastic rate, and European agriculture is lavishly, if not always economically, established, the poverty of 7 million Africans is the greatest social problem, and very little is being done to resolve it.

The official argument is that economic expansion will of itself solve the problem. It does not matter that it is all European. As the economy expands, the number of jobs will increase and rates of pay for all races will go up. The country has sufficient resources to maintain the whole population at a high standard of living and if its exploitation by European skill and resource goes on as it is now, Africans will participate in its benefits as well as Europeans. Very soon, many more will earn enough to get a vote and assume leading positions and gradually both political and economic inequalities will painlessly disappear.

The justice of allowing the economic development of a country to be dictated solely by an immigrant thirty-sixth of the population is questionable. Do the Africans want Kariba or the magnificent sky-scraping office blocks that are going up in Salisbury or Lusaka? Is this the way they want their country developed? Should they have a share in the profits that are being made by Europeans at the moment, or is it enough for them to participate—if they will—indirectly in a gradually rising standard of living? And apart from all this, the argument is vulnerable. Economic expansion has been going on like wildfire since 1953. A few tens of thousands of African workers on the copperbelt enjoy rather higher wages—enough to allow them a good instead of a bad African standard but nothing like enough to bring them near the lowest European one—but the general African standard has not altered at all. Social and economic changes happen quickly in the twentieth century and considering the speed of development, some result should be perceptible. Economic expansion *has* in fact taken place and has *not* affected the African standard of living. Still less has it done anything whatever to bridge the gap between the races and it is hard to see why it ever should. A high standard of living for an African is a three-roomed house, electricity if he is lucky, one suit of clothes and a cotton dress or two for his wife; enough milk, tea, sugar and carbohydrates for his family and not enough meat; and bus tickets or a bicycle. For a European, a luxury dwelling with modern conveniences, two cars and no need to worry about food, drink and clothing. The Europeans start with an enormous lead and the expanding economy will do nothing to reduce it; but unless it is reduced the division of society along racial lines, with all its discriminatory political implications, is likely to survive. This is why a government that was in earnest about the spirit of the Constitution would devote all its energies to improving the African standard and, without levelling down European standards, insist upon a really significant African advance as its major objective.

The place of new European immigration in this ideal scheme is hard to understand. Africans are poor and underdeveloped. They need access to the many opportunities and jobs at present taken up by Europeans. They have given a good deal of evidence of their ability to succeed in them if allowed equal chances. A means of remedying their poverty would be to give them such chances. But the Government is vigorously encouraging the immigration of Europeans into the Rhodesias,[1] largely in order to increase the proportion of Europeans to Africans.[2] New immigrants inevitably take up jobs or land that would otherwise be open to Africans and thereby increase the country's racial problem. They all expect and demand a European standard of living and constitute an increased charge on the country's economy whatever contributions they also bring. They will all qualify for the vote and will vote for the Federal Party and European supremacy and this, alas, is the main reason for bringing them in. A government seriously devoted to promoting Africans to European economic standards, and giving them an equal position in society would, as its first move, stop all immigration and expedite the

[1] Figures for European immigration into the Federation are:

1956–57	1957–58	January to October 1958
24,217	16,951	14,784

[2] There is no immigration into Nyasaland but as long as it remains in Federation it will be under a Federal government controlled by Europeans. The population ratio in the Rhodesias concerns it intimately.

advancement of Africans to equality. That the Federal Government does not is the ultimate demonstration that its professed objectives are not its real ones.

White Rhodesians are in a dilemma. They see some objections to the crude racialism they observe in the Union and wish to find another, more elegant, way of organizing society. But they cannot face the fact that "there are only two end-points, total *apartheid* and total integration". They are seeking a middle way, a way which does not exist, a means of perpetuating white privilege and at the same time relieving the black man of some of the insupportable burdens it places on him. They cannot see that unless they are prepared for total integration, they are bound to slip into the practice of *apartheid*. This stood out again and again in Sir Roy Welensky's address to the Federal Party Congress in September 1959, which we have already quoted. "I am convinced that our approach to the problem of a mixed community is the right one and I lose patience with those people who see in the removal of racial pinpricks the doom of the white man in Africa." Racial pinpricks—restaurant cars and public lavatories—are not the point. Political and economic discrimination are and their removal means political and economic integration. Social integration is much less important. Sir Roy went on: "Poverty in Africa is a living reality and the Federation is part of Africa. Therefore we cannot ignore it or delay the task of eliminating it. And because we of all people must be realists if we are to survive in Africa, we cannot afford to pretend that there is any solution to the racial problems of Africa which does not embody betterment of the living standards of the African. Therefore," he said, "while I will never be prepared to concede the European standards of the Federation to political expediency, our task here is to do all we possibly can with all the outside help we can gain, to raise the standards of our African people and to raise them as quickly as possible."

This is all very exemplary and one hopes that Sir Roy will do it. But why depend only upon outside help? Why not divert to African development some of the Federal funds now spent on maintaining European standards—on European education, on social services, for instance—or raise the very moderate rate of European taxation, in order to prove the Federation's sincerity? Why not put an end to European immigration since Europeans take out of the economy more than they put in and use cheap black labour to do so, since the argument that more immigration produces more prosperity for the benefit of Africans will not bear examination, since the Africans do not get a fair share of what prosperity there is and since more Europeans are a barrier to their political emancipation? Will Sir Roy attempt not only to raise the living standard of African people but to bring the franchise within their reach? For, besides the definition of partnership, which has never been given, there is another and even deeper question behind the theory and practice of the Constitution, behind professed interracialism and actual European supremacy. It is the sixty-four thousand dollar question for the Federation. It is the riddle of the Sphinx and no one has ever been found to answer it. Are the Europeans, who profess that there are no racial politics, no real colour bar, and equal opportunity for all in the Federation, prepared to envisage the day when black voters outnumber white on the ordinary roll, and political control passes from white into black hands? Or will they continue as long as they can the present shuffling rearguard action, giving Africans the appearance of the vote and withholding real political power, paying lip service to African advancement and clinging to European privilege?

Sir Roy made some illuminating remarks on this question. Those who favoured extreme measures to satisfy their desire for power, he said, should realize that extremism was not going to be allowed. They must realize that leadership was not an easy task. It required acceptance of responsibility as well as readiness to subscribe to the essential laws and rules of the community. Is European supremacy one of the essential laws and rules of the community? Is it extremism to challenge it? Did the Congress leaders whom he was criticizing fail in responsibility to their own African community or to the European oligarchy which dominates it? What is extremism and who is not going to allow it? Even if Congress leaders did favour extreme measures to satisfy their desire for power (rather than executing their own responsibility to their own community), who has power now and who desires it?

The Europeans have the power, as we have seen, and they have laid down the essential laws and rules of the community. Until they are prepared to alter them, to mitigate their claim on decisive political power and abandon their stranglehold on the means of representation, the only way of protest open to Africans will be extremism tending to defiance and violence. Raising the African standard of living, necessary though it is, is only a groundwork for the willing extension of African political rights. The opposition to this is centred in the European electorate of Southern Rhodesia. It is the largest white group in Central Africa and it has set the tone of political life and race relations for the whole Federation. It is still essentially *apartheid*-minded and shows so far no disposition to change its prejudices or its privileges. Unless it can do so, it will be impossible for the Federation to survive in any manner consonant with Britain's undertakings and responsibilities to Northern Rhodesia and Nyasaland. And if it survives in breach of them it will sooner or later be dismembered by African bitterness and discontent. However good the intentions of the Federal Government might be it can, as Mr. Savante said, "only do a limited amount unless it is genuinely supported in its measures". It can in fact as now constituted do nothing to destroy African poverty, banish discrimination and promote African political advancement without the support of Southern Rhodesia. It looks at present as if it would be a long time before it has this support. But until it has, any thought of Federal independence of Britain is out of the question. A reassertion of Britain's right to legislate for the Federation and to govern the northern territories would be more to the point. Sir Roy Welensky said, at the Party Congress on 17th September 1959, that he was convinced the 1960 Constitutional Conference would end in full independence and nationhood. If the Federation's Government continued to accept its responsibilities, he was convinced its record and programme would make this outcome inevitable. He can hardly believe it in the early days of 1960 and anyhow it is hard to see what he means. How do the Federation and its government accept their responsibilities? What is there that is reassuring in its record and programme?

CHAPTER IX

Southern Rhodesia and Federation

The Federation has failed to achieve anything the British Parliament expected it to because of the fallacy that the Constitution and the doctrine of partnership were strong and precise enough to bridge the Zambezi and provide a creative opportunity for the principles (even if they were not always practised) of the Protectorates to modify the white supremacy of Southern Rhodesia. The tensions inherent in the situation have proved too strong. The responsibility is Britain's for imagining that Federation could possibly work in tune with British policy and thinking on colonial affairs. But it is mainly due to Southern Rhodesia that the Federal Government has proved to be a settlers' government, none the less because the Federal Prime Minister during the decisive years has been a Northern Rhodesian.

It was not that the Southern Rhodesians set out deliberately to infiltrate and dominate the Federation, but that with Southern Rhodesia as a focus, or a rallying point, the various white groups united to acquire a much greater power, over a much greater area, than any had possessed individually. Southern Rhodesians, as the largest, most homogeneous and well-established group, set the key and the tone. They simply could not help doing so. The settlers of Northern Rhodesia and Nyasaland were no more liberal, nor more enthusiastic about African paramountcy, but, in spite of their influence over their local legislatures, their isolation placed limits on their power. They would have liked independent settler government but they knew they had no chance of getting it. They were subject to the same slow-footed, faltering but ultimately decisive Colonial Office power that for fifty years has been protecting Kenya from becoming another Southern Rhodesia. Federation, however, loosened the grip of the Colonial Office if it did not altogether break its hold. It gave Europeans in the northern territories the backing and support of Southern Rhodesian tradition and Southern Rhodesian numbers. It gave them fresh confidence and made it possible to envisage a single co-ordinated European policy, independent of London, for the whole Federation, to entrench white supremacy in Northern Rhodesia and adapt Nyasaland's rate of progress to European wishes. The Federal Government's job was to carry out this policy. It is not so much that Southern Rhodesia is constitutionally over-represented in the Federal Parliament, as that the Southern Rhodesian system fulfils the inmost desire of the majority of settlers and offers them what they have always wanted. Inevitably most of them line up with Southern Rhodesia. This is exactly what the Africans knew would happen. They opposed Federation because they knew that the Federal Government would be a European-dominated government standing for white supremacy with the support of the whole European population. It is useless to blame Southern Rhodesians for the influence they have had. Their history and tradition makes them complacently certain of the absolute justice of total white supremacy and their sense of insecurity makes them irrationally and fetishistically attached to the preservation of all its trappings and symbols. But the fact must be faced that they hold the dominant influence in Federal politics. No Federal Government can survive long if it offends them on racial issues; and their influence is contrary to all that Britain has promised and stands for.

It is ironical that the only people who do not see all this are the Southern Rhodesian Europeans. The majority of them are perhaps the only people in the world who take Welensky's interracial professions *au pied de la lettre* and genuinely believe that the Federation and its constitution as at present interpreted represent a serious threat to European privileges. The Dominion Party is so afraid lest even the shadow of the Colonial Office's "sentimental" Native policy should fall over Southern Rhodesia from the north that it is demanding Southern Rhodesia's secession[1] from Federation and re-establishment as an independent self-governing white colony unless the whole Federation is granted complete self-government and independence of Britain at once.[2] Mr. S. Aitken-Cade, then leader of the Dominion

[1] Sir Edgar Whitehead, the Federal Party Prime Minister, also began to talk seriously of secession unless Britain was prepared to guarantee the rule of "civilized men" only in the northern territories, in January 1960.

[2] The D.P. reiterated this demand when Mr. Macmillan visited Salisbury on 20th January 1960. It took particular exception to the Prime Minister's assurance that his Government would not withdraw protection from Northern Rhodesia and Nyasaland till they desired it and said: "This clearly indicates that no recommendation from the Monckton Commission can change the U K. Government's determination to establish African-controlled governments in the northern

territories. The only conclusion that can be drawn from this is that the Federal Government will duly be controlled by the African electorate. In this case, and unless the security of the European in Southern Rhodesia and the country's natural wealth are assured, the colony will have no alternative but to secede." If this is how it thinks it clearly does have no alternative. A Federal Government responsive to African opinion is the only kind of Federal government compatible with the intention of the Constitution, Britain's responsibilities and the survival of Federation.

It is irresistible to compare the D.P.'s expressed belief that government by an African majority must be intolerable to Europeans and deleterious to the country's economic and natural resources with a letter written a week later, on 27th January 1960, by Sir Robert Kirkwood to *The Times* from Jamaica.

"The fears that are expressed by white settlers in Africa were widely held in Jamaica until quite recently. When first I came here 20 years ago, the average white Jamaican openly and vociferously argued, and genuinely believed, that the 'black man' was quite incapable of running the country. And even conservative coloured and black Jamaicans averred that universal adult suffrage 'could never work here'.

Yet look at us now. More economic progress has been achieved in the short years since Jamaicans elected under universal adult suffrage took over the Government than in the previous century. Incidentally, two white Jamaicans were recently elected to the Federal Parliament, and two more to the Jamaican House of Representatives; and this under adult suffrage in a country where coloured voters outnumber whites by one hundred to one.

When one explains this to the average European resident in Africa he replies that our circumstances are quite different from his; our electorate much more advanced, etc. This misses the point that in backward communities, particularly, it is not the electorate but the leaders who run the country. And, although I have not visited Africa myself, experienced and reliable Jamaican friends of mine who know the leaders in Kenya, Nyasaland, the Rhodesias, etc., tell me that most of these men, though dedicated and even fanatical nationalists, are, for the most part, far from holding radical views in economic matters. My friends consider that once elected to power these men would seek advice and assistance, and govern with a sense of responsibility and attention to what is best for the economic development of their respective homelands.

This is where the European comes in. West Indian leaders know that we can help, and they take us into counsel. We unreservedly acknowledge, and help to sustain, their leadership. They, in turn, feel the need to inspire confidence in the western countries if they are to obtain much needed know-how and capital for development. This they could not do by penalizing white minorities and expropriating European capital. Nor have I ever detected that our politicians felt the slightest inclination to penalize capital of any description going about its legitimate business.

From my talks with Jamaicans who know Africa I am convinced that the present Central and East African leaders will still turn to the western countries for economic aid, and not to Russia, provided we take prompt steps to join with them in a rapid advance to self-government on the basis of a common roll. The Africans are the majority; the majority must govern; and they must govern during the lifetime of their present leaders. Every year that passes without an acknowledgment of this fact and related action thereon will increase the chances that the African leaders will turn to Russia.

I am certain that most of our present West Indian leaders, who have earned general commendation from Europeans resident in these parts, as well as in their missions abroad, would have been capable, only a few years ago, of leading revolutions, bloody revolutions, if their rightful ambitions to govern in their own homes had been indefinitely and unreasonably deferred. Within 10 brief years a mighty and beneficial transformation can take place in the economy of a backward country under the spur of nationalism and leadership. And a decade of wasted years is a frustrating, embittering experience for a zealous patriot and his followers."

Party, the opposition in the Southern Rhodesian Parliament, brought a motion before the House in July 1959 asking for a referendum to find out whether the people of Southern Rhodesia (he meant, of course, the Europeans) wanted to stay in the Federation. The questions which should be put, he said, were whether Southern Rhodesia should remain part of the Federation in which during the past two or three years it had lost the initiative or whether it should regain its independence. The motion was defeated by only sixteen votes to eleven, after the Prime Minister, Sir Edgar Whitehead, had said that while the country must "continue to fight for dominion status and independence", the economic implications of secession were altogether too serious. The importance of this is that the Dominion Party is the *majority party* in Southern Rhodesia. Sir Edgar Whitehead's Federal Party government is a *minority government* which won the 1958 territorial election only because of the distribution of seats and the system of the alternative vote which is in force. A majority of Southern Rhodesian electors actually voted for the Dominion Party, and if Mr. Aitken-Cade's referendum had been held, it might easily have decided for the Dominion Party policy. It may seem almost incredible that a majority of Southern Rhodesia's white population finds the exiguous, almost imperceptible moves that have been made towards African emancipation so alarming that it would prefer giving up the copperbelt to accepting them. It is not easy for those who believe that the Federation should be dismembered, or at very least fundamentally overhauled, because it is unfair to Africans, to gauge the value of this strange and unexpected support from allies who believe it is unfair to Europeans. But, in view of its dominant position, as well as the oddity of some of its attitudes, a more detailed examination of Southern Rhodesia must be the next stage in our study of the Federation.

PART THREE

Partnership in Practice

A Study of Southern Rhodesia

CHAPTER X

Southern Rhodesia Today

We left Southern Rhodesia on the verge of Federation at the end of the first chapter—a small shoal of coeloacanths sheltering in an amiable backwater from the storms ahead. Federation brought a generous infusion of rich food into the pool and re-established its connection with the affairs of a wider world. Commerce, industry, public enterprise and development of every kind forged ahead at a great pace. A great deal of building has gone on in Salisbury and Bulawayo and they are becoming every day more like sleek American capitals and losing all appearance of pioneer bush settlements. The Kariba Dam—the largest in the world —was begun immediately and is already in full operation. The European community felt increasingly prosperous and secure as new enterprise, new capital and new immigrants came in. It might have been short-sighted to move so far and so fast on the single foundation of Northern Rhodesian copper.[1] But this was not necessary. A great variety of industry has begun or been extended in Southern Rhodesia since 1953—cigarette factories, steel, motor-car assembly plant, light engineering, for instance—and diversified the economy. Private investment and government support have been concentrated in Southern Rhodesia to the detriment of the other territories. (Sir John Moffat referred in the Northern Rhodesian Legislature on 27th January 1960 to "the obvious bias of the Federal Government for the development of Southern Rhodesia at the expense of the north".) It has been a purely material development and has not brought with it any new, detached or enlightened consideration of the country's situation and problems nor of the place of two and a half million Africans in this expanding society.

The result is that in Southern Rhodesia today we find a society

[1] Cf. John Gunther, *Inside Africa*, H. Hamilton, 1955, p. 615. "If a visitor asks what will happen if the price of copper should fall catastrophically, people blanch and change the subject. Among other things practically all social services (those that exist) would have to be drastically reduced. Seldom has any country hitched its wagon to such a single star."

committed by its Constitution to "racial partnership" and actually preoccupied with little but maintaining the privilege of its white members.[1] We find the Federal and territorial governments simultaneously trying to persuade Britain that they are advancing, and actually moving backwards, or at least sideways. We find that the only people who have learnt anything in the past fifty years are the Africans and that, as they demand, even now with surprising moderation, genuine participation in the life and government of the country, the majority of Europeans retreat in shocked horror into a quite unnecessary State of Emergency.

There are lots and lots of very nice white people in Southern Rhodesia just as there are in South Africa, or Little Rock. Strictures on a tradition or a system are not condemnations of individuals. But there is no avoiding the fact that, with the exception of a few dozen really independent thinkers, the white population of Southern Rhodesia is enslaved by its history, bound by traditional attitudes, and blinded by one of the most powerful of all human lights—the gleam of a large steady income.

The position of the few genuine liberals is probably more isolated and difficult even than in the Union, because there are not enough of them to give each other support. The monolithic structure of society constitutes almost as good a thought police as the more obvious repressiveness of the Nationalist Government or the Broederbond[2]—in some ways a more insidious one because its influence is unconscious and oblique. You cannot be declared a statutory communist and deprived of civil rights by the Minister of Justice (though you can now be shut up for five years without trial on mere suspicion of association with Congress). But it would be social and professional suicide to proclaim in Southern Rhodesia that the inevitable implications of partnership, in however remote a future, are an integrated society, universal suffrage, the abolition of racial discrimination and restriction, and control of government by an African majority; or to declare much sympathy with the African National Congress and its aims. Very few jobs would be open to anyone who

[1] "In some respects segregation is more pronounced in the Rhodesias than anywhere else in Africa, even in Kenya and the Union . . . racial discriminations in the Rhodesias are among the most barbarous, shameful and disgusting in the world." John Gunther, op. cit.

[2] The secret society of Afrikaner intellectuals—mainly teachers, Dutch Reformed pastors and university lecturers—which is the inspiration, and to a great extent the master, of the Nationalist Party and the fountain of Afrikaner orthodoxy.

Sir Roy Welensky

Kenneth Kaunda

JOSHUA NKOMO

SIR EDGAR WHITEHEAD

professed such views; if he were a professional man his practice might diminish. He would lose friends. He would be carefully watched by the ubiquitous and efficient C.I.D. who take a particular interest in thoughts they cannot understand and who proved in the 1959 Emergency to have very well-filled dossiers concerning the private thoughts and words of liberal Europeans. He would seriously endanger the well-being and social position of his wife and children. And he would feel that his voice found no resonance, that he was accomplishing nothing. One achieves little but self-destruction by battering against the granite block of Rhodesian prejudice. And life can be agreeably ample if one accepts things as they are.

Perhaps the only way a real liberal can at the moment be effective is as a lecturer at the University College of Rhodesia and Nyasaland. A few European members of this society belonged to Congress until it was proscribed and continued to demonstrate their practical sympathy with it afterwards and were not arrested or muzzled, as they could have been. But Salisbury City Council, as well as the Nyasaland tobacco growers' association, withdrew substantial grants of money they had promised to the College in 1959 in protest at the political views of some of its members. Taken in conjunction with the far more serious actions of Sir Edgar Whitehead's government in passing the most arbitrarily repressive legislation into law with the unstinted agreement of a vast majority of public opinion in 1959, this kind of thing seems a disappointingly inadequate response to the challenges of Southern Rhodesia's future. It unquestionably makes the expression of liberal—or even unconventional—opinion dangerous rather in the way it is in General Franco's Spain than in a Western democracy. And Guy Clutton-Brock's detention shows where participation in African movements leads to.

It is widely claimed that the 1959 Emergency has stimulated liberal thinking in Southern Rhodesia and that a truly progressive public opinion is crystallizing among Europeans; but one looks in vain for signs of it in the actions of the Government or the words of the opposition. Certainly the Emergency, and the not very favourable world publicity it attracted, has made quite a lot of Rhodesians who never thought about it all before see that there is something wrong. But what evidence is there that they recognize what must be done to put it right or are ready to urge the necessary measures upon the unyielding majority of their fellow citizens? When there is a substantial body of European opinion in favour of abolishing land apportionment and extending the African vote, it will be time to talk of a progressive movement. The 1959 Emergency and the suppression of all African political organization is an historical fact.

In Kenya violence was forced upon the Europeans by the Africans. Mau Mau demonstrated in a sinister and terrifying way the effect of continued frustration, subordination and exclusion from rights in their own country upon a vital and emergent African people and the irresistible power of an African majority to claim attention for their grievances by force if they are driven to sufficient exasperation. Exasperation was intense, pent-up and well-founded; the outburst of violence was unusually barbarous and revolting. Unfortunately, nothing else was enough to bring Kenya Europeans to a fundamental re-examination of their own position, making constitutional change and political reform of a kind that could not have been dreamt of ten years ago a practical possibility. It is no use blinking the unpleasant fact, that despite the poisoned and distorted forms assumed by Mau Mau, and despite its military defeat, violence has produced results for the Africans in Kenya, even though it was violence of an unusually disgusting kind, which did more harm to Africans than to Europeans, and was detested by most of them. The fault lies with the Europeans for having neglected peaceful protests for so long.

There was nothing of this sort about the 1959 Emergency in Southern Rhodesia. It was forced upon the Africans by a European government. There was no threat of force from Congress and not the slightest menace to public order. The events of 1959 caused no inconvenience to Europeans and have not brought them to re-examine their position or the structure of their society. The Government determined to use the disturbance in Nyasaland as an excuse to carry out plans long conceived to nip Congress in the bud and reaffirm white domination. Congress was a legal political party, not a secret society like Mau Mau. It was pledged to work by constitutional means and any sort of violence was as much beyond its capacities as its wishes. It was suppressed on the assumption—which stands out very clearly in the territorial Prime Minister's speech in the House on 13th March presenting the Preventive Detention Bill[1]—that anything Africans did for themselves was bound to be misguided and wrong; they must accept their position as wards of

[1] For a description of this measure see page 200.

the Native Affairs Department—a government within a government, which administers African life according to European decrees through a system separate from the political, economic and social processes set up for Europeans. Congress was condemned as subversive; but it has never been explained why, if it really was, none of its leaders or members have been prosecuted according to the existing, and very stringent, laws against subversion and sedition, nor why special legislation permitting imprisonment without trial was necessary to "deal with it".

Unless Southern Rhodesians recognize that Africans have legitimate grievances in full measure and set out to put them right by steps that seem to them at present out of the question, the future will bring more, not less, "subversion". The demand for social justice can only be resisted by tyranny. Cleaning up Congress and stamping out African protests is to cauterize the symptom and ignore the disease. The disease is the relegation of two and a half million Africans to a second-class position in society and it makes all professions about "partnership" hypocritical. The only cure is to abolish such measures as the Land Apportionment Act, the Native Affairs Act, the Native Land Husbandry Act and the pass laws, to get rid of legalized discrimination of all kinds and to revise the electoral system. African interests must be represented in fair proportion to the number of Africans and Congress and other African organizations that may arise must be admitted to the counsels of the country. When Rhodesians today talk about social integration, they conceive it in the narrow sense of restaurant cars, public lavatories and interracial hotels, the granting of minor social privileges and, though they do not much like it, they still imagine it will do something to meet the situation. This is a dangerous illusion. Africans care very little about this kind of integration and it does nothing to solve their problems. It gives them nothing of substance. Political and economic justice and equality before the law are what they want and these are the only things that will do any good. If white Rhodesians can find the strength and courage to disown exclusion, segregation and discrimination they may find even now that they can live in peace with Africans and avoid being "swamped by a black flood". If they are determined, under the insignia of partnership, to perpetuate a condition of helotry for Africans and supremacy for Europeans, the events of 1959 can only prove to be the prelude to a real convulsion that could cause Central Africa slowly to disintegrate into chaos.

he saw his African friend waiting for the same train and walked up to greet him and shake his hand. But suddenly he recollected that he was in public. Several Europeans whose good opinion was important to him were watching. Changing his tone in mid sentence to the stridency reserved for natives he said: "Come, boy. Get out of my way," and stumped off to the end of the platform pretending the whole thing had never happened.

The Press is full of curious instances of preoccupation with race. The *Citizen* (Salisbury) of 26th July 1957 had the following item on its front news page. (Admittedly the *Citizen* is rather a *News of the World*, but the *News of the World* does a lot to express and to condition public opinion in Britain.): "Rumours growing in length as they spread reached the *Citizen* this week. The informants were perturbed about what they described as 'the thin end of the wedge' or 'the beginning of the end'. They had heard that four European women in the accounts section of the Rhodesian Labour Supply Commission had had two Native clerks put in the same office with them. They alleged that the women now had no privacy at all and strongly objected to having two Native men staying in the same room as themselves all day long. On investigation it was found that the facts were true but the fears—that the time had apparently come when European women were to be forced to work with African males whether they liked it or not—were groundless. The whole affair was a time and labour-saving experiment. Endeavouring to facilitate the women's work on the posting machines, it was decided to see if their work could be speeded up by employing two African clerks to do the elementary but time-wasting job of sorting out the cards and preparing lists for the day's work. During my investigation, an official told me that a decision was pending to remove the African clerks from the girls' room if they were taken on as permanent."

An elderly lady said to me the other day: "They're giving education to the Natives now—Africans as we have to call them. But it's not right you know. They can't do it, they just can't do education as we can. I'm told that only one in a hundred who begins education gets to the end." She didn't know what kind of education she meant nor what "the end" was nor what happened to the ninety-nine who failed to reach it.

Whether this form of delusion is preferable to a more realistic approach to the racial problem is hard to say. Younger and more hard-headed people certainly take a different line, which Sir Roy

Welensky expressed admirably when he said lately that the white races were not going to take any risks, "we have too much to lose"; or again in a speech on 18th July 1957: "The role of the European is not to bring this great country out of the darkness and savagery that has clouded it for centuries only in order to hand it over to someone else." This is the classic over-simplification you encounter daily. Those who propound it must be either dishonest or stupid and it is not easy to know which they would prefer to be thought. No one has ever suggested that the European should hand over to someone else. Even the manifesto of the African National Congress of Southern Rhodesia, before it was suppressed, pledged itself to the principle of equality between black and white. I have never heard anyone in Congress suggest, even in long private conversations with its leaders, that they want the white man to "hand over" completely or to "get out". There is no anti-white movement among the Africans nor even much anti-white sentiment—yet. There is a strong and growing demand for a removal of some of the disabilities the black population suffers in relation to the white, for an approach to something like fair representation. It would be no compliment to Sir Roy Welensky's intelligence, nor to his intelligence service, to imagine that he was not perfectly aware of this when he suggested that he might be asked "to hand the country over to someone else", but he has to say this kind of thing to please his electors.

The social situation between the races was excellently described by the African barrister, Mr. H. W. Chitepo, in an article entitled "*What the educated African feels on being addressed as Boy*" in the *Rhodesia Herald* of 16th July 1957: "What in fact happens at the frontiers of contact leaves much to be desired. In offices the African must not use the lift or the main staircase—he must use the fire escape. A special messenger is employed in many buildings to prevent Africans from using lift or staircase. And when he has found his way up by the back stairs he is met at the reception desk by a cold indifferent voice. If he replies in a cultured voice and correct English she (the receptionist) gets even more furious and out comes the kitchen kaffir:[1] 'Ena busy maningi steriek. Come tomorrow.'

In the shops the situation is often much worse. The African must wait until every European has been served. In some cases he must wait until even the Indians and Coloureds have been served, including

[1] A bastard mixture of European and African languages in which it is considered proper to address black servants.

those who came in after the African has stood at the counter and waited. When the assistant is in a very good mood she will say, 'What can I do for you, boy?' Occasionally she gets the shock of her life from the retort: 'I am not your boy.'

The African determined to get what he wants has to wait with fury and anger bursting out of him. Next morning he reads in the *Herald* the Minister's speech in Parliament, 'our record in race relations is one of which we can be justly proud. Nowhere in Africa have relations between African and European been so good.' The African is expected to echo this sentiment after yesterday's experience at shop or office. The African M.P. is expected to speak in glowing terms of how well partnership is working. The African leader who after such experiences denounces partnership as a sham, a mask to conceal from the outside world the true intentions of the Europeans, is a political demagogue, irresponsible and dangerous.

The sixty or so years since settlement of Southern Rhodesia by the Europeans have brought and left many complexes, prejudices and deep-seated irrational assumptions in the relation between African and European. The most significant of these is that the Africans do only menial tasks. Both custom and convention have seen to it that contact between the European and African is the contact between master and servant. . . ."

By contrast, think what it would be like to try and argue with the European M.P. who said this (also reported in the *Rhodesia Herald*):

"Over-emphasis on academic education combined with the wrong type of teaching and over-stimulation of unsuitable and irresponsible political comprehension in African schools is laying the foundation of future friction. 5 per cent of the revenue is contributed by Africans, and 20 per cent of it is spent on him,[1] more than half of it on academic education. Academic education is not to the advantage of the Africans at their present stage of development. Too many African teachers seem to think they should impart a political flavour to their teaching. Pupils at Goromonzi [the first, and till 1957 only Government secondary school for Africans] were asked to write an essay on what they hoped to achieve and 90 per cent wanted to be M.P.s."

[1] This is a convenient simplification which overlooks African contribution to revenue through indirect taxation, fines and in various other ways; as well as the fact that European incomes are so much higher than African that it would be reasonable for European taxation to make a much larger contribution to African welfare than it does. If African wages were higher, there would be less profit, so really the Africans pay the tax.

A self-styled "antiquarian" wrote, in a letter to the Press:

"The Bantu first crossed the Zambezi into this country in about the fourteenth century. The idea that the Bantu inhabited this country from time immemorial and consequently have a claim to it is a dangerous myth." Argument will never get far with racial prejudice of this kind. The foundation of the whole thing was tragically summed up in a conversation with a thoroughly nice, intelligent young woman, the wife of a rather despairingly liberal Federal civil servant in Salisbury. She said that Kwame Nkrumah made her flesh creep; she found him altogether alarming. "But why?" I asked. "Well, it's all this Pan-African stuff he talks—the Africans working together to get control of the continent and so on." "Well, isn't that just what Cecil Rhodes was telling the white man to do a little time ago?" "Yes, I suppose it is, but I don't mind that." "Why not?" "Because it doesn't affect my children's future."

Certainly, white Southern Rhodesians are faced with a difficult decision—whether to take the obvious, short-sighted course or to look ahead to the long view, whether to cast their bread upon the waters or to try and hang on to their cake. They can only provide a future for their children and grandchildren by coming to terms with African nationalism before it is too late. But, in the words of the Tredgold Report,[1] "Only a man of exceptional moral fibre can be relied upon to press for the long view, involving compromise and concession of immediate benefits by his group, especially as this course must lay him open to a charge of disloyalty to his group." It would be complacent to blame them if they do not possess this exceptional moral fibre nor produce leaders who do. But this does not make it any easier to accept mere professions of "partnership" as evidence that white society as a whole *is* taking the long view. "After all they *can* buy beer and spirits now and educated Africans are more or less exempt from passes." "Education is going ahead like anything." "You wouldn't believe how quickly things are changing." When one is asked to believe that genuine liberalism is in the ascendant, one is asked to listen to the whisperings of a few uneasy consciences and to close one's ears to the continuous rumble of conservative prejudice.

Some liberals may be ready to cast their own bread upon the waters but it is not easy for them to exhort other people to do the

[1] Report of the Franchise Commission, p. 5, ll. 265–8, Government Printer, Salisbury, 1957.

same. To do so brings them within the orbit of a law which declares it criminal "to utter words or do any act or thing whatever to promote hostility between one or more sections of the community and any other section or sections or encourages anyone to break the law". Widely interpreted this might punish by a £100 fine or a year in prison or both almost any move to give justice and respect to African nationalism—telling a black man he had a raw deal from the whites, encouraging African Trade Unions or political organizations. It could certainly convict the organizers of any defiance campaign against segregation such as Freda Troup, Helen Joseph and Patrick Duncan organized in Johannesburg: and their only crime was to enter an African Municipal housing estate.

CHAPTER XII

Rural Partnership

Many of the laws of Southern Rhodesia seem to exist to make justice impossible and are as discriminatory as anything in the Union of South Africa. The Land Apportionment Act, 1941, was a rather stronger version of the original Land Apportionment Act of 1930, which in its turn only summarized and recognized practices which had been progressively sanctioned by custom since 1898. Various additions and amendments to it have been passed by the territorial parliament since 1941. The Act is not very different from the celebrated Group Areas Act in the Union, except in its effect upon the Asian and Coloured people.[1] It divides the whole country into large separate parcels for Africans and Others and provides that no African may under any circumstances own or occupy any land or premises reserved for Others and vice versa. It is so strictly applied that special Acts of Parliament were needed to enable Mr. H. W. Chitepo, a bencher of the Inns of Court, to occupy chambers in Salisbury and to allow African students to live and work in the University College of Rhodesia and Nyasaland which is in a European part of the town. A European may be given rights in a Native (African) area by a white Native Commissioner, (the African chief's agreement is required in rural areas, but since he is a civil

[1] In most respects, the same laws apply to Asians and Europeans. This reflects the fact that Southern Rhodesian law is not founded upon the near-religious Afrikaner conception of racial purity but upon the desire to preserve economic privilege. The Asians are too few to threaten this seriously. But there is a perceptible tendency to extend legal discrimination to Asians. Social discrimination against Asians is enforced by custom. Legally an Asian may buy a house or land wherever he wishes, but the European landlord who sells or rents premises to an Asian incurs the obloquy of his fellow Europeans. No Asian except the diplomatic representatives of India and Pakistan have ever lived in Salisbury's European residential areas. Asians live in the Indian quarter, by a convention which is as unbreakable as a law, because there they can buy real estate which was in Asian hands before the present stratification set in. They may, and do, occupy business premises anywhere, which Africans may not. A few of the less desirable European farms have been sold by their owners to Asians but this is rare.

servant subordinate to the Commissioner, he could not well withhold it), while an African may never be given rights in European areas save by Act of Parliament. When Apportionment was made law, the Act accepted all existing European holdings as equitable, presupposing that the Founding Fathers and early settlers had acted justifiably when they occupied[1] the country. But Mrs. Millin in her by no means hostile biography of Mr. Rhodes writes: "It was to Mashonaland rather than the (geographically) more convenient Matabeleland that Rhodes sent his pioneers because he knew he had no right to the land and preferred to argue the matter if necessary with the humble Mashona rather than with the arrogant Matabele." The early settlers took what they wanted, not what they needed, and left the rest to the "Natives". You see the pattern wherever you go in the country today. Drive north-east from Salisbury tomorrow, through Banket, Senoia and Karoi on the road to Kariba. As long as the country is flat, open veldt, easy to work and not too stony, the whitened plough discs mounted on the road side proclaim the names of fortunate people farming between 2,000 and 20,000 acres—"A. B. Puttock, Glenivet," X.Z. "Slivovitz, Steppeland Farm" or "J. G. van der Bult, Oud Oranje"—and point the way through herds of Friesians or Afrikanders, crops of maize and tobacco and much uncultivated land to pleasant homesteads where the gathered tractors and show jumpers eavesdrop the clink of sundowner glasses. These people have built up their herds and bought their tractors by their own hard work and capital risk and should not be blamed. Their company can be as good as their hospitality as long as you keep off the Native Question.[2] But the law establishing their privilege puts them, like everyone else in the country, in a false position. As soon as you reach the stony red mountains leading up to the Zambezi escarpment all this stops, and it is Native Reserve. Drive east to Umtali and for over a hundred miles the picture is the same; large open farms, each with its irrigation dam built round a good spring as a reservoir against the long, dry winter; fine herds and fertile crops, so that people say: "Look how well the white man farms. This is the prosperity of our Great Country." There is a little ridge just beyond Rusape and off the main road where what was St. Faith's

[1] Occupation Day is a Southern Rhodesian national holiday. The use of the military term is rooted in tradition.

[2] "We've had to give up maize and concentrate wholly on dairying," one hostess on a hard working farm said to me. "Why? Baboons?" "No, worse," she said. "Human baboons! The path to the Reserve passes through our fields."

Mission Farm used to abut on the Makoni reserve. You can stand there beneath the precipices of a kopje and near the grove containing the burial places of the Makoni tribe's ancestors. You look west over these flourishing, flat European farms, east into a strange depression like a big bowl of sugar loaves where dry, rocky hills spring up below your point of vision. It looks like an aerial view of the high Apennines. Clusters of beehive huts on the hillsides are joined by long curling trails and through the central valley an unmetalled road winds along, slow and pot-holed. The mountains begin with an exciting suddenness. You are standing on the border between the European Reserve and the Makoni Reserve for Natives. The flat land is European, the mountains are Native.

Rhodesians wriggle a good deal on this land question. "The land in the Reserve is just as good as our land," you will be told, "only the Munts don't know how to use it." This is as true or false as you want it to be. Most of Southern Rhodesia consists of high, dry sand veldt with occasional patches of damp vlei[1] and calls for large scale farming to make it productive. A soil sample from the Reserve and one from a European farming area might yield the same results in the laboratory. But the Europeans have most of the country where the soil is spread out in expanses of hundreds and thousands of acres. In the reserves it lies in small patches broken up by rocks and outcrops, on the sides of steep hills in rough intractable country. You cannot get at the soil to work it and there is less good vlei land; instead the choice is between arid slopes or occasional sodden marsh. There are plenty of places suitable for building dams, but too little money available to build them; and without dams, intensive cultivation is out of the question in a country where it scarcely rains at all for six months of the year. Erosion is harder to control in hilly country and it stands to reason that Africans in the Reserve will not work so hard at their contour ridging when it is an incomprehensible thing that they are roughly ordered to do by the Native Commissioner, as the Europeans who have had the opportunity to learn that their future livelihood depends upon it. These are the things to remember when someone says to you "The Natives are hopeless farmers. They can never achieve what we can. Look at the state of the reserves—in spite of all the work the Native Commissioner put in."

Remember that it is owing to the Land Apportionment Act that

[1] Flat land which is watered for at least most of the year by its own springs.

there is too little land in the reserves for the Africans and too much in the European areas for the Europeans. Nearly all the land is poor light sand veldt and this must be borne in mind when considering the following figures. The relative densities of population are: African reserve land, 33·3 to the square mile; European areas, 4·0 to the square mile. There are 48 million acres allotted to 219,000 Europeans, and 39 million to 2,800,000 Africans. The Constitution and the Land Apportionment lay down that the only places where an African may live are in the reserves or Native Purchase Areas; in a specially segregated part of a town so long, and only so long, as he is employed in that town; or on the land of a European master while he is in his service. The overcrowded reserve is the only place where he can enjoy anything like the peace and security of a home of his own, unless he is one of the very few lucky enough to get a farm in a Native Purchase Area.

There is an acute shortage of reserve land because the size of the reserves has changed hardly at all since 1930[1] and the African population has nearly trebled. Consequent overcrowding, the very grave exhaustion of the soil and the tendency inevitable in such circumstances to split up the available land into ever larger numbers of smaller holdings is forcing the Government to do something. The obvious thing is to make some European and unassigned land, held in trust by the Crown for future white immigrants, available to Africans. But no Government would survive "taking our land for the Munts". So we have the Native Land Husbandry Act 1951[2] and the Native Land Husbandry Regulation 1956, which outline the future of African land tenure. It would be unfair to say, as one is tempted to, that these laws are *designed* to deny any sense of security to Africans, to keep them altogether subservient to the Native Commissioners and to perpetuate the utter difference which exists between the condition of European and African husbandry. They have the benevolent intention of introducing reforms into the reserves for the improvement of agriculture and of raising the standard of living. Many of their provisions would be beneficial,

[1] Certain tracts of remote and economically poor Crown land (e.g. in the Zambezi Valley area) have been reallocated to African use since 1955 in order to accommodate "native squatters" thrown out from better Crown land. Between 1949 and 1957, 80,000 Africans who had established "squatters' rights" on good Crown land were deprived of them.

[2] For a full study of the effects of this Act and of Land Apportionment on African and European agriculture, see K. Brown, *Land in Southern Rhodesia*, Africa Bureau, 1959.

desirable and necessary if they could provide the inevitable prerequisite of more land for African occupation. Without this they make no sense at all. The Government's attempts to claim them as a successful means of revolutionizing African agriculture are contradicted by the report of its own Natural Resources Board in 1954, which said: "The time for plain speaking has now arrived, and it is no exaggeration to say that at the moment we are heading for disaster. We have on the one hand a rapid increase taking place in the African population and on the other a rapid deterioration of the very land on which these people depend for their existence and upon which so much of the future prosperity of the country depends." The deterioration is caused by overcrowding and there has been no change in Land Apportionment since these words were written.

The aim of the Act is to provide larger, and permanent, holdings for a smaller number of Africans so that they can feel secure in the occupation of acreages big enough for profitable farming. It does not work because the shortage of land puts an economic fallacy at the roots of the whole undertaking. For his minimum subsistence, an African farmer needs at very least eight acres and, better, twelve of arable land to grow maize for himself and his family and winter fodder for the cattle. He needs eight oxen—four for ploughing, two young ones coming on, and two cows for breeding. Ten acres of grazing per beast per annum is necessary on this poor sand veldt, so he needs eighty acres of grazing. Under the Act, the unit assigned to him in a farmer's right is six acres of arable (though recently plots of eight acres have sometimes been given, and forty acres of grazing. The basic unit of land is not viable even for subsistence farming. A man may, with the consent of the Native Commissioner, buy up to three additional farming rights from fellow Africans (this is what is meant by transfer of rights) so that the maximum legal holding is twenty-four acres of arable and 160 of grazing—enough for sixteen beasts.[1] As well as limiting the Africans' opportunities for expanding both agriculture and living standards, the compulsory smallness of their holding is disastrous to the conservation of reserve land. The main objection to the Native Land Husbandry Act from the point of

[1] This at least appears to be the maximum in the Act. The Government's explanatory document, "What the N.L.H.A. means to the African", says ambiguously, "an individual may acquire title to an area equal to not more than three times the standard area". In practice, N.C.s generally restrict an individual's arable holding to eighteen, not twenty-four, acres.

view of land use is that it enforces and perpetuates the system of continuous cultivation on land which is for the most part quite unsuitable for it,[1] and suffers accordingly. The minimum unit of European farming land sold by the Government to new settlers is 750 acres because it is considered the smallest area that is an economic proposition for European farming; there is no upper limit to what a European may buy and all European land is freehold.

De-stocking as it is called—the compulsory reduction of the number of cattle in the reserve by order of the N.C.—shows again how the shortage of land and the way the Act is applied defeats its own good intentions. African cattle are in the main too many and too poor. To decrease their number and increase their quality is an excellent thing. But to many Africans cattle are still a symbol of wealth, not an economic utility, and the number you own is all that matters. They are four-footed bank-notes, walking credit balances. If the authorities are going to order a man to give up six cattle—which to him are currency—in order to improve his grazing and turn a smaller number of beasts to more profitable use, they must be able to prove to him the paradox that he will be a richer man without his six bank notes mooching about his land than with them. If de-stocking reduced the permitted number of cattle to eight and taught him something about dairying and cattle breeding, he might find that paradox worked in practice and accept the compulsion gratefully. Since in fact he is compelled to de-stock down to six, and then finds them insufficient to meet his needs and manure his land—that he has lost six bank notes and gained nothing—he bitterly dismisses the whole thing as just another bit of the Europeans' tyrannical chicanery and, more important, rejects the idea of improved farming methods. If he could be given more land, none of this need be so; but he cannot because all the spare land is European. Ten thousand Africans are at present on the waiting list for farming rights and some of them have been waiting ten years for land—since before the Bill was passed. Yet the Government goes on encouraging white immigration as vigorously and intensively as it can and allotting European land in 750-acre plots to all of them who want it.

Land reform such as the Act intends is a necessary part of the adjustment of every African community to the cash economy of the modern world (though it should not be forgotten that their own systems of land tenure, and their own methods of shifting cultivation

[1] See K. Brown, op. cit., pp. 8–9 and 11.

were ideally suited to the welfare of their communities and the conservation of their lands before the Europeans revolutionized their environments). But considering that agriculture is the traditional African occupation, that occupation of land is the only security most Africans know, while to many Africans *ownership* of land is an alien conception, and that suspicion of European land-grabbing is the deepest preoccupation of all African minds, it is essential for any reform of land tenure, to enjoy the confidence and understanding of Africans, to be done with their consent and co-operation and, as far as possible, by their own traditional authorities. The way in which it is done matters almost more than what is done. The Act fails in its psychological approach as well as in its agricultural economics. Here, even more than in Kenya, land reform is to be steamrollered through by the white authority.

The Act, when applied to any area, is to be carried out by the Native Commissioner or his representative. He will assign to each applicant the land he is to occupy and may even "point out to him a dwelling site where the farmer or any other native shall reside". The penalty for disobedience is £5 or a month in prison. Landholding is a right granted to the farmer by the Commissioner. It may, if he is thrice convicted of bad farming, be revoked. The native farmer may be moved from one holding to another, even from one area to another, by order of the Commissioner and if he does not go, his stock and crops may be seized and sold. He may not erect any fence without the Commissioner's permission. Disobedience of the husbandry regulations or of any order of the Native Commissioner is an offence punishable by fine or imprisonment.

A landholding right is not negotiable. It cannot be "pledged, attached, sold in execution", nor mortgaged nor used as security *nor may be left in the holder's will.* The right expires on the holder's death. He may indicate to the Native Commissioner the person to whom he wishes it to pass, but the Commissioner may refuse to assign it as requested and either pass it on to an heir he considers more suitable or withdraw it. Any transfer of rights between natives must be registered with the Native Commissioner and the parties "may be asked to appear in person before him". The effect of all this is to emphasize that a native is not, and never can be, a landowner as the European farmer is, to deprive him of the security either of tribal communism or of European ownership. He is there on the Native Commissioner's sufferance and is almost completely defenceless and subservient to him. (The Act provides for various appeal rights but in general the Native Commissioners do not encourage their use and many natives are not bold enough to invoke them.) Farming and landholding are regulated with a mixture of paternal despotism and brusque authority by a white official. It is not on such foundations that a sturdy independent peasantry or a landholding middle class is built.

The Act provides for the enforcement of good farming practice and the authorities may prescribe not only anti-erosion measures but the manner of preparation for sowing, the rotation of crops, manuring and fallowing, levelling, drainage and irrigation and the use to which any land may be put. They have similar powers over stock and may order the reduction and limitation of the number of beasts on any land, the culling of inferior beasts, grazing control and the growing of fodder.

These are all the most urgent necessities and their accomplishment will be a boon. It would be ludicrous to object to them or to criticize the use of wide compulsory powers to enforce them. The War Agricultural Committees in Britain could do nearly as much and possessed in wartime the power of eviction. The British agricultural revolution owes much to them. But in a traditional, conservative agricultural community, compulsion is very little use without simultaneous education in Western methods. You must explain to the farmer in a way that he can understand why it is to his advantage to do as you tell him to. The Act makes no provision for this and it is unfortunately the case that few Southern Rhodesian Native Commissioners possess the confidence of their subjects enough, or have enough sympathetic contact with them, to be able to do so. The Act places far too much power in the hands of the Native Commissioners instead of going to the expense of setting up an independent advisory service with avowedly educational aims.

Many government officials will privately admit the deficiencies of the Native Land Husbandry Act. "But if you want to see the best we are doing for African farming,"[2] they will say, "look at the Native Purchase Areas where we have provided for qualified Native Master Farmers to buy freehold 200-acre farms, if the Native Commissioner approves their farming methods and if they can afford to buy land. This land is quite as good as the average European land and, furthermore, some of these chaps are getting jolly good results from their husbandry. Many of them have built their own European-type houses, have their own cars and tractors and even electric generating plants."

The idea behind the Native Purchase Area scheme is a good one—in so far as any idea conceived within the limits of the Land Apportionment Act can be good. If you visit Native Purchase Areas, you will find that the soil, spoonful by spoonful, is often as good as any in the country. But the bush is only partially cleared. The roads are never tarred and generally abysmally bad. The nearest telephone, railhead, main road and petrol pump are generally many miles away, not because remote areas were chosen out of malice for the Native Purchase Areas but because established European farms have long been clustered round these vital services and it would not pay to extend them for Natives. (Company's electricity is rapidly reaching most European farmers, who no longer need their own generators.) If I wanted to make money farming, I would choose to be in a European area, not a Native Purchase Farm. The fact that many African Master Farmers have done extraordinarily well on the few hundred acres allowed them seems to prove that they could do at least as well as the European amid the amenities and facilities of a European area.

Incidentally, an African, to be allowed a 200-acre farm, must be a qualified Master Farmer, while a European can buy an unlimited quantity of land, and use it with a very much greater degree of freedom, without giving any proof at all of his ability.

Native Purchase Areas have to be carved out of the existing African land and so do nothing to relieve the ultimate problem of the overcrowding and land hunger of an expanding African population. They create a new class stratification within African peasant society, and a new class of African—an agricultural middle class whose interests Europeans rather vainly hope will coincide with their own. But they do not alter the inflexibly rigid delimitation of African land as a whole though this is the only thing that can solve the problem. Until it is changed, no more than an insignificant number of Africans can hope to farm on the scale of the Purchase Areas and a smaller and smaller proportion of the whole African population can hope to farm at all.

What is needed is a radical scheme of Land Reapportionment to control the present wasteful extensiveness of the European areas into the reasonable limits of modern intensive agriculture. Certainly there is a necessary place in Southern Rhodesia for large farms and their occupants should be the best farmers regardless of race. If they were making the maximum contribution to the economy, it would not matter if they were all European. This would be acceptable even to the most "extreme" African opinion. But a wasteful European agricultural industry,[1] occupying large acreages that are half-farmed, or not farmed at all, and excluding from them on racial grounds Africans to whose welfare they are essential is not acceptable. Thousands more African smallholdings are necessary and could be provided with no detriment to European farming. And it might even be a positive advantage to Europeans to be forced to reduce their acreage and have to get down to the study of modern high production methods.

White Rhodesians, however, are quite unprepared to consider any reapportionment of land and as long as the present electorate retains its stranglehold on political power no government will be able to undertake it. "Keeping our land"—the Europeanness of the European areas—is a fetish. There is more European farming land on the market today than anyone knows what to do with. Its value has fallen seriously and the Government cannot import immigrant settlers quickly enough to take it up, let alone to settle on as yet unassigned land reserved for white settlement. Supply is well ahead of demand and to sell European land today is to sell at a loss of up to 20 per cent of its value in 1950. But the Crown will not allow Africans to buy it, and restricts them to congested and worn-out reserves.

White ideas about land are luxurious to the point of prodigality. 750 acres may be the minimum unit but farms of 20,000 or 40,000 are common and by no means all of them are the cattle ranches in poor dry areas which might justify these acreages. There are some very good big farmers in Southern Rhodesia just as there are some under-capitalized hard-working men struggling to make a living single-handed on 1,000 sandy acres. But the standard of efficiency is in general low.

[1] The report of the Select Committee on Unimproved Land in Southern Rhodesia, 1957, stated that only 1·1 million acres out of 31·7 million of European land was under crops. It described this as "deplorably low". Allowing for all the special pleading about the requirements of tobacco cultivation, the nature of sand veldt and the fact that the figure is for land under crops and excludes ranching and natural pasture, to find only about 3·5 per cent of European land under crops is fantastic. A report issued by the Southern Rhodesia Ministry of Agriculture in 1951 says: "The great majority of farms in the Colony are under-developed," and went on, "No body of men complains more about the inefficiency of native labour than the farming community. They can expect little else so long as the guiding strength is lacking at the top."

Two hundred acres of tobacco bring in enough to live on for the year and you find people simply shifting tobacco crops of this size round their farms in a twenty-year rotation and leaving much of the remainder idle. Some of the best agricultural scientists in the country will tell you that a careful farmer could do as well on seventy acres as many Rhodesians do on 2,000 and that the average level of land utilization and productivity is grotesquely low.

African farmers do not enjoy unrestricted access to a free market for their products. The European may sell maize—the staple crop—to the highest bidder of any race, or to the Grain Marketing Board at a guaranteed price of 38s. a bag—a device for protecting agriculture from the effects of price fluctuations and national overproduction.[1] An African may sell to a European (for which he needs the permission of the Native Commissioner) or to the G.M.B. His produce is then subject to a levy of 3s. 9d. per bag for the Native Development Fund plus 3s. 9d. "trader's handling margin" and 5s. "transport equalization fund charge". He gets 12s. 6d. per bag less than a European would, of which 3s. 9d. is a form of taxation paid to the Ministry of Native Affairs for the maintenance of the reserves, and the rest are compulsory payments to middle men.

In an identical deal, a European farmer would get the full guaranteed price of 38s. per bag in his pocket, and an African only 25s. 6d. An African farmer may not sell beef or cattle on the European market without the permission of the Native Commissioner, but pigs, poultry and vegetables are allowed freely through the fence of separation.

The worst objection to the levy is that it penalizes the successful progressive African farmers with a surplus to sell and does not touch the man who is only out for subsistence, although it is agreed that *the* most important thing for African agriculture is to get away from the subsistence mentality and start growing cash crops as part of a money economy. The inequity of a different price for the same product according to the grower's race is psychologically and economically indefensible.

The official justification for it is that the African population is under-taxed and that this is a good way of getting those who can afford it to contribute to the cost of African social services and the maintenance of the reserves. It is true that very few Africans

[1] Overproduction of maize is a considerable problem. The G.M.B. holds at present thousands of tons which it cannot dispose of.

pay income-tax because their incomes are very low. But every adult male has instead to pay £2 per annum Poll Tax, which does not apply to Europeans. Considering their general economic position it is questionable whether Africans are under-taxed. The majority of male rural Africans earn perhaps £35 a year. The average African income per head in the whole country was £10·7 a year in 1949[1] and may now be about £15.

Africans are subject to all the same indirect taxation as Europeans and make a significant contribution to the exchequer in fines for breaches of the Pass Laws. Income-tax is low. A single man with £800 a year pays £6 5s. 0d. A married man with £1,200 pays £32 10s. 0d. Sometimes one wonders whether it is not the European who is under-taxed rather than the African although the *volume* of European tax is greater because European incomes are incomparably higher.

It is symptomatic of the European tendency to confuse *apartheid*, or separate development, with partnership, that government, Press and public like to emphasize that a proportion of European taxation is spent on African welfare—education, urban housing, social and medical services in particular. The principle that taxation of the rich helps to pay for the welfare of the poor is so fully accepted in Europe as not to require comment. What is surprising is that all such services are provided separately for Africans, and at a standard which would be considered completely inadequate for Europeans. Communications, facilities and amenities in the reserves are maintained at a level which Europeans would never accept (there are no tarred roads, for instance). They are very largely paid for by the people themselves and kept up by their own labour on the orders of the Chief, who is instructed by the Native Commissioner. The volume of European taxation spent on developing the reserves is relatively minute.[2] Proportionately, a very much larger demand is made upon the low average African income than on the higher European.

I heard a Minister in Parliament in July 1957 defend the expense of improving one of the Salisbury African housing areas by assuring the House: "It will not under any circumstances cost the country

[1] C. T. Leys, op. cit., p. 21. See also footnote on p. 89 and Postscript.

[2] African levies pay for about 60 per cent of maintenance and development in the reserves. The £2 poll tax is supposed to pay for police and administration and to cover about 20 per cent of the cost of African education. Poll tax was doubled when the educational five-year plan came in.

anything. . . . I know many will object to so much being done for African housing but it is necessary. . . . Beer profits [from the monopoly the City Council then held of selling liquor to urban Africans] can be used for African housing if the Municipality agrees." But if one is going to talk about partnership and to claim to be advancing towards it, economic equality, fiscal unity and equal and shared social services for all are as essential as social integration and equality in law.

Of course there are enormous difficulties in raising income-tax equally from 2½ million people living on ten or twenty pounds a year, and a quarter of a million on a minimum of seven or eight hundred.[1] These difficulties would diminish with a progressive rise in the African standard of living to a point when they no longer occurred. This will never be achieved by doling out separate social services to each racial group, still less by putting a heavy burden on enterprise and success among Africans. It stands to reason that the richer group must be ready to contribute to the advancement of the poorer. This could be a way out from the impasse of discrimination, competition and distrust into the only future which can safeguard the security of all concerned—one of mutual co-operation and respect in an integrated society.

It would be hard to find better words to sum up the rural Africans' position than some written in a pastoral letter by the Roman Catholic Bishop of Umtali in 1959: "Can you in conscience blame the African if, eking out a tenuous existence on poor soil in an overcrowded reserve, he is swayed by subversive propaganda, when close beside him lie thousands of acres of fertile soil which he may not occupy nor cultivate nor graze because, although unused and untended, they belong to some individual or group of individuals who perhaps do not live in the country, but who hold the land in the hope of profitable speculation?"

[1] C. T. Leys, op. cit., gives the European income *per caput* as £487·2 in 1950. See table in Postscript.

CHAPTER XIII

Urban Partnership

The shift from subsistence farming to a cash economy is a difficult adjustment to make in a community whose traditional pursuit for centuries has been agriculture and whose only conception of security is the occupation of land. It seems to be inevitable that all African societies must, if they are to improve living standards and support their rapidly increasing population, undergo some sort of industrial revolution and rationalize their system of land tenure. Agriculture must be adapted to provide a profitable occupation for one section of society, instead of a bare living for the whole of it. Those for whom there is not room on the land must find other ways of living. This has been the pattern of change in Europe over the last three centuries and we are very familiar with the process of rural enclosure and mass urbanization. In Africa its problems are only just beginning to appear. Their existence is not the fault of white supremacy or the Native Land Husbandry Act. Indeed insofar as this Act promotes a form of enclosure it is trying to serve a necessary socio-economic purpose, and the objection to the Act is not its aim but the fact that other laws prevent it from attaining it. We have learnt by bitter experience in Europe that when enclosure drives large numbers of peasants from the land into the towns proper provision must be made for them to lead their new lives and to form a viable urban society. But in Southern Rhodesia, while the Land Husbandry Act is causing landless Africans to try and change to an urban industrial life, the Land Apportionment Act is making it impossible for them to do so with any dignity or ease and so making sociological nonsense of the whole process. Its provisions completely prohibit any African from acquiring the secure membership of a satisfactory urban community which is an essential feature of industrialization.

The Land Apportionment Act, 1930,[1] and other legislation such

[1] It was amended in 1941 and various revisions and additions have been passed since then. This is the basic instrument.

as the Native Urban Areas Act, 1951, associated with it provide for the complete segregation of Africans in all towns in Southern Rhodesia. They may only live, or occupy any sort of business or professional premises, in areas designated by the European town council as African locations. The land in the location remains the property of the Town Council and no African may ever possess it. An African may live, in a town, outside a location, only if he is in the domestic service of a European who provides his accommodation. He may only work outside a location in the employment of a European master. This means that an African doctor cannot take a consulting-room in the main part of any town to see his patients, and that an African shopkeeper cannot set up a little tobacconist's shop to serve Europeans. Both are rigidly confined to the location and a special Act of Parliament would be needed to alter this in any individual case. No European is allowed to enter a location without a special permit. Africans need a special permit to live in a location and they will only get it if they satisfy the European authorities that they are suitable people to do so and have jobs in the town concerned. If they lose their jobs, they are ejected from the location which means there is nowhere they can legally stay in town. The only thing they may then do is to return to the Native reserve in the country where, if they have left because they are landless, they will have no means of subsistence except to sponge on their kinsmen.

Every location is controlled by a European municipal official, who has an office in the location and is called the location superintendent. All Africans living in the location are under his discipline and he enforces a rigid and multifarious set of laws, which apply only in the location. They naturally do not apply to any European outside it. Parliament delegates to the town councils the precise framing of laws for locations under their control but they follow a more or less regular pattern. It is so hard for anyone who has not seen the system in action to believe that such laws can exist in a society dedicated under the British Crown to "partnership between the races" that the best thing is to list the main provisions of the regulations in force for the Harari location in Salisbury, Southern Rhodesia, the Federal capital.

No one not an African may enter the location at any time without permission from the location superintendent. Africans not living there may enter it only between 6 a.m. and 6 p.m. (So you may *never* receive a European visitor, and may not have even an African from outside for the evening, or to stay the night, without leave from the location superintendent.) The Superintendent may prohibit anyone of any race whom he "considers undesirable" from entering the location. Anyone of any race present in the location who fails to produce his permit on demand is guilty of an offence.

None of your children may live with you in the location after they are sixteen.

You will be turned out of the location:

If your wife is not recognized by the white official as your legal wife.

If you and your family go away for more than a week (in some places it is two weeks) without telling the Superintendent; or if you want to go away for a period which, in his opinion, is "unreasonably long".

If you cease living under the conditions of family life or are convicted of subversion or sedition, *or cease to be employed in the town where your location is situated.* (Quite simply, if you lose your job, you not only lose your home, but the right to stay in the town at all.)

You will be guilty of an offence (the penalty is £10 or 3 months) if you

Do not comply with a lawful, reasonable order, request or direction authorized by the bye-laws or given by the Superintendent.

Obstruct the Superintendent, or contravene any bye-law.

Carry on any business, trade, or calling in the location without permission of the Superintendent.

Convene or address a public meeting without applying 48 hours in advance to the Superintendent.

Carry on a public meeting later than 9 p.m. anywhere except in the location Public Hall.

Carry on a meeting in the Public Hall which is not educational or religious or for a purpose specifically approved by the Town Council. (You cannot hold a political meeting the authorities do not approve.)

Fail to send the Superintendent in advance the agenda of a meeting to be held in the Public Hall.

Collect money at a meeting in the Public Hall for a purpose that is not religious.

Have anyone to live with you in your home except your wife, and children under sixteen, without permission, which may not be given for visits of more than two weeks.

Fail to display in a prominent position a certificate from the Superintendent giving details of the authorized occupants of your house.

Leave the location between 9 p.m. and 5 a.m. without permission signed by your employer or the Superintendent.

If you build your own house in a location—you may do this with permission, but may never own the land it stands on—and later wish to leave, you *must* consent to sell your house to the Town Council at a price fixed by a European arbitrator, if they want it.

The Superintendent or any of his staff are empowered to enter your house at any time for any purpose and the medical authorities have unrestricted rights to make inspection "which shall be carried out without undue harshness".

The Superintendent has legal power to prevent you:

Keeping a dog or any stock which is *in his opinion* habitually a nuisance.

Taking part in or permitting others to take part in any game or activity so as to cause a noise or disturbance.

Erecting any fence (likewise the white official may remove any fence of yours which in his opinion is dilapidated or unsightly, *at your expense*).

Acquiring a site for any religious purpose unless you can prove that your sect has a "substantial enrolment of members, a college or other adequate means for the training of ministers and sufficient funds to carry out the purposes for which the application is made." (Christ and his twelve apostles would satisfy none of these conditions.)

To get most of the permissions required by the regulations you must "appear personally before" the Superintendent.

You are only allowed to live in the location by a Certificate of Occupation issued by the Superintendent, after he is satisfied that you fulfil all the necessary qualifications. He can withdraw it if, *in his opinion*, you cease to fulfil them. And all this applies to every single African, educated or simple, rich or poor.

If you work as a servant in a European or Asian town house, and go to work daily, you may live in the location or your employer may apply to the Town Council for a licence to accommodate a Native in private premises. You may bring your wife to live in his private premises if your employer employs her too and if the Council's licensing authority *in his discretion* allows you to. If your employer agrees and the licensing authority in his discretion does not, you may not bring her. For you to live a married life as a domestic servant, your wife must be recognized by the local authority as your "approved" wife and the Act goes on inscrutably: "For the purposes of this Act there shall be a competent authority who shall be appointed by the Governor."

You need the licensing authority's permission to have any children living with you on your employer's premises.

You are—and this is a good thing—protected from the draughty insanitary pigsties that are considered good enough for the "boys" even in some well-to-do quarters of South African towns and which disfigured Nairobi before the Emergency. The local authority has a duty to inspect domestics' accommodation and does insist upon a decent standard.

If you want to come into a town from the reserve, to look for work, to see your friends and relatives, to visit the sick or for any other purpose for longer than the twelve daylight hours of one day, you must get a pass from the local authority. You will be given this pass for a minimum of three days and a maximum, in exceptional cases, of twenty-one. It authorizes you to live *only* in the Native Hostel in the location.

You will not get a pass to look for work if you are under an unexpired contract of service to any employer in Southern Rhodesia.[1]

If you do not find work, you will be sent away after *at most* three weeks and not allowed to enter the town for more than twelve hours in the next three months.

You may not enter any town for more than twelve hours for any purpose—not even to visit the sick or see a new-born child—without a pass. In "urgent cases of a lawful nature" you may get one from any magistrate, native commissioner, European police officer or other white officer who may "if circumstances warrant it" even issue you with a permit to spend the night outside the location hostel. But when the urgent call reaches you, these gentlemen are often at the club or otherwise inaccessible and cases are not infrequent where Africans are kept away from a deathbed by the lack of a pass.

[1] Masters and Servants Act.

Under the Pass Laws, if you are an African outside the rural Native reserve, or employed in a town or employed on a European farm, or on a journey, you must always carry a piece of paper (often you must carry several different kinds but the technical ramifications are too tedious to go into) signed by a European saying that you have a right to be where you are. If you are in work, it gives details of your job; if you are not, it says what you are doing.

The Pass Laws are, on the whole, enforced. They are certainly not honoured in the breach, though there are too many Africans about for every disobedience to be detected. The police carry out very frequent checks and every evening one can see in Salisbury a sight that is familiar in Johannesburg too, and seems more appropriate there—hundreds of Africans being stopped by African police under European officers and being asked for their passes; dozens being driven off under guard in jeeps to the police station to be charged, fined or imprisoned for what is surely the most technical offence that incurs criminal procedure in any country in the world.

Southern Rhodesia claims to have modified the Pass Laws by exempting large classes of "educated and civilized" Africans from their operation in recent years. It is true that a bill to this effect has passed the House, and that the Minister of Native Affairs has anyhow the right to exempt any individual or any class of Africans from carrying a pass. It is true that if you are one of these, you are spared the tiresomeness and humiliation of having to appear before a European every day or two to get permission to go on existing. But it is ironical that Rhodesians think they have in this way conceded something of value. "Educated and civilized" Africans do not agree with them, because if you are exempted, you are still required to carry your certificate of exemption—a kind of identity card—and may be challenged by the police for it at any moment. No European is required to carry any kind of identity card. Europeans still believe that by tinkering with the machinery of discrimination, they are promoting "partnership" and advance. But Africans cannot see the difference between being obliged to produce a pass and being obliged to produce a certificate of exemption from being obliged to produce a pass. Unfortunately Rhodesia is still unable to abandon the belief that an African's life in a white-dominated world is like a railway journey from birth to death. He is always on the European Company's premises and it is only fair that he should always carry his ticket.

All towns are purely European settlements. The locations are always well outside the town, sometimes miles away. Supervision and insecurity of tenure prevent the development of an urban class of Africans with any sense of membership of the community. They instil a sense of subjection and inhibit the growth of self-respect though simultaneously they are producing a deep solidarity based on a shared resentment. The object of the system is largely to keep the Minister of Native Affairs and the police informed of all that is going on among urban Africans and to prevent their having any unsupervised contact with the outside world. It effectively inhibits social relations between Africans and members of any other race. It makes it impossible for African family life to take real root in the towns. It provides a useful control over the dissemination of information among Africans and over the development of trade unions or political parties.

It is doubtful whether any state except Nationalist South Africa in the whole of history has ever infringed the personal liberty and human dignity of a group of its citizens as much as these fantastic laws do. Hitler's racial legislation perhaps approaches them. They read like a Dickens parody of the regulations of a poor law institution. They create the kind of second-class citizenship that was imposed by medieval Europe on the Jews. It is the Ghetto that the locations call to mind—with perhaps a dash of the open prison thrown in, for there is not always the physical squalor of the Ghetto. It is the spiritual squalor of the whole system that is shocking.

Southern Rhodesia has none of the shanty towns of South Africa (and there too they are being cleared up under a system of *apartheid*). Physically the locations are often better than the slums of the East End in 1939, and do not always compare too badly with some of our post-war council estates. The new ones are clean and inexpressibly drab with the gloom that comes from an utter absence of amenity, a failure to consider anything but utilitarian economy—row upon row of identical repetitive plaster bungalow boxes covering in some places the area of a fair-sized town, sometimes just a small village, and facing a dusty, pot-holed track. In the superior new Salisbury locations "for upper class Africans" each box has a plot about twenty feet square at the back, with the identical w.c. and single water tap. The older ones are mere slums with little or no surrounding land and taps and lavatories are shared. There are no hedges or fences between the houses. There is no street lighting of any kind except on main roads[1] and electricity is not so far available in most location houses. The public halls are adequate but inexpressibly dreary. The local pub or "native beer hall" run by the town council—at a profit which is ploughed back into improving, or more frequently enlarging, the location—shows an almost inconceivable lack of cosiness. The open front of a shed of steel girders with a corrugated iron roof gives on to an expanse of sand the size of a football field where you sit at concrete tables on fixed concrete benches and drink. The whole is surrounded by a high chain link fence to separate the drinkers from the general public of the location. There is not a blade of grass, not a flower has been planted, there is not the slightest bit of comfort or adornment, not even a pin-up calendar anywhere. It is an area for drinking in, not a place to spend a sociable hour. The natural result is that drinking advances and social life does not. The hostels—where single men must live and visitors must stay—are the same; dismal steel and concrete, clean but grim, rudimentary and comfortless with no vestige of any civilized or civilizing environment. There is a clinic, clean and reasonably equipped, in the bigger locations and it is usually possible to get a doctor's attention for urgent cases in daytime though very hard at night. Also in the bigger ones you find a good sports stadium—an oval rampart of earth terraced into seats on the inside surrounding playing fields and running track. The location embodies a carefully calculated minimum necessary to keep industrial workers fit as cheaply as possible and to put no ideas into their heads.[2] It has also to be inhabited by Africans making a thousand a year or possessing high professional or academic qualifications.

Perhaps the worst thing about the whole system is that so much is left to the caprice of the individual location superintendent; there is so much unlimited authority and personal rule. The worst possible training for responsible citizenship is to live under irresponsible officialdom. It is the law of the bad boarding school or the totalitarian reich that is taught in the location, the law that is not consistent or impartial, and in whose eyes all are not equal, and we should have only the Europeans to blame if this were the only law the Africans knew when they got political control. There could hardly be a greater

[1] In South Africa this is a deliberate policy in order to make it difficult for people to visit one another and plot "treason", but here I think economy is the only motive. It is good enough for natives without.

[2] Small town locations are often squalid and smelly through bad management, and without any amenity but the beer hall.

condemnation of this whole business than the fact that it is universally admitted that things are much pleasanter and easier for Africans in Bulawayo than in Salisbury because the head of Native Welfare in Bulawayo is the humane and progressive Dr. Ashton, who interprets the regulations leniently. It is preposterous that the legal rights of a whole adult community should depend upon whether an official is humane or not.

CHAPTER XIV

Native Affairs

The extent to which discrimination is written into the law, and *apartheid* is being increased by current legislation, is illustrated by a study of the powers of the Native Commissioners and the conditions of African Local Government. The Native Affairs Act, 1928, from which the quotations in this chapter come, must have been out of date almost before it was passed. A native commissioner is placed in every district as superintendent of natives. He has all the powers of a magistrate for civil and criminal cases and the ordinary magistrate's courts which try Europeans and others are excluded from jurisdiction over natives. It is an indication of his absolute power that "nothing contained in any law shall be deemed as debarring a native commissioner from trying and punishing any native who has been guilty of insolent or contemptuous behaviour to, or of failing to obey and comply with any reasonable order request or direction of such native commissioners". The Native Commissioner is executive, policeman and judge, tax collector, electoral returning officer, and director of agriculture and land tenure in one person.

Beneath the N.C. is a strict hierarchy: the Chief, deprived of his independence as the ancient traditional tribal authority, is appointed by the Governor and responsible to the N.C. for "the general good conduct of the natives under his charge"; and "no chief shall leave the district in which he resides without the authority of the N.C." "Any chief guilty of insolence or of contemptuous behaviour is liable to £20 or six months and loss of his position."

The N.C. assigns land to natives for occupation and farming and may prohibit new cultivation or the building of new huts where he thinks fit and may enforce eviction from such huts and the demolition and abandonment of such cultivation. He has the power also to order any native to move his place of residence from wherever it may be to any place he specifies in his own or any contiguous district.

Further, the law lays down that "no native shall move from one district to another without the consent of the native commissioners of the districts concerned" and if he does he may be "ordered by the N.C. to return to the district whence he came".

These are the kind of laws which were made everywhere all over the continent before people realized that Africans were by no means as childish as they looked to Western eyes, and that they would in any case soon begin demanding advance as a right. Today they are irrelevant and insulting. One can understand the origin of such legislation in its historical setting, but with the mentality that is determined to keep it in force, no longer as an instrument of paternalism but as a means of suppressing a developing community, one must have at least a difference of opinion. The rule of the Native Commissioners today is the best possible illustration of the truth that paternalism which outlives its historical context turns to tyranny. But no legislation has been introduced since Federation and "partnership" to alter or mitigate it. The tendency has been to tighten up.

It was paternalism turned to tyranny that caused the government to declare the Southern Rhodesian Emergency in 1959 on little or no provocation. Its intention was to nip African political movements in the bud. It was by challenging this paternal tyranny that Congress incurred the charges of subversion and intimidation brought against it at that time. Congress reflected and represented the resentment of all Africans against the system of rule by Native Commissioner. The official picture of thousands of peaceful Africans in hundreds of contented villages being intimidated by small numbers of Congress agitators into protesting against the rule of a kind and beloved father is unconvincing.

The modern N.C. is a born Southern Rhodesian with family and financial interests in the white community. He has not the detached paternalism of the old style Colonial Office D.C., and has quite a different attitude to Africans. He has come to see himself as a defender of white rights against the black menace and does not hold with natives getting uppish. He is not easily accessible and to see him means a journey to the local town and a great deal of waiting before you get to him. It is by no means impossible that, if he considers you insolent when you get there, he may take you from his office to the courtroom, assume his capacity as magistrate and sentence you to a fine or imprisonment. I know a university graduate who went to see the N.C. "Sit down," said the N.C., in Shona.

The graduate looked round the room and saw no chair, only a block of wood in the corner. "Excuse me, sir," he said in his most respectful English, "do you wish me to sit there?" "Get out at once!" roared the N.C.—and carried him off to prosecution for insolence because he answered in English when addressed in Shona, and did not sit down when ordered to.

The whole system has ceased to work in contemporary conditions. As soon as Africans move towards the modern world—and this happens very quickly—the white man's possession of such powers becomes oppression, and tutelage becomes victimization. The system needs to be changed and replaced by one which would bring Europeans and Africans under the same laws, the same administration, and the same exercise of democratic rights, both in central administration and in local government.

The Native Councils Bill (1957) does not do this for local government. Instead it provides for the development of African local government for African communities and areas separately from white local government for Europeans. Africans will elect responsible councils which will enjoy considerable powers in African areas (under the supervision of the N.C. or location superintendent) but no attempt is made to associate them with local government in European areas. The Bill gives no glimpse of any future day when all areas shall be one and a single council shall contain African, European and Indian members sitting together to run a single community. They are to be for ever apart. The late C. W. M. Gell wrote: "It is possible to believe that the Rhodesian Native Councils Bill was genuinely intended to develop local self-government among Africans. But one must seriously question its methods. Why, in a society nominally dedicated to multi-racialism, introduce the principle of 'separate development' for African town councils? African townships are not in any case more than dormitory suburbs of the main town they serve; surely they should be treated as wards of that municipality, sending their representatives to sit on its council? This is what Rhodesian Africans themselves desire."[1]

Mr. Garfield Todd, when he was Prime Minister, recognized the ability of Africans to take part in a modern society and genuinely wished to give them a chance to achieve civic responsibility and integration. But the electorate would never have accepted such measures as establishing integrated town councils. In most of his

[1] *Central African Examiner*, 22nd June 1957.

undertakings, he was simultaneously urged by his own conscience to go forward and by his electorate to go backward and it is not surprising that the attempt caused him to lose balance and fall from office without achieving anything he desired. By increasing the powers of African Local Councils in African areas only, for instance, he increased their separation from European society, and a measure intended to be liberal emphasized the prevailing *apartheid*. Since Mr. Todd has been succeeded by Sir Edgar Whitehead recent legislation has increased discrimination. No measure has yet passed Parliament which significantly diminishes it in any liberal sense. The removal of minor social inconveniences and insults which the Government is so fond of advertising does nothing to alter the system and does not impress the Africans who live under it; while the Industrial Conciliation Bill has been shown to be a two-handed engine, doing more for European control of trade unions than for the benefit of African members.[1]

[1] See footnote on p. 76.

CHAPTER XV

Education for Partnership

THE SCHOOLS

The Africans of Southern Rhodesia are calling for release from the kind of restriction and discrimination described in the last few chapters. The European Government rejoins that they are not yet civilized enough for a change in their status and that the country's economy will not support it. It offers them educational opportunities which it claims are second to none in the continent, and asks them to make use of them to increase their civilization while giving the Europeans time to expand the economy. It promises them a dignified and prosperous position in a flourishing partnership in a generation or two on condition that they will wait in tutelage till then. The theory is that as more and more well-educated Africans come forward they will quietly and gradually take their place beside the white man; a continually increasing number will be able to earn £720 a year in a continually expanding national economy and will qualify for the franchise; a few will be unspectacularly elected to Parliament by multi-racial constituencies and unobtrusively one will be inserted into a ministerial post. As they prove their worth and their civilization, both the need and the desire for discrimination, segregation and colour bar will wither away. Partnership must be allowed to unfold slowly and one day the full flower will be seen. It is no good forcing things. The fears and prejudices of the whites are too strong, and a head-on collision will be deleterious. It is a theory which a study of the educational programme makes it hard to sustain.

The Southern Rhodesian Government introduced its five-year plan for African education in 1955, when Mr. Todd was Prime Minister and Minister of Education. It has been continued, and even slightly expanded, by his successor Sir Edgar Whitehead. Expenditure on African school education has risen from £1,835,000 in 1955 to £2,807,000 in 1959. The greatest obstacle the plan faced was the shortage of trained teachers. Of the 10,000 teachers in African schools in 1955, only one-third were trained.

The aims of the plan were:

(*i*) To provide a minimum five-year elementary schooling for the whole African population of school age—400,000. (Sir Edgar Whitehead states that 80 per cent of African children are now entering the bottom forms of primary schools. He does not say how many of them complete the first five years—the shortest full primary course; but for a variety of economic and other reasons, the proportion that does not is regrettably high.)

(*ii*) To provide eight-year courses in all urban areas and to increase their availability in rural ones also, because this is the minimum qualification for training as the humblest form of teacher (the Primary Teachers' Lower Course).

(*iii*) To increase the facilities for the Primary Teachers' Lower Course so that the number of teachers with this minimal training may rise from one- to two-thirds of the teaching body over ten years.

(*iv*) To increase the number of lower grade secondary schools, offering courses of between two and four post-primary years leading, at the highest, to a School Certificate. These courses afford entry to various forms of trade and technical training but not to university education within or outside the Federation. All such schools are comparable to English secondary modern schools at best. None of them does sixth form work or has any relation to a grammar school. There are now twenty-three of them in Southern Rhodesia.

(*v*) To establish one more full secondary or grammar school, with three hundred places. This means that there are now two such schools in all in Southern Rhodesia, with 600 places for both sexes, serving 2½ million Africans with 400,000 children of school age; and virtually all access to higher education is through them alone. (Later plans envisage a few hundred more.)

(*vi*) To establish post-primary trade courses in building, carpentry, leather-work and metal-work, lasting three or four years. There are now ten such courses in the country with an approximate enrolment of five hundred pupils.

(*vii*) To establish one technical college in (Bulawayo) providing a five-year post-junior secondary course in technical subjects for teachers of technology, in 1960. When trained teachers begin to emerge, it is proposed to open technical schools for Africans on the lines of English senior technical schools.

All this is being undertaken by the Southern Rhodesian Department of Native Education, and paid for from the territorial budget. European education, it will be remembered, is a Federal function, organized by the Federal Ministry of Education and financed from the Federal budget. The Federal Ministry does not impinge upon African education until it reaches university level. It is not easy, therefore, to compare what is being done for, or spent upon, African and European education in Southern Rhodesia. But Federal expenditure on education in 1958 was £6,200,000 exclusive of buildings for all three territories, with an estimated additional expenditure of £1,624,110 for buildings—a total of £7,824,110. Southern Rhodesia has by far the largest European population and it is fair to assume that not less than £3,500,000 can have been spent there on education for a total European population of 219,000 as against £2,161,000 for an African population of 2,800,000. Even if a reasonable amount of the European £3,500,000 is assumed to have been spent on the interracial university college, the difference remains striking. In the same year, there were twenty-two state secondary schools serving a quarter of a million Europeans and twenty serving 2½ million Africans.

A large number of the schools for Africans at all levels below grammar school are government-aided mission schools. The Department of Native Education pays the salaries of all teachers in them and the missions provide the premises. No fees are charged in government primary schools, but all mission schools charge a nominal fee which, though small in European terms, is a significant item in the limited budget of an African family. Small fees are charged in government secondary schools, whether African or European, below grammar school level. The two African grammar schools—Goromonzi and Fletcher High School—are boarding schools and attendance there costs £22 a year. European boarding schools charge rather more. African industrial and trade schools cost £10 a year. Small though school fees are, the economic differences between African and European are so great that the Roman Catholic Bishop of Umtali was not wrong to say in a Pastoral Letter in 1959: "There could scarcely be two more violently contrasting systems of educational opportunity; the European child has everything provided for him freely; the other must struggle and pay for everything he has."

But it is not for economic reasons that the theory of developing social integration through education is hard to reconcile with the practice of the Native Education Department's five-year plan. It is because the plan offers an education which affords a strictly limited opportunity and very few chances of reaching the higher income levels necessary for an ordinary vote. The most it will give Africans is continued social and political inferiority at a slightly higher level of training. It will not materially alter the racial balance of the franchise nor enable the Africans to compete seriously with Europeans in the professions or more highly skilled trades. It provides them, for instance, with technical training in building, carpentry, leather-work or metal-work, which never carry a high rate of remuneration, but not in motor engineering, aircraft maintenance, accountancy or commerce, though Africans who have started from exactly the same background and standard of civilization are performing all these functions successfully over the border in the Congo—and far higher ones a little further afield in Tanganyika. It does nothing to alter the fact that it is hard for any African to earn £720 a year and qualify for the only kind of vote that decides elections, and almost impossible for any European not to. There is, unfortunately, no incompatibility between educating a large number of Africans to the level of artisans or lower primary teachers (whose salaries will nowhere near reach the level of enfranchisement) and depriving them of any influence upon the society they live in.

The Department of Native Education says that its policy is to build the educational system from the bottom on the sure foundations of primary and trade schools before advancing to over-ambitious expansion at university level. On general educational and social grounds, in normal conditions, this is sound; but it is a slow method of advancing a community. It is hard not to conclude that the Government which laid down this policy was motivated by other considerations than purely educational ones. At least, there is no question but that the Department of Native Education was frequently consulted by the Government in planning the new franchise. Its prognosis of the results of the five-year plan were carefully collated with the educational and economic requirements for the vote before either were made public. Educated and politically conscious Africans—and some Europeans—believe that the

Government wishes to make a good show over education while actually refusing to advance Africans to power or responsibility. The Government answers that in leading a "backward" people on, it is more important for everyone to learn something than for a few to learn a lot, that secondary and higher education are an extravagance when there are still villages without a mud-walled, grass-roofed, primary school. But it is hard to see why the one should preclude the other if the will for both is present. Undeniably the five-year plan will produce a large, semi-skilled, relatively poor class, able to serve but unable to compete economically or politically with Europeans. What it, or any future development on the same lines, cannot produce is an appreciable number of highly educated Africans within foreseeable time.

To reach controlling positions, or even to get the vote, Africans need a grammar school education and widespread opportunities for university education. Experience in East Africa (at Makerere College) and in the West (at Ibadan and Achimota) shows incontestably that a "primitive" African population can produce an almost unlimited quantity of "graduate material" in a period of fifteen or twenty years. The controlling factors are the number of grammar school and university places available. But the Southern Rhodesian educational programme offers a school-going population of 400,000 about 1,000 grammar school places as its sole means of access to university education. Under twenty Africans were admitted to the University College of Rhodesia and Nyasaland in 1958, under forty in 1959, and the number is expected to stabilize at round about sixty for the whole Federation in 1960 for a good many years to come. The College authorities would be glad to accept as many more as presented themselves with suitable qualifications. It is the educational policies of the territories—and of Southern Rhodesia in particular—that prevent their emerging. They offer a very wide entry at the bottom and an extremely narrow exit at the top.

Sir Edgar Whitehead, Prime Minister of Southern Rhodesia, is fond of advertising the five-year plan. He claims that access to the university is open to all who can attain the entrance qualification without distinction of race, and that every African capable of benefiting from it has the opportunity to go there. He claims that his Government is establishing new secondary schools every year to provide this opportunity. When he was asked a short time ago whether he thought that two secondary schools, with six hundred places, provided sufficient access to the university for a population of 2½ million he answered that there were not two, but twenty-three secondary schools in Southern Rhodesia. He did not appear to recognize what his Director of Native Education could have told him, that twenty-one of these schools were secondary modern schools, offering no prospect of advance to university education and that only two, with six hundred places between them, would offer courses qualifying for university entrance.

The five-year plan might, in an impoverished and underdeveloped African country, be a not unworthy attempt to lay the foundation of a developing educational system. As an advertisement for partnership it fails and proves to be no more than education for subordination—a means of giving Africans the equipment for more useful servitude without the opportunity of increased influence in society. It is sad that a scheme good in itself is vitiated by failure to provide its necessary corollary of rapid extension of grammar school facilities; and that the humane and painstaking efforts of the many members of the Native Education Department are defeated by the setting of segregation in which they take place.

THE UNIVERSITY COLLEGE

A great deal is made of the power of the University College of Rhodesia and Nyasaland to pave the way to partnership but it is doubtful whether enough Africans will be able to get there for it to do so. It is a lamp of liberal enlightenment but its beams may not be strong enough to pierce the surrounding darkness. It was initiated by a committee of European sponsors from the three territories at the time of Federation. The British Government offered it a sizeable grant of money on the condition that it was constituted as a college for all races on an equal footing. Plans were nevertheless prepared for separate facilities for whites and others in different parts of the town but the British Government insisted that all students must live and work on the same site and this was conceded, not very willingly. An all-European College Council was set up and in 1955 Dr. Walter Adams, Secretary of the Inter-University Council for Higher Education Overseas, in London, was made the first Principal. The University College of Rhodesia and Nyasaland came into existence in 1956 and was formally opened by the Queen Mother in 1957. It was financed, apart from the

British grant, by the Government of the Federation, and by public subscription. Early in 1960 it had 169 students; 133 Europeans, thirty-five Africans, and one Indian. Two of the Africans were women.

The College is attempting to do something that has never been done before—to create a genuinely interracial university. (Achimota in Ghana, or Makerere in East Africa are interracial in name, but over 99 per cent of their students are black.) The English and Afrikaner universities of South Africa are white universities, which consider only the attainments and requirements of the white populations, and in the few which still have a minority of African students, the Africans must struggle along as best they can behind the white man. Fort Hare, the South African Native College, is a segregated institution for blacks only. Luvanum and Elisabethville in the Congo, and Roma in Basutoland, serve a population virtually without permanent white residents. Salisbury follows none of these patterns. It is seeking to incorporate all races of the Federation in a single residential community, not simply to provide degrees for Europeans nor simply to extend university education to as many Africans as possible. It is at present in special relationship with London and it teaches for London external degrees, but its eyes are on the future in which it hopes to become the Oxford or Cambridge, or the Yale or Harvard, of an integrated multi-racial society. It is devoted to the higher education of the Federation generally and its academic staff is for the most part aware that one of its functions in its socio-political context is to be a school for genuine interracialism. Its aims are noble but whether, in view of the deterioration of political relations between the races, they are realistic must remain an open question.

It was felt from the outset that the real difficulty would be to get white students to come where they might have to work, play and live alongside Africans. If all, even of the fairly small number of Africans in the Federation who could qualify for admission to the London general degree course, were admitted the institution would be dubbed a Kaffir college and avoided by Europeans who would continue—and could afford—to go to South Africa or Britain for university education. But if the College could, without recourse to discrimination, open with a majority of white students and a sprinkling of black, and could provide a challenging academic standard, its reputation and the reputation of interracial life would grow,

Europeans would come in increasing numbers, and the gates could gradually be opened to Africans later on. The College believed it could only be true to its long-term interracial vision by keeping out the Africans to begin with, a paradox which, in the circumstances, cannot lightly be dismissed as casuistry.

The best way of ensuring a white majority without openly admitting any racial distinction was to put the entrance qualifications and academic standards beyond the reach of most Africans. The minimum requirement for entrance to Salisbury is a good Higher Certificate (or G.C.E.), leading immediately to three years' work for a degree. The Intermediate Examination, designed to bridge the gap between School Certificate and true university work, is not done. This sets a higher entrance standard than most other universities or colleges in Africa. The standard of academic study and performance required for a degree is above the minimum requirements of the London external general degree and above those in force at, for instance, Makerere, although the final degree given is exactly the same. Salisbury has adopted this rather austere standard not least in order to assure white students that they are not being fobbed off with anything second rate.

The College was severely criticized in Westminster, in the British universities and elsewhere, for segregating its students racially in its halls of residence, when it was first opened. It has now developed to a situation where both races live in the same building on different floors or corridors, and feed in the same dining hall. There is no segregation in teaching, sport or any other official activity. To have got so far so soon, and to have established so much harmony within the College, is a great achievement. It would be hard to exaggerate the compromises demanded of a liberal academic administration in starting such a college and the difficulties it has had to face regarding the theory and practice of interracial life. It is not the College that deserves criticism but the society which finances it and which it serves.

It is particularly unfortunate that it is not financially self-supporting. It has to collect a large sum by public subscription in order to provide itself with independent funds to eke out government grants. The bulk of subscriptions can only be collected from the wealthy class, the Europeans (though many African communities have subscribed generously according to their means). Not only must the College temper academic policy to meet the prejudices of European opinion and to get white students to come; it literally cannot afford to offend them beyond a certain point if it is to survive financially. To ask a Rhodesian to contemplate the end of segregation and the social colour bar touches all the most tender and neurotic areas of his sense of insecurity. It hacks away his traditional symbols of stability and leads him forward into an alarming and amorphous unknown. To suggest that it is his duty to assist such a process is to invite an hysterical response. One can understand how, after the first party in the College to which Europeans and Africans were invited—a party at which a dance band played all the evening but no dancing took place for fear the races might dance together—a European girl was found sobbing in a corner and explained that the reason for her collapse was that she realized she had actually been enjoying herself among Africans.

The College has handled troubles of this kind, and much greater ones, with humanity, tact and outstanding success. Africans as a whole have probably underrated its difficulties and overrated its powers. It is hard for them to understand that the liberal academic spirit, although a European immigrant, must manœuvre for a secure footing in Rhodesian society with as much delicate circumspection as an African entering an "interracial" hotel. Unfortunately, therefore, the College has to a great extent sacrificed the confidence of the majority of Africans in its necessary attempts to gain that of Europeans. Their expectations of it were perhaps naïf and their belief in the virtue of university education exaggerated. In the early days of partnership, it was widely thought that the College would be a sort of Makerere (whose fame and reputation in Central Africa is amazingly widespread considering that it is nearly two thousand miles away) where hundreds of Africans would quickly be admitted to equality with Europeans and the privilege of a degree. A suspicious reaction set in when it proved to be a fairly exclusive affair. One hopes this will prove a temporary phenomenon.

The early difficulties in establishing interracial residence received a lot of publicity and Africans, not understanding the delicacy of the College's own position, concluded it was not in earnest on the matter. They could not help seeing that the high entrance standards were designed at least partly to keep them out, and could not appreciate the long-term intention behind the decision. They know that the College is supported by, and is in close relation to a Federal Government which they increasingly distrust and dislike and they are not used to the idea of disagreement on points of principle between European authorities.

The Federal Government has taken the legal power to prohibit admission to the College of any student, however academically acceptable, without giving any reason for excluding him, and all overseas appointments to the staff can be vetoed by a refusal to grant an unacceptable person an entry permit. (What should we think in any British university if government security authorities controlled admission of students and recruitment of staff to this extent?)

University education is more expensive for Africans in the Federation than in East Africa, where virtually any student who is admitted to Makerere has his full expenses paid by his territorial government or local council. The Federal Government provides only eighteen bursaries of £150 for members of all races. (The cost of a year's residence and tuition at the College is £150 a year.) A very limited degree of help is available from native authorities or other sources. Africans cannot be blamed for concluding that the College respects the racial policy of the Federation, making university education available to a large number of Europeans and only to an élite of certain selected Africans (which is how the majority of Europeans probably do see it) nor for overlooking that there is no stronger opponent of this policy than the College itself. It would like to admit many more Africans but can in this respect make haste only slowly.

It is fashionable to represent the University College of Rhodesia and Nyasaland as both the herald of the new age of Federal interracialism and as a panacea for all the troubles of the mixed societies of the three territories. Mr. Macmillan did so in his visit to the Federation. Sir Roy Welensky and Sir Edgar Whitehead have commended it in the same terms in Britain. This is understandable enough. It is, since St. Faith's Mission Farm was disbanded and sold as Native Reserve by the Diocese of Mashonaland, pretty well the only instance of genuine interracial partnership in the Federation. But it would derogate from the College's real achievement to imagine that it has become this as a pilot project for the future with the full support of public opinion and the Federal Government. The College is swimming against the stream and it has got as far as it has by a firm, if discreet, insistence upon values that are not those of the European community. It will go on swimming, one hopes with increasing strength, but it is an illusion to suppose that it can ever by itself reverse the flow of the current. A single university institution with a few hundred members cannot hope to alter, or even seriously to influence the outlook and attitudes of a large society, whether African or European, distributed over an enormous area. It can only remain the custodian of liberal values and hope that the current of opinion will turn in its direction. To count upon the College to transform race relations and to teach partnership to the whole Federation is to place it in a false position which it cannot sustain and to absolve the Governments and the public from the responsibility of changing their own outlook by hard thought and action. It has an influence, of course, and this will become stronger. It may be a decisive one in the lives of a few individuals. Twenty or thirty undergraduates, of both races, will learn every year that close personal relations with the other race are a much simpler and more satisfactory thing than they ever imagined; and will at the same time receive a broad liberal higher education. They will carry this knowledge, and whatever conclusions they base upon it, into their lives and jobs. But neither they nor the College can have a decisive influence upon race relations in a society of 7 millions, nor upon the prejudices of 300,000 Europeans, the majority of whom will have no first-hand experience of the College and very many of whom will continue to view it with suspicion.

In his speech in Salisbury, in January 1960, Mr. Macmillan was bold and wise enough to point out that the College was only a beginning and that a logical consequence of its existence was for all races to have the same education and go to the same schools in the course of time. He was perfectly right. Drastic changes of this nature, not only in education, but in the economy, in land tenure, in the law and in habitual ways of thinking are the only means of transforming race relations and promoting partnership. They cannot be initiated by the University College but only by governments and by public opinion. His remarks gave great offence to many, though not all, Rhodesians and were mentioned by the Dominion Party as one of the three reasons why Southern Rhodesia must leave the Federation if Britain maintained her present attitude. Most of the European public, especially in Southern Rhodesia, does not desire the extension of what the College stands for. They expect it to remain a privileged and ornamental exception. It is useless to expect the College to be able to change their minds single-handed.

CHAPTER XVI

Partnership and the Expanding Economy

When you ask people in Southern Rhodesia what is being done "for the African" they first of all say "Oh, education, of course". If you persuade them that what is being done is not enough, nor the right thing, even if some money is being spent, they say, "Well, the expanding economy. He can cash in on that."

The extent to which he can is seriously limited by the discrimination he suffers in general. It offers him little more than the chance to be a better-off helot rather than a worse-off one. The belief that economic expansion alone will abolish discrimination, segregation, under-privilege and political impotence for Africans is sufficiently prevalent to need some consideration. It is the cornerstone of the racial policy of the present Prime Minister. The argument runs that the economy is expanding; primary production from agriculture (including tobacco) and mining (the temporary setback to Northern Rhodesia copper is not too important and many other minerals are now being discovered in the south) is forging ahead; diverse secondary industries are booming; new factories are springing up daily and capital is pouring in to finance them; skyscrapers and office blocks are shooting up in the great cities; a considerable number of immigrants are coming into the Federation and need housing, services and the satisfaction of their daily needs. Colossal sums are being invested in the Kariba hydro-electric scheme, which can satisfy all our own needs for power and still export it profitably over half the continent. There is masses of money in circulation and more on the way. Let the African have his fair whack of it. Indeed, he is bound to. There cannot possibly be enough Europeans to do the jobs and as more and more of them leave artisan's work and go into management, not only the menial tasks but jobs as foremen, skilled artisans, master plumbers, master builders and master farmers will open up to Africans. We look forward to the day, very soon, when a really large class of Africans with families in the locations will be earning up to £30 or £50 a month and an immeasurably larger number will be pouring money back to their relatives in the reserves by earning £10, even £15 a month in industry. "You know an African can *live* on a few pounds a month. He has few needs."

"Yes," a critic may reply, "but why only £50 a month—£600 a year? The minimum qualification for the ordinary, inalienable vote is £720 a year. Nobody seems to intend any significant number of the present generation of adult Africans to achieve political influence through sharing in economic expansion, and if the likelihood of it arose the qualifications could be raised once more. And I see you take it for granted that Africans will go on living in locations and that a great many will be uprooted migrant workers from the reserves. As long as you go on thinking that an African is well off on £15 a month and rich with £40, and a European poor with £70, the Africans will be justified in saying that all this talk of partnership is bunk. As long as you promote European immigration, your motives will be suspect.

"As long as you retain a political system that is operated by Europeans, and artificially limit the influence of the special vote, the only one that will be within the economic reach of many Africans for a long time to come; as long as you keep Land Apportionment, residential and educational segregation, separate social services and the Native Affairs Department and all the other things we've been talking about, you'll be practising *apartheid*. Economic expansion by itself is not a machine for ensuring social progress. It is simply a means of giving the poorer classes the power to take from you what you are not prepared to allow them. Africans are not nowadays ready to wait for economic advance alone to emancipate them within the arbitrary restrictions of the present system and at the snail's pace it imposes. They are going to demand something very much more rapid and if you won't let them have it, you're going to have to keep them down by more and more violence and repression—whatever is happening economically—as Whitehead has had to do already with the banning and arrest of Congress, the Preventive Detention Act and all the rest of it. Economic expansion without planned social and political reform is a sure recipe for protest and repression."

We are not far from the Limpopo and across it is Nationalist South Africa—*apartheid*, unconditional *baaskap*, the Treason Trial; the shanty towns, locations and mine compounds of Johannesburg and the muddy misery of Cape Flats; an atmosphere of repression and suspicion unequalled since the Third Reich. The economy of the Union of South Africa has been expanding rapidly for the last ten years but this expansion has brought no improvement in race relations. It is firmly based upon black labour, but this foundation of the economy is subject to *apartheid* and severe discriminatory legislation which is steadily increasing. It is not free to organize itself, nor to make any kind of protest and Africans have no prospect of gaining any political influence. Their social position is that of relatively well-paid helots kept in their place by the white man's police. They can only advance to self-determination in the face of the white man's guns and this they are not yet strong enough to do.

The standard of African earning and African living as well as the general level of African education is a good deal higher than in the Federation. There is great poverty in some rural reserves and appalling living conditions in urban slums, but it is not unusual for Africans to earn £30, £60 or even much more per month. There are Africans of considerable wealth in business and of great distinction in the professions. There are large classes of highly educated, widely informed and aware Africans—citizens of the world confined by the bars of *apartheid*, such as Anthony Sampson has described in *Drum*. But neither by wealth, education nor economic importance have they the remotest chance of escaping from the position of second-class citizens. Until Southern Rhodesia abolishes its discriminatory and repressive legislation, which is hardly less harsh than that of the Union, there will be no reason why the same conditions should not apply there.

An increase in the spending power of Africans can easily lead to demoralization in present circumstances. What is a wealthy African to do with his money? He cannot buy a house in the town and settle there.[1] He cannot buy a place in the country and live there.[1] His opportunities for going into farming are sorely limited.[2] He may have a vote, but he can only vote for the Federal, Dominion or Central Africa Parties if his vote is to count at all. No Africanist party has a chance of winning a seat. He must continue carrying his identity card and produce it to any policeman who stops him. He can stay in a good hotel in Salisbury if multiracial hotels are ever started. He still cannot take his wife out to drinks and dinner in a good restaurant because "the management reserves the right of admission". He can-

[1] Land Apportionment Act.
[2] Native Land Husbandry Act.

not live in the location unless he persuades the superintendent he has good reason to—and can never own his front-garden patch there. He cannot live in the reserve unless the N.C. allots him land under the Native Land Husbandry Act. Even if he is allowed it, or qualifies for a purchase area, it will be years before he gets occupation, given the present enormous waiting list. He can buy motor-cars and drink (in a native bottle store) and consumer goods. The effect of economic expansion without the will of the ruling class for change and advance is more likely to be an increased consumption of Coca-Cola in the reserves and increased instability and demoralization in the towns than the arrival of the millennium.

It is the old tragic question of time and pace. Probably no white man in Africa doubts in his inmost thoughts that *one day* every country in Africa will be ruled by Africans. Even Dr. Verwoerd and his followers know it. Their insistence that they are fighting for the *survival* of the white man—this is the word always used, not his triumph—indicates a forlorn if infinitely protracted rearguard action. Certainly everyone in the Federation knows it. But always they seek to stave it for a generation. "Not in my time," is the ultimate denial of hope for the future. It is the motto of the man who will not plant an oak tree for posterity. A nice old retired colonel was kind-hearted enough one day to give some Africans a lift on the road from Umtali to Salisbury and open-minded enough to talk Southern Rhodesian politics with them. As it happened, they were some of the leaders of Congress, and they put the Africanist point of view vigorously, forcefully, if politely. "Yes," he said, as they left his car, "I know you boys are going to win in the end. But, by God, if it happens in my time you'll find me with my back against a wall and a gun in my hands, shooting you down till I drop."

CHAPTER XVII

The African People

If one goes to Southern Rhodesia from anywhere further north one is above all struck by the extraordinarily large number of Africans who appear to have assimilated European ways and a European outlook, by the high standard of spoken English and by the friendliness, patience and discipline of African people. You meet neither the obvious dislike, suspicion or fear of Europeans that can be met in Kenya, or sometimes in Uganda, nor the lawless criminality and nihilism that despair has begotten of enlightenment in South Africa. You meet the resilient gaiety and high spirits with which most Africans accept their second-class lot—a highly civilized, Mediterranean quality which the inhibited Anglo-Saxon in his business suit takes for uncivilized. You meet courtesy, restraint and ability.

There are some primitive communities in the reserves. There are also many individuals of considerable moral stature and great ability. In some remote areas, along the Zambezi for instance, where people have just been moved to make way for the Kariba Dam, traditional ways have changed as little as almost anywhere in Africa. Polygamy, paganism and sorcery persist. People lead a primitive tribal life in the present and take what to the European appears irresponsibly little thought for the morrow. Few of the methods of modern hygiene, agriculture or economics prevail. Yet these communities have survived for generations before the white man came. To write them off as simply inferior, feckless and "uncivilized" is the judgment of ignorance. They have survived by means of a high degree of organization well adapted to their environment but in no way part of the white man's civilization, above all by a formal understanding of human rights and human relationships based upon the family and the chieftainship. They have their own clearly codified morality, which may be quite different from ours. Thousands might die from natural causes but none starves unless all starve. This is hard to equate in any way with our system where few die unnecessarily but many are poor or miserable in isolation. It is only when the traditional organization is broken up by the white man, and nothing put in its place, when detribalization sets in, that these communities become chaotic and unviable. Nowadays nearly everyone wears shirt and trousers, often very ragged, and spends his spare cash, such as it is, in a store that sells Stork margarine, Coca-Cola, Sheffield jack knives and Manchester cotton. The majority has ejected the sorcerer and the superstitions of witchcraft. People resort to them only when they have nothing else to believe in; they regard them as an evil influence, hostile to the best interests of the people and they want to escape from them completely. The witch-doctors themselves are on the run and have been driven underground into furtive secrecy, knowing they have lost their power. Nothing could reverse this process except to bottle up the reserves in physical and spiritual frustration; nothing could encourage it so much as an advance to responsibility and acceptance in society as a whole.

The reserves are best described as a traditional society of poor peasants, a conservative society accepting its lot with all the peasant's suspicion of innovation and the peasant's shrewd judgment of character. As detribalization goes on, and the ideas of political nationalism flow in, as they inevitably will, this conservatism will disappear and be replaced by an inchoate and disruptive awareness of grievance. It would be wise to profit by the conservatism and remove the grievance before it is too late.

The majority of the African population lives in the reserve, but the centres of political power and potential revolution are among the fully detribalized Africans working in the towns. They would be unique if they were all angels but they are so fantastically unlike the average settler's opinion of them that one often wonders whether one can be discussing the same people. This is because very few Europeans ever know any Africans except as workers or servants on a basis of second-class citizenship, which is not conducive to mutual respect. I do not think the detribalized Africans of Southern Rhodesia, as a whole, are any more unreliable, irresponsible, gullible or injudicious than a good many enfranchised electorates in the world today, or even in Europe. I even doubt if they are any more "uncivilized", ill-informed, unenlightened or incapable of exercising wise and moderate judgments than the British working classes who came to power in the nineteenth century. Electoral theoreticians tend to take an altogether too exalted view of the attainments of the voters who make democracy tick over today. There is a grave danger, owing to the prevalent belief in the possibility of measuring civilization, that a man is judged by the façade he presents, by the clothes he wears, his ability to eat with a knife and fork, or to offer a fellow a drink. If the state sets out to judge its citizens' quality, the façade should be of no importance.

But even the façade Africans in Southern Rhodesia present is a good deal less discouraging than one would think from the way many Europeans talk. Superficially at least the Africans in Southern Rhodesia look civilized enough. The very poor wear very poor ragged clothes, like the very poor anywhere. As there are very many more very poor people than in any European country one notices them more. Like the very poor anywhere, the very poor in Southern Rhodesia are sometimes dirty and smelly, dishonest, stupid, and, when they have a few pennies, drunken. The pattern is familiar from Cork to Vladivostok. So many people are near or below the bread line that the white man on his £2,500 a year says: "Look at the Munts. They all smell—they all drink—they all steal—and they can't do a damn' thing right." He forgets that he puts his life into the hands of the black chauffeur who drives him to the office; that his children are cared for by a black nanny; that if he takes a bus it is driven by a black driver; that the telephone exchanges are manned at night by black men (in the comfortable hours of daylight it is a white prerogative); that the non-commissioned ranks of the police are full of Africans directing the traffic and running in their fellow Africans for pass offences; that the C.I.D. employs lots and lots of plain clothes Africans who may, if occasion demands, be set to watch Europeans; that many an up-country general store with its varied stock and innumerable small financial transactions is run very efficiently by a black manager for an absentee European who comes round once a month to check the books and take the profits; that the kitchens and dining-rooms of most hotels are organized solely by Africans while the manager serves in the bar;[1] or that some Africans whom good fortune or education have raised above the bread line are making thousands in trade or business (with natives only), or farming 200 acres, or working with efficiency and success as clergy, mission superintendents, primary and secondary school teachers. He forgets that

[1] It is a shibboleth that a black man may not serve behind a bar. Clubs in the remote country employ a full-time white bartender at £1,000 a year rather than put a black man there.

Africans are successfully doing pretty well everything the law allows them to[1] and, in the few cases where they have made the opportunity, have become doctors, lawyers or journalists with first-rate professional qualifications. The respectable, well dressed, quietly industrious Africans are naturally less noticeable than the poor and ragged. But as a community Africans have accepted the change to European society. They have given up tribal ways, tribal dress and tribal thinking. They are poised for advance. It is up to the white man to decide whether it is a peaceful advance brought about by generous understanding or a destructive one caused by frustration.

The myth of the unusual backwardness of the Southern Rhodesian Africans is widespread. So many even well-intentioned people told me: "I'm afraid you will find them very backward. It'll be a long time before education makes any headway here." I did not find this. I found them in general more advanced, better educated, readier for peaceful progress and more reliable than many African communities I know well, and I found large numbers of people of great ability. What I did not find is a large highly-educated class at the top, because opportunities of secondary and university education have been extremely limited in the past. They are far from adequate today.

Three generations of white domination have, for the most part accidentally, prepared a uniquely favourable foundation for interracial integration and done much to diminish its risks in Southern Rhodesia. Complete economic dependence upon the white man has produced a knowledge of English, even among those who have not been to school, which is unrivalled anywhere to the north. (It is as good in the Union.) This is not only because English is the language of instruction after the first three years of primary school, though it has a lot to do with it. You have to know English to earn money at all, even if you do not go to school, and there are generally several members of your family who know it. The importance of a widely disseminated common language to the whole process of integration and electoral reform cannot be exaggerated.

The white man has never been challenged at all—until the last year or two—and his position and prestige are taken for granted.

[1] They are in practice excluded from the administration of the country in any but the lowest grades; from nearly all highly skilled and highly paid employment; and from all but limited participation in the railways. Such jobs belong to the white man. It is still true that the train from the Congo is brought to the frontier by a black crew and taken over by Federal whites because engine driving becomes too difficult for blacks in Northern Rhodesia.

There was, till 1959, practically no anti-white feeling in Southern Rhodesia. The situation is accepted with a singular absence of bitterness not altogether easy to account for. The lack of secondary education—the first government secondary school at Goromonzi was started in the 1940s—the complete absence of university education till 1956, and the conservative paternalism of the missions, have a lot to do with it. The Administration has not at any time exactly laid itself out to encourage the spread of information and ideas. No one has ever thought of getting the white man out, nor challenged his right to be there. This makes the talk of "handing the country over to someone else" that Sir Roy Welensky indulges in particularly mischievous.

Any European working class of the past two centuries would have rebelled long ago against the grievances that Africans suffer. But Africans have far greater patience than Europeans. The white man is mistaken in taking it for the dumb patience of the ox. It is a more civilized quality, the easy going patience of a humility that does not like trouble. It can be taxed too far. I have never heard anyone in Southern Rhodesia say: "We must get the white man out. This is a black man's country." But I have heard people say: "I think we have a harder job educating the white man than he has had educating us. How can we teach him to share the country with us? Will he force us to make Mau Mau before he will learn?" And this is the feeling of a growing number of Africans today.

The aim of white policy for over fifty years has been to prevent the development of a united African front and of a corporate sense among Africans. Locations, reserves, passes, and native commissioners have been pretty successful in this until the past few years. The educational situation has delayed the growth of a publicly enlightened *élite* who might preach liberty, equality and fraternity to their fellows, and the lack of a free African Press has held back the growth of public opinion. All newspapers and periodicals for African consumption, in English or the vernacular, are owned by Europeans and their African editors are allowed just enough freedom of expression to maintain circulation. The Press has never become the leader of African opinion and it is difficult not to believe this is European policy.[1] In consequence of these things, and of their general

[1] Sir Roy Welensky, as Federal Prime Minister, in 1957, opposed the sale of the largest group of newspapers for Africans to a London company but did not object to a South African one.

subjection, the African population, rural and urban, was almost completely unorganized till 1957. It was too difficult to start political parties, movements or organizations. Charles Msingelis's worthy but minute Labour Party never made any real headway. The Congress Movement had collapsed entirely. There were no African political leaders with a popular following. This could have given responsible European leadership its greatest opportunity. To collaborate with the latent forces of Africanism in laying the foundations of a really interracial democracy, and to help emergent leaders of Africanism to become the colleagues of the white man for the advancement of the whole society, might have changed the aspect of half the continent.[1] But Rhodesian Europeans could not seize their chance and preferred to emphasize the polarity between black and white and to force the leaders of Africanism to become either their "stooges" or their foes. When Congress was resurrected in 1957, the African masses were no longer lethargic. The failure of four years of promised partnership to offer them anything of value made them look for leadership and political organization. Congress provided it and African political life became a new and vital force. The Europeans and their Government, by cold-shouldering Congress, left it to develop on its own lines and sacrificed all chance of collaborating with or influencing it. They chose by the 1959 Emergency to alienate it completely. The claim that Congress did not really represent Africans but only intimidated them is self-contradictory. If this had been so it could never have drawn large crowds to its meetings or wielded the influence it did. Sir Edgar Whitehead attached great significance to the fact that when he outlawed Congress, he had fifteen personal letters of support from Africans. But fifteen letters from a population of 2½ million seem to prove the opposite point to the one he was trying to make.

[1] A writer who foresaw the Europeans' failure, in Rhodesia, has pointed out that their success was the only thing that might have had any influence on South Africa. "It is likely that opposition (to the idea of partnership) . . . will gain ground first because of white Rhodesians' growing apprehension about black–white partnership (whites are outnumbered by thirty to one in the Federation) and secondly because of the normal democratic swing of the pendulum against the party in power. Even if a party openly devoted to *apartheid* does not come to power, there is no doubt that the Nationalists' task in the Union would be eased by the existence of such a party north of the Limpopo. The success of partnership would on the other hand make the future of *apartheid* and Nationalist Afrikanerdom difficult if not impossible." S. Patterson, *The Last Trek*, Routledge, 1957.

CHAPTER XVIII

Partnership and Electoral Reform

The myth of colour difference today is just the same as the nineteenth-century myth of class. A threatened governing class needs a belief in its own intrinsic superiority to justify its privileges. The upper classes of mid-Victorian days accepted the comfortable truth of their right to *baaskap*. God made men rich and poor. "The rich man in his castle, the poor man at his gate." "The poor are always with us" (misquoted and grotesquely misinterpreted).[1] They are irresponsible, dirty, lazy and dishonest. They must be kept in the station in life to which it has pleased God to call them. They could not possibly do most of the things we can do. We must keep our distance from them in order to maintain our position. If need be we must use force. Such are the views behind Peterloo and Tolpuddle. There were dissentients but it was the dominant upper class myth. The recorder and poet of this myth is Charles Dickens, and however caricatured his figures may sometimes be, his delineation of social attitudes is accurate. *Hard Times* is a penetrating study, of universal scope and truth, of the "we/they" myth. It is uncanny to read it in Southern Rhodesia today. The unconscious heartlessness and inhumanity, the guilty knowledge of self-delusion, the subordination of generous impulse to material convenience, the dehumanization and moral collapse, are in the ambient air. It is a book about Africa. The gulf in human understanding and charity between Dickens's rich and poor is the gulf between black and white today.

At the dark bottom of racial prejudice in Africa or the U.S.A. there is nothing but the sterile theme of privilege. It gains currency and ramifies into innumerable variants with generations of repetition.

[1] The Bishop of Llandaff published a treatise in 1793, "On the Wisdom of God In Making Men Rich and Poor." He was Professor of Chemistry and Regius Professor of Divinity at Cambridge.

It is absorbed by the young as an unquestioned part of the truth. And all it amounts to is "what we have, we hold". It is *ex post facto* rationalization of motives the conscious mind is ashamed of. The belief that the meeting of black and white is in some inscrutable way different from the meeting of any other human beings, that there is some obscure biological repulsion—or attraction—between them, or that the black races are inherently inferior is the precise equivalent of Mr. Bounderby's beliefs about the poor—an excuse for economic class antagonism. It is evolved and accepted with passionate subjectivity to conceal the fact that the difference between black and white is a difference of wealth and is to remain so. It is natural that its home is South Africa where a white governing class has committed itself longest and most deeply to dependence on black helotry. "European civilization" implies simply white privilege and the words are heard most often in mouths that most often betray what it really means. It was Mr. Strijdom who called for "the closest co-operation between all countries who have interests . . . in the preservation of white civilization" and it is the Dutch Reformed Church which has made discrimination into a principle of Christianity.

Africans are no more "different" from white men than Italians from Scandinavians or Czechs from Britons except that their skins mark them as different. When one knows them, at any level of development, the striking thing is how exactly the same they are in their basic preoccupations, in all humanly important ways. The difference is one of history. It is customary to describe them as primitive in settler countries and to claim that it will be centuries before they attain "European standards". This is because they are poor and look poor. But they are no more basically inferior or less capable of rapid development than our ancestors were. After all, only a century ago Highland and Hebridean peasants were living in windowless "black houses" with an open fire in the middle, dwellings every bit as "primitive" as the African villager's hut.

There is nothing in the meeting of black and white as such to cause hostility between the races. The first Europeans felt none of it. Contempt, patronization, revulsion and exclusiveness are not found in the writings of the early travellers, missionaries or prospectors. They found no difficulty in taking race relations naturally. Even van Riebeck planted his celebrated hedge for defence, not for racial segregation. Livingstone, Baikie, Ashe and his colleagues in Uganda, and all the others who came into contact with black men before white exploitation had begun, found them what they are—a collection of people with vastly different customs from our own, people of infinitely varied individuality. They made great friends with some, and felt respect for many. They thought that they lacked the religious enlightenment and educational opportunities the West was considered to possess and in consequence often harboured cruel beliefs and erroneous habits. But it never occurred to them that it degraded them to sit down with a black man, that it "felt" different to shake hands with one and so should be avoided or that black men were intrinsically inferior to white men.

It was only where it became profitable for white men to live in Africa on land which might have been occupied by black men, to enslave them or to use their cheap labour to make great profits from farming or mining, to impose a foreign way of living on their country—it was only in fact when the economic exploitation of Africa began—that the myth of black inferiority sprang up. It was invented by the white man as an excuse for a situation which filled his pocket while his conscience obscurely blamed him.

All belief in the difference between "them" and "us" is the product of class antagonism, irrespective of racial difference. Mr. Bounderby talking of the "hands" is indistinguishable from any conventional settler talking about the natives; and much later in Britain we have Lord Curzon who expressed surprise, when he saw some troops bathing, that "the poor have such white skins". The trouble in Africa is that they have not white skins—that social mobility and the consequent change of class structure is inhibited by the fact that whatever a member of the lower class achieves, wherever he is, he is recognizable as a member of his class. Nevertheless one wishes that the Southern Rhodesian public could see its political and electoral problem as the class problem it is, not the race problem it is not (except in so far as thinking about race makes it a frankly intractable factor in a development at best difficult enough); that it would learn the lessons of the Reform Bill and the Trade Union movement by example and not insist upon learning them the hard way in practice. For what happened when the oligarchic myth of the eighteenth and nineteenth centuries was broken down in Britain proves some Southern Rhodesian fears to be ill-founded.

Three things stand out in the history of nineteenth-century Europe. First, a newly enfranchised populace does not necessarily use the vote for revolutionary purposes.

Second, the harder it is for the populace to get the vote, the more revolutionary it becomes.

Third, the vote is not *bestowed* upon a lower class by a benevolent oligarchy when it is judged ready for it. It is taken, seized if you like, by the lower class when it is powerful enough to destroy the myth of its own inferiority. Yet the basic principle of Southern Rhodesia is "only the civilized will be given the vote", and no part of Mr. Rhodes's legacy has been more fatal than the misinterpreted slogan "equal rights for every civilized man" both because it asserts a principle of development that is opposite to all historical precedent and because it suggests that there is in the hands of skilled technicians some means of calibrating civilization.

The nineteenth century in Britain saw the transfer of political power from a small property-owning oligarchy to an industrial and agricultural proletariat. Concessions were not made from any particular idealism nor with any particular graciousness. Their only merit is that they were made in time. The transfer of power was accomplished without revolution or economic disaster, without the development of insuperable antagonism between the classes, and the governing classes were not overwhelmed. On the contrary, they were able to retain the substance of their property and political influence. By making limited material concessions and accepting, more or less reluctantly, the rising leaders of the poor into their ranks, by gradually abating their exclusiveness, they remained the leaders of the country. The working class was ready to vote to a great extent for members of the upper class. The upper classes were not swamped by the extension of the franchise. Universal suffrage did not cause revolution though the majority of those enfranchised would not, *mutatis mutandis*, have qualified for the ordinary vote in Southern Rhodesia.

The Tredgold Report rejects universal suffrage because it would mean "that the overwhelming majority of votes would be African". It would mean "racial representation of the worst type because, for practical purposes, only one race would be represented".[1] The result would be "to place the European minority in the hands of the African majority, a majority for the most part uneducated and backward. . . . So large a section of the population is backward and

[1] Report of the Franchise Commission for Southern Rhodesia, Government Printer, Salisbury, 1957, p. 5, ll. 291–2. For practical purposes only one race—the white—is represented under the existing 20 per cent rule.

illiterate and completely lacking in political background that the effect of adult suffrage would be to place political control in the hands of people sadly unequipped to exercise it".[1] These words might have been uttered by Lord Melbourne, or Mr. Bounderby, with this difference—that when it came to the test, they had enough opportunism and freedom from prejudice to accept working class emancipation instead of rejecting it. They understood that the process of industrialization *must* place the wealthy or educated minority "in the hands of a majority for the most part backward and uneducated" and that if the minority wishes to keep leadership it must manipulate this process so as not to lose it. The essence of Western democracy is precisely its tendency to give more and more power "to a majority for the most part uneducated and backward" and to rely upon the upper class to lead the majority by flexibility, understanding and skill. The nineteenth-century British just pulled this off. They showed the pliability of the reed in a storm and kept their roots.

Southern Rhodesia is choosing the way of the oak. It wishes to become a great industrial exporting country in a short space of time, supplying the markets of all Africa. Kariba is being built to this end. The present intention seems to be that the African masses should participate in this programme and its benefits simply by providing an endless supply of cheap, disenfranchised labour from the location while government remains a prerogative of Europeans.[2]

But to make a substantial concession of political rights to Africans now, and to guarantee more in the near future is the only way in which the whites can avoid being swamped. "To place the minority in the hands of a majority for the most part uneducated and backward" is inevitable; it had best be done at a time chosen by the minority. There is not the slightest chance that the masses will wait until they are what the settlers consider sufficiently educated and "civilized". If offered any real prospect of advance, Africans would at least till lately have been ready to seek it constitutionally in the framework of the established order. They are very patient people.

The British upper classes just saved their bacon—and also the country's. If reform had met more resistance in the nineteenth century, we should never have won the Battle of Britain.

[1] Ibid., ll. 295–7.

[2] In a society where the lowest paid white artisan gets nearly £1,000 a year and pays little income-tax, one can only regard the whole white population as economically upper class.

In Germany, where resistance was stronger and the behaviour of the governing classes more curmudgeonly and inhuman, socialism has been a Marxist organ of bitter class warfare and antagonism, to the detriment of the working class and the country as a whole; class and labour relations have been bloody and embittered; weakness at the hinges of class contributed heavily both to the rise of Hitler and the 1945 collapse.

And in Russia where the extreme refusal of any kind of concession took place, you have the October Revolution. South Africa has already chosen the path that leads there. Many of Professor Keppel Jones's predictions[1] have already come true and a complete disintegration of the country appears nearly inescapable. History shows clearly that the only alternative to violent revolution is to offer the populace real partnership and that, if it is done in time, the sacrifices and risks are not great. Sheer repression cannot pay. It is inherent in the numerical balance of forces in Southern Rhodesia that a quarter million whites cannot go on holding down ten times as many blacks for ever either by force or by juggling with figures. To refuse to face this is to run away from reality. In an industrial economy power flows into the hands of industrial workers. There seems everything to be said for conceding a good deal of power before it is demanded.

The working classes in nineteenth-century Britain did not get the vote because they were judged sufficiently educated and civilized. The seventeenth and eighteenth centuries did not witness their intensive education and preparation for advance into civilization; they witnessed the growth of their numbers and of their importance to a developing economy. When they were strong enough they forced the ruling class to take them increasingly into the real partnership of legal and economic equality. The franchise is neither a right nor a skill. It is a means of power which is seized by a group which can no longer be resisted. The art of government in a developing society is to judge the right moment to yield and the survival of a governing class depends upon its ability to do so. Western Democracy is a rather clumsy machinery, the best so far devised, for reflecting the balance of forces in a community. It is concerned with the strength of those forces, not their degree of civilization. To deny any powerful force its electoral reflection is to ensure that it will sooner or later smash the machine. One misses in Southern Rhodesia, and in the

[1] A. Keppel Jones, *When Smuts Goes*, Shuter & Shooter, Pietermaritzburg, 1947.

Tredgold Report, any objective consideration of the question: "Are the Africans, or will they soon be, powerful enough to demand the franchise?" though it is a far more important question than: "Are they civilized enough to be given it?" It is one to which, in a country aspiring to rapid and comprehensive industrial development among ten times as many Africans as Europeans, the answer seems very clear.

It is ironical that in fact the degree of an African's officially recognized civilization depends not upon his personal accomplishments but upon where he happens to be born or to live. A peasant of no education living by subsistence agriculture is civilized enough for the vote and full civic rights in Nigeria or Ghana; civilized enough to be promised them shortly in Uganda; he is becoming civilized enough to vote in Kenya a lot quicker than in the Federation. He is not civilized enough in Southern Rhodesia unless he has educational standard IV and £300 a year, *but* civilized enough to have one-sixth of the other voters' power if he has passed educational standard VIII. There is no objective difference between these people at all. In the Union of South Africa Professor Z. K. Matthews is not civilized enough to vote because he is black; in Uganda he would be offered a Ministry in the Government. Africans may be forgiven some scepticism about the nature of a civilization test which so clearly reflects the interests of those already enfranchised.

A man enfranchised in time, however backward an illiterate, is less dangerous than a man disenfranchised *sine die*. A limited franchise inevitably becomes the instrument of group interests and it is so hard for human beings to give up an exclusive right that it is better for the whole state that they should never possess it.[1] The franchise has developed as a means of representing a whole community, not a civilized majority of any or all races, and any other use of it is unlikely to work well. Those who are not ready to respect the interests of the majority of their fellow citizens in the society they live in have really no alternative but to look for another where the majority agrees with them.

Any enlightened and imaginative government in Southern Rhodesia would proclaim immediately that its objective is universal adult suffrage, thus gaining the indispensable confidence and

[1] Cf. Tredgold Report, p. 5, l. 256. "Only a man of exceptional moral fibre can be relied upon to press for the very long view involving compromise and concession of immediate benefits to his own group," already quoted on p. 136.

goodwill of the disenfranchised masses. It would need at the same time to indicate the stages by which full enfranchisement might be achieved. A government prepared to do this would enjoy an enviable freedom of movement to advance further in its own time, choosing its own ground, to the only solution of the problem that can make sense in the long run. Unfortunately, it would, at the moment, lose the support of the dominant European electors and fall from office.

CHAPTER XIX

Political Parties in Southern Rhodesia

THE CENTRAL AFRICA PARTY

Mr. Todd's modestly liberal paternalism as United Rhodesia (later Federal) Party Prime Minister of Southern Rhodesia estranged him from his cabinet colleagues and the electorate and he was forced by a very unedifying conspiracy of his ministers to resign at the beginning of 1958. He later became leader of the Central Africa Party, which is described in its Federal context on pages 95–7. Its policy in Southern Rhodesia is the same as for the Federation. It has chosen its name astutely, implying devotion to the welfare of Central Africa as a whole and not committing itself on the issue of Federation or Dominion status as its more powerful rivals, the United Federal and Dominion parties have done. It would choose to continue Federation on the more liberal terms it wishes to introduce and believes these would be acceptable to Africans generally. Being opposed to the United Federal Party, it does not adhere to its policy of Federation at any price, indissolubly imposed by Europeans.

THE DOMINION PARTY

The Southern Rhodesian general election of June 1958, in which 50,000 Europeans and 1,650 Africans were registered, confirmed the United Federal Party's rule under Sir Edgar Whitehead. He was elected by an absolute minority on the system of the alternative vote used in Southern Rhodesia. Had the election been held on the system used in the United Kingdom, the Dominion Party would have got in and formed the government. That is to say that more electors wanted the D.P. as their first choice than wanted any other party; but when second choices were transferred from ballot papers whose first choice had been another, and wholly unsuccessful, party, the U.F.P. had a majority. Whichever system more accurately reflects the will of the electorate, the Dominion Party commands enough support to justify examination. The party operates in Northern as well as Southern Rhodesia, and sometimes talks of doing so in Nyasaland. But its centre is Southern Rhodesia and it favours that country's secession if the privileges of its European inhabitants cannot be safeguarded within Federation.

The Central African Examiner, while still an independent paper, described the Dominion Party as "reactionary, segregationist, and travelling, even if it has not yet awoken to the fact, towards a South African solution to a Rhodesian problem". Its objective, in its own words, is "to establish in Central Africa a Great Nation[1] of fifty or sixty million inhabitants by A.D. 2000, half of them European, half of them African, with full justice to the two main components". Its policy statements during the 1958 election called for:

(*i*) Dominion Status at once, if necessary in defiance of the Constitution and Her Majesty's Government.

(*ii*) The consequent elimination of British responsibility and Colonial Office protection for the Africans of Northern Rhodesia and Nyasaland.

(*iii*) Rejection of the idea of "partnership" and its replacement by a system of political separation and racial segregation entrenching white supremacy and very like *apartheid*.

(*iv*) A franchise based on separate racial rolls, strongly weighted in favour of the European.

(*v*) The protection of the white standard of living against African encroachment.

(*vi*) An "unprecedented" European immigration scheme to raise the white population of the Federation from 300,000 in 1958 to 3½ million by 1975 and to 25 million or 30 million by the end of the century, changing the present ratio of one European to thirty-six Africans to one to four by 1975 and one to one by A.D. 2000.

Native policy was said to be to keep "control in European hands for the foreseeable future and to assist the development of the African in the manner most suited to his capacities". He was to be "encouraged to help himself", to be given "training in honesty, loyalty, responsibility and hygiene" and "vocational courses to fit him for his proper place in the development of the Federation". There were only two references to African education in the party's programme, though there were elaborate plans for "safeguarding the

[1] The capitals are the Dominion Party's.

future potential" of European children by extending their educational facilities and "subject to the limitation of the smaller funds available, the education of Asiatic, Eurafrican and coloured children should be guided by the same principles". No education transcending the boundaries of race was envisaged.

Few openings were expected to exist for white-collar or academic Africans. It was assumed that the best jobs naturally belonged to Europeans (in spite of the few African barristers, doctors, journalists, teachers and clergymen who are working in the Federation and who prove African ability in these directions). But the party was "opposed to the exploitation of African labour to the detriment of the European worker". This was a way of saying that even African artisans would be discouraged from competing, at an economic wage rate, with the uneconomic rate demanded by Europeans. The immigration programme, designed to secure white supremacy by force of numbers, would see to that. "The population is to be increased many times over" by immigration, party policy says. "Nothing could so safeguard civilization and, incidentally, African advance. Such a swift migration is unprecedented in world history. We are in a situation where the unprecedented is essential to success or even to survival."

The party desired "to foster a spirit of mutual confidence and co-operation between the races while making it possible for each group to maintain its identity". It proposed to allow Africans to own their own homes in urban locations and "to manage their own townships with all amenities owned and managed by Africans". But it was unshakeably opposed to complete integration. "Social development should be left to follow the wishes of the electorate" (which was over 90 per cent European). It accused the U.F.P. of "enforcing all forms of integration by law", though all it had done at the time was to make a law that Indian diplomats might not be expelled from public houses. It said that "the lessons from neighbouring territories were to be studied" on this subject; and promised "consultation and co-operation with all neighbouring States in solving common problems".

The doctrines of white supremacy, *apartheid* and the *assimilado* system meet in the Dominion Party's franchise proposals. There are two rolls; one for civilized people and one for Africans. All non-Africans go automatically on the civilized roll, because they have "for some generations shown themselves fair, tolerant, reasonable and liberal-minded". This roll is to include Africans "adjudged qualified to use" the franchise. But most Africans "have had no opportunity of showing themselves fair, tolerant, reasonable and liberal-minded. The idea of a tolerated opposition is entirely alien to them, certainly for the present and possibly for some generations to come." So, in order to qualify for the "civilized" roll, an African was required to produce testimonials from ten registered "civilized" voters and from a magistrate or Native Commissioner, guaranteeing "that he has lived in a civilized way for ten years, is educated and understands the implications of liberal democracy and is of good general repute". He must then appear before a board of five State-appointed examiners to prove his "civilization". An adverse decision from two of the five disqualified him. "What is in question is character and of this a Board of Examiners would be the only satisfactory judges until the verdict of history is passed." This roll will elect over 80 per cent of members.

The Dominion Party is anti-Asian. It speaks of "hungry eyes waiting to direct here the teeming millions of Asiatic countries only a short distance, comparatively, from the shores of Africa". It seems to feel an almost equal hostility towards the British Government and Colonial Office. It would "take such steps as are necessary to attain independence", in spite of "yielding to none in allegiance to the Crown and being determined to remain within the British Commonwealth", and would "denounce any international instruments that deprive the Federation of its sovereign rights". It remarks ingenuously that Northern Rhodesia, the white copper-miners' stronghold, "must recognize a future for *all* races, not only the black", that "the contrast between Northern Rhodesia and Southern, where the Colonial Office has no authority, is most marked", and that "co-operation of all races will be easier without the interference of a foreign government". Regarding Mr. Lyttelton's promise that the Federal Constitution would not be changed, nor Colonial Office protection withdrawn from the northern territories without the agreement of "a majority of *all* the inhabitants" (including Africans), it argued that "it was generally accepted that this was intended to allude to *a majority of voters* if only for the reason that it is a practical impossibility to obtain the opinion of 'a majority of the inhabitants' ". Apparently if we do not "adhere too strictly" to the precise meaning of words and promises, "inhabitants" can mean white inhabitants and the Great State may arise.[1]

[1] This account of Dominion Party policy is taken entirely from propaganda issued by the party up to the 1958 election.

Since 1958, the Dominion Party has added Partition of the existing Federation to its programme. It advocates the replacement of Federation by what it calls the Central African Alliance. It proposes the establishment of a Dominion of Rhodesia ruled according to Dominion Party policies, and including all areas of the Federation which have a considerable population of white settlers; that is, Southern Rhodesia, the copperbelt in Northern Rhodesia and the line of rail, several hundred miles of it, joining the two. The rest of Northern Rhodesia (including the Barotseland Protectorate) and Nyasaland are to become a primarily African country. This African area is to have a large measure of independence and self-determination, but to remain in alliance with the Dominion of Rhodesia and share a variety of functional services with it. It will not come officially under its political control.

The apparent realism of this scheme is deceptive. It could never work, unless the African state were kept under the actual domination of the Dominion of Rhodesia as Dr. Verwoerd's Bantustan will be under the Union Government. It places virtually all the known natural resources, including the copperbelt, and all the industrialized or developed areas, in the white Dominion and leaves the African state with an enormous area of uncleared, unproductive bush. It leaves about 3 million Africans as compulsory citizens of the Dominion of Rhodesia, subject to the Dominion Party's native policy. It is naïf to imagine that the African state in the north would acquiesce in either of these conditions, or consent to remain in alliance with the Dominion unless the deeds of alliance forced it to—unless, that is, "alliance" meant in fact political control.

If the alliance left external affairs, defence, currency, customs, communications or any form of taxation with the Dominion, it would be political control—the political control of a Bantustan by a white government more openly repressive than the present Federation and even less responsive to African opinion. If it did not it is hard to see what the point of the alliance would be. No free African state would stay in it. Alliance with Tanganyika or the Congo (which would have the copper and uranium of the Haut Katanga)—or perhaps with both—would be far more attractive. And a hostile, Africanist state of this size and importance would be an unwelcome neighbour on the northern borders of the Dominion.

The Dominion Party is still worth watching. Its policy is the natural one for the existing Southern Rhodesian electorate and it polled the majority of its votes. It is an Algerian type of policy, diametrically opposed to the one laid down by the British Parliament as the basis of Federation.

THE UNITED FEDERAL PARTY

It will be interesting to watch the development of relations between Sir Edgar Whitehead's Southern Rhodesian wing of the U.F.P. and the central party under Sir Roy Welensky during 1960 and 1961. Theoretically they stand as one man for maintaining the Federation in its present form, for the evolution of "interracial partnership" on a basis of "European standards", for Dominion status for the whole Federation at the earliest possible moment and for the interpretation of the Federal Constitution described in Part II of this book. But as the inconsistencies of the conception of Federation become clearer—and they have become very much clearer since the 1959 Emergencies, the Devlin Report, Mr. Macmillan's African tour and Mr. Macleod's installation at the Colonial Office—so too does the incompitability of Federation in any form acceptable to Britain with the preservation of the existing interests and privileges of Southern Rhodesian Europeans. Sir Edgar Whitehead is responsible electorally to them, but as a party man to Sir Roy Welensky. These two different loyalties will conflict more and more. The absolute indissolubility of Federation is the cardinal point of Sir Roy Welensky's policy. It cannot have been much more agreeable to him when Whitehead, after Mr. Macmillan's visit, said that if Britain pursued a strongly pro-African policy in the Northern Protectorates, Southern Rhodesia would have to secede than when Dr. Banda talked of Nyasaland's secession a year previously. The Southern Rhodesian U.F.P.'s policy on Federation is at present obscure.[1] Its internal territorial policy is fairly clear.

Sir Edgar Whitehead proposes to expand the economy by the most intensive industrial development possible and simultaneously to

[1] On 10th February 1960 Sir Edgar Whitehead told the territorial Assembly in Salisbury that he would not be a party to any agreement reached by the Federal Constitutional Review unless Southern Rhodesia's own independence were increased. He said he was negotiating for the removal of Britain's remaining reserved powers over Southern Rhodesia. (That is, the right which has never been used, to veto in particular legislation and certain other powers of a discriminatory nature.) He fears that the Review may enlarge African power over the Federal Government and is seeking to secure Southern Rhodesia's position. It is hard to see, however, how a Southern Rhodesia with increased power to discriminate against Africans could remain in a Federation over which they were gaining more control.

extend African education as fast as he can by means of the five-year plan described in Chapter XVI. He claims that economic expansion will provide ever-increasing opportunities, and that Africans will emerge from the educational system equipped to take them, from the highest political, administrative and managerial positions down to the lower reaches of artisans' work and agriculture, on an equal footing with the Europeans. By reason of their education, they will be acceptable to the Europeans as work-mates, as fellow citizens, as voters—in a word as partners. Sir Edgar believes in the enormous, almost unlimited, industrial potential and promise of Southern Rhodesia and of its mineral deposits. He believes that the greatest steel industry in Africa can be set up there. And he believes that the almost unlimited prosperity which, he says, can be based on all this will of itself solve all racial problems, if the necessary capital and the necessary time can be found. He admits the supreme need for time to carry out this process. While industrialization and education are raising the African standard, while Europeans are learning to abate their exclusive prejudices and privileges, Africans must accept discrimination with understanding and equanimity. The process may take one or two generations. But no one must rock the boat or distract the attention of the man at the economic wheel while this difficult and protracted landfall is being made. African political movements which ask too much for Africans too soon are endangering the ultimate interests of Africans as much as everyone else's. If they are given their head, this will cause the Europeans to shy away from "partnership" into increased racialism; if they want too much jam today they won't get any tomorrow. This justifies their ruthless suppression in general and the imprisonment without charge or trial of 495 members of Congress in the spring of 1959 in particular. "It is a very ancient tradition of the British people that a Government should defer action against subversive movements until actual rioting or bloodshed has taken place. My Government does not subscribe to this tradition." He justifies the legislation he introduced at the time to "deal with" Congress or any future African movement. It is necessary, even if it is the most repressive in existence in any country in the world. It does not seem to the U.F.P. ironical or contradictory that as strong measures should be needed by a British power in the name of "partnership" and democratic development as have been required by the Afrikaner Government of South Africa to enforce *apartheid*. They are the only means of buying the time necessary to deliver the *Wirtschaftswunder* lying nascent in the womb of "our country".

The Preventive Detention Act, 1959,[1] provides for the arbitary arrest, and detention "during the Governor's pleasure" of anyone who *appears* to have been associated with any organization that led to the 1959 Emergency, or *appears* to be concerned in any activities which might necessitate the declaration of another Emergency. No charge and no trial are needed to shut up indefinitely anyone who appears to fall into these categories. The Act sets up a non-judicial secret tribunal of one judge and two Members of Parliament to inquire into every case of detention and advise the Governor as to the necessity or otherwise of its continuation; it remains in force for five years from its original passage but there is nothing to prevent its prolongation.

The Unlawful Organizations Act, 1959, allows the Government to proscribe any organization it wishes. This, as well as preventing the continued existence of such an organization, brings individual membership of it under the terms of the Preventive Detention Act. These laws are not, in theory, discriminatory. They could as well be applied to the Dominion Party or the Central Africa Party as to the Congress movements. The Amendment to the Native Affairs Act, passed at the same time, is, however, openly discriminatory. Since the Native Affairs Act itself is discriminatory the Amendment could not be otherwise. It awards a fine of £50 or six months' imprisonment to any native who does or says anything to undermine the authority of any officer of the Federal or Territorial Government, from the highest European functionary down to the humblest African head-man or kraal head. And it punishes in the same way the offence of bringing any such authority "into disrepute or contempt". It forbids any meeting of twelve or more natives for which prior permission of the Native Commissioner, in writing, has not been obtained. The European public remains free to criticize the Government and hold political meetings as it wishes.

Finally, the law provides that no court action of any kind may lie against any government official with regard to anything done *in good faith* while applying the provisions of these Acts. A policeman who exceeds his duty, an administrator who inflicts financial or personal

[1] A very similar Act exists in Ghana under Dr. Nkrumah's Government. This is equally contrary to the values of Western democracy. Its sanction is that it was passed by a government elected by a majority of the whole population, not by a tiny minority as Sir Edgar's is.

damage through misapprehension or false identification, is indemnified in advance against any action by the subject.

These laws must be regarded as part of the policy of the Southern Rhodesian U.F.P. since it regards authoritarian control of African political life as essential to the execution of all its other intentions. Anyone who has studied the Southern Rhodesian security laws of the last twenty-five years,[1] and noticed their ascending scale of severity, will be surprised that it was necessary, or indeed possible, to find measures more draconian. They read like the legislation of a tyranny becoming increasingly aware of its precarious position and they seem always to be attempting to forestall a Mau Mau type of rising—a thing which in the psychological and geographical conditions of Southern Rhodesia is quite out of the question. And anyone who reflects upon the number of distinguished and respectable people who are members of the Prohibited Immigrants Club lately founded in London will wonder that yet more could be done to protect innocent African minds from dangerous thoughts.

But the U.F.P.'s recent legislation has gone a good deal further than anything before it and the fact that it is the culmination of a long line of notorious ancestors, stretching back well before the days of Federation and partnership, indicates that U.F.P. policy represents no real departure from the European supremacy of earlier days. It is not easy to take people into partnership by laws of this kind.

"Political problems are unimportant," says Whitehead. "It is the economic ones that matter." This may seem an odd view for a politician but he is not a politician; he is a technocrat and master planner of formidable ability. The rigid enforcement of a master plan for economic development, the subordination to it of all social and political forces, of all accepted conceptions of freedom and human rights, and of all considerations of present happiness and feeling; the reliance on purely material development coupled with a predominantly utilitarian education for backward peoples—the faith in the Moloch economy, if given enough human sacrifice for a long enough space of time, to return its nourishment with a thousand-fold increase to the whole of society, is his policy. It is almost indistinguishable from Stalinism.

Can he, by these methods, buy the time he says he needs? It is unrealistic to hope that the African population of Southern Rhodesia

[1] The Sedition Act, 1936, the Subversive Activities Act, 1950, the Peace Preservation Amendment Act, 1953, the Public Order Act, 1955, for instance.

will refrain from further attempts to rock the boat on account of the 1959 Emergency, or that Congress will accept its defeat as final. They have little confidence in the Government's promise of a better future and it is hard to see how they could have considering the legislation and treatment they have been subjected to.

Further organized attempts to express African opinion are inevitable in the next few years. These will lead both to further and more savage repression of Africans, and to further disturbance and discontent which will impede the unfolding of Sir Edgar's *Wirtschaftswunder*. It is impossible to expect Africans, whose feelings are now fully aroused, to wait a generation, even a quinquennium, for benefits which, rightly or wrongly, they do not believe they are ever intended to receive. The only hope of persuading them to do so would be to give them some immediate earnest of good faith—a substantial increase in the African minimum wage, many new grammar schools, more university bursaries, a revision of Land Apportionment, and a significant extension of the franchise. But the European public would not stand for this. The government which attempted it would give way to the Dominion Party. It seems to be the almost inevitable fate of any Southern Rhodesian government to lose the confidence of its own electors if it does even the minimum necessary to gain that of Africans and to lose the confidence of the unenfranchised Africans if it offers the Europeans their minimum demands. It really matters very little who governs Southern Rhodesia in existing circumstances. Every Prime Minister will be subject to the stranglehold of a tiny electorate of Europeans, largely artisans, who are not yet enlightened enough to recognize that clinging to their traditional fetishes and privileges is the one sure way to disaster. The tolerant, wealthy farmers who appear on the platforms at U.F.P. meetings and who genuinely accept the inevitability of African advance in the same way as Sir Edgar himself does, whether he likes it or not—under European control, of course, and above all not too fast—are as much an impotent minority as the Central African Party or the "extreme" liberals on the staff of the University College. Sir Edgar's Stalinism is Stalinism with a difference. It is as though Stalin had attempted to force his economic revolution through under the necessity of respecting the rights of the Tsarist landowners and capitalists, with dictatorial powers only over the peasants and workers. It is hard to foresee any future for Southern Rhodesia except what has taken place in South Africa—successive moves to the right at every general election until a completely reactionary government finds itself in a state of irreconcilable antagonism with a completely embittered populace.

The deficiencies of the U.F.P. African educational programme as education for partnership have been discussed in Chapter XVI. It may produce a better trained working class; but it cannot hope to produce the degree of opportunity and advance which Sir Edgar Whitehead regards as a necessary accompaniment to economic expansion if his party's policy is to achieve the integrated and undiscriminatory partnership it professes to aim at.

CONGRESS

The Southern Rhodesian African National Congress is at present a prohibited organization and its leaders are in prison or exile. A successor to it, which at present is still legal, has been founded under the name of the National Democratic Party. Its aims are roughly identical but it is not easy to see what it can do in the strait-jacket of preventive legislation in force. There was a Congress movement in Southern Rhodesia before the war but it perished for lack of support. African political consciousness had developed a lot when the African Youth League was founded in Harari location near Salisbury in 1955, and immediately began to assert itself in defence of Africans. It surprised and disconcerted the authorities in getting various grievances redressed by the kind of concerted action among location dwellers which they were not prepared for.

Congress grew out of it. When it proclaimed its official foundation in September 1957 it issued a statement of principles and policy[1] which also surprised and disconcerted the authorities. It declared itself an interracial party and appealed to Europeans as well as Africans to join it. It pledged itself to constitutional methods and disclaimed violent or revolutionary intentions. It said that it had no racial hostility and no desire to dispossess Europeans or drive them out of the country. It demanded justice for Africans and a realization of the equal partnership in the political and economic life which had been promised to them. It called for universal adult suffrage, the end of Land Apportionment and of the Native Affairs Department and the abolition of all discriminatory legislation and of industrial and occupational colour bar. It made hardly any reference to purely

[1] This is reproduced as an Appendix on pp. 235–47.

social colour bar but it did ask for equal rights for all races in all public places. It was a sober, moderate, reasonable petition of rights.

Congress was inexperienced but vital and its leaders were realistic. They did not imagine that under any conceivable circumstances, all their proposals could be accepted and introduced at once or all together. The manifesto was the design for twenty-five years of reform, not a political programme for immediate fulfilment. Congress had put all its cards on the table knowing that each one would at best have to be picked up separately by the other side with a lot of bargaining and manœuvring.

The Congress leaders were not wild men, though they have been treated as such. They were, rather, like the proletarian section of the early Labour movement, men with a deep experience of a kind of life that is unknown to established politicians—the life of the poor—but little enough knowledge of the ways of the great world. They know poverty and subjection at first hand and founded Congress while living under the rule of location superintendents and native policemen. They were ingenuously idealistic in their hopes, harshly realistic in their judgments; affectionate, shrewd and resolute. They were vital and volatile, tough, often hilariously humorous.

Four or five individuals each, in Salisbury and Bulawayo, were the nucleus of Congress. Those I knew well, who are all now in prison, were polite, laughing men in a little house in the location with two pictures, of the Virgin and saints, on the wall and a pressure lamp snorting on the table because there was no Company's light—a neat room with simple European furniture where they sat drinking tea, talking and inquiring endlessly, their minds sparkling as odd people walked in and out, unannounced and unexplained, friends, sympathizers, hangers-on, inquirers. A grave old chief from the reserve, who listens and says nothing, a fat trader who talks nonsense, earnest and intelligent young men, came in from the shadows, drank tea and faded out. The dispersed atoms of African consciousness were slowly coming together, cohering to form a means of collective expression. Bigger results have sometimes come from such men and such beginnings than from more sophisticated politicians.

Congress and its leaders were very closely, if generally courteously, watched by the police. They were given a fair hearing by the *Rhodesia Herald*, but the run of European public opinion could not get beyond derision, contempt and the cry for suppression, born of fear and guilt.

It was remarkable, and to an outside observer a little laughable, how much public excitement and suspicion these first tentative stirrings of African initiative excited. It was convenient for the Government and the Europeans to be able to believe that communism was at the back of Congress, but there was no evidence for the belief. Without access to secret files in either Moscow or Salisbury it is impossible to deny categorically that communists may be active in Southern Rhodesia. One can only say that one has never seen any sign of it and that, in a country where the mildest liberal egalitarianism is often described as communism, one requires proof. It is perfectly certain that Congress owes nothing to communism, that its leaders are not communists nor inspired by anything remotely approaching communist ideals or ideas and that neither its supporters nor the inarticulate mass it represented were susceptible to overt communist propaganda; though to drive African movements underground by repression is the ideal way of manuring the seed bed of poverty, disillusion and despair where communism grows best. The Europeans themselves are creating the conditions which communism can most easily exploit.

PART FOUR

The Future of Federation

CHAPTER XX

The Future of Federation

Nobody really believes any longer that the Federation can go ahead to the future once planned for it. The Bandas, Kaundas and Nkomos, the irreconcilable European pretensions and African grievances, the absence of consent on the part of most of the population to the political system they live under will all be there after the Monckton Commission and the Constitutional Review of 1960–61. The failure of Federation became clear in the first half of 1959 when the governments concerned could think of nothing better to do than to describe an almost universal outburst of popular feeling as the work of a few unprincipled agitators practising intimidation; and to arrest the leaders, and suppress the following, of a movement as irresistible as the French Revolution. Guy Clutton-Brock[1] describes the failure of Federation when he says that, after the 1959 crisis, "the Federal Government hastily opened to all races the public side of counters in the Post Office. It appointed an African as a Parliamentary Secretary to the Ministry of Home Affairs. It promised the removal of interracial 'pinpricks'. It gave no indication that it would seek to ease the real causes of deep disquiet but stated rather that 'its sympathies lie with the policy of the Southern Rhodesian Government'.[2] At a moment when Federal statesmanship could have achieved a major advance in the territories, it backed a policy of repression throughout the Federation. Why did it do this? Because it is a white colonists' government and the ideas of the majority of colonists throughout the Federation are those of Southern Rhodesia."

Southern Rhodesian attitudes to race relations are, as we have seen, concentrated on white supremacy—at best, on equal but separate development of the races, at worst on a more oppressive form of *apartheid*. Fair political representation for Africans is dismissed as "mere head counting", in some way different from the principles of democracy; it is believed that it would result in the white man and all

[1] *Dawn in Nyasaland*, Hodder & Stoughton, 1959, p. 158.
[2] Reported in *Rhodesia Herald*, 27th February 1957.

that he stands for being swept away.[1] The African population on the other hand are prepared to share the country with the existing Europeans on terms very advantageous to them and to accept favoured and safeguarded European participation in government for a long time to come, because they recognize that the Europeans have made their homes there and brought capital and skill; that they are a necessary and irreplaceable element in the economy; and that the advance of the whole community needs the aid of European knowledge.[2] They are no longer prepared to suffer the political domination of a racial minority group or its consolidation by further European immigration; and they demand the evolution of a political system that represents all races and sections of the population in some relation to their numbers. Britain has the most binding obligations to prevent any form of white supremacy in the northern territories and has still, if she cares to exercise it, a very considerable degree of control over their futures, though practically none over Southern Rhodesia's. The argument that it is unfair to withhold independence, or Dominion status, from the Federation with its European standards, and to give this privilege to a less advanced black country like Nigeria can hardly impress anyone; for it is clear that, what-

[1] The principle of African representation has been accepted for Nyasaland since the Emergency, though nothing has yet been done to introduce its practice; but no one has suggested that the few hundred European farmers and few thousand European settlers there will suffer this fate when it comes. This can only mean either that it need not happen to the quarter million Europeans in Southern Rhodesia either in similar circumstances or that the Federal Government proposes to assert its power over the Nyasaland Government to prevent it. Europeans need not in fact be swamped in either country. Southern Rhodesian fears are the familiar rationalization of the desire to keep the country white and buttress European privilege.

[2] Independent African governments (e.g. Ghana or the Federation and regions of Nigeria) show the greatest possible readiness to welcome European assistance in every branch of life—the police, the law, commerce, education, etc.—and to pay it very well indeed, so long as it comes as partner and not as master. No African politicians aspire to govern without employing Europeans in the civil service at high levels and high salaries. The opportunity every African government has of doing so makes nonsense of the view so often repeated—and, for example, by Sir Robert Armitage, Governor of Nyasaland, on 1st December 1959—that African independence is impossible because "there are not at present Africans with academic, professional, technological or even technical training to run government services, let alone the non-government side of commerce, industry and all the activities that make a modern state". Certainly the money would need to be found to pay Europeans to do these jobs. But it would need to be found for qualified Africans too. If Britons were unavailable, or unacceptable, the United Nations is developing an international civil service for work in underdeveloped countries. As for commerce and industry, Booker Bros., for example, could operate just as well, and with as much benefit to the economy in Nyasaland, under independent government as they do under the present system or as they do in the Caribbean Federation.

ever rivalries and struggles for power may develop in Nigeria, 9 million voters, a representative electorate from 30 million people, are being given the opportunity to express their will in controlling the country's future. If independence were given to the Federation of Central Africa, less than 100,000 Europeans would control the future of 7 million Africans.

The doctrines of Federation and partnership have not proved strong enough to bridge the Zambezi or to bring Southern Rhodesia and the northern Protectorates into any kind of unity except the unity of minority rule and European privilege. The whole flimsy structure has collapsed into the river where it is becoming increasingly distorted by the pressures it is subjected to and is dangerously impeding the free flow of the current. There is an unanswerable case for removing the wreckage and creating a less fateful course of development.

Ironically, political Federation has produced the exact opposite of the aims of the British policy which imposed it. It has created disturbance, discontent, and instability, which can only increase as long as Federation endures and which present the strongest possible temptation and opportunity both to South Africa and to Communism, instead of the peaceful, powerful bastion of liberal interracialism and graduated progress which Britain intended to found upon the wealth of the copperbelt. Political Federation is not necessary to these aims. It is positively inimical to them. They can only be attained through government by consent and respect for the will of the majority.

A year or two ago, it was taken for granted in London and in Salisbury that the 1960 Constitutional Review would lead to Dominion Status—that is to say to complete self-government for the European inhabitants—on the assumption either that they could be trusted to fulfil Britain's responsibilities towards the Africans of the northern territories or that Britain was not in earnest about them. Today not even Sir Roy Welensky professes to believe that Mr. Macmillan will give the Federation independence in 1961 and the British Government clearly recognizes that it is out of the question; it is not yet evident how much more it has recognized nor how far it is prepared to go. But the present omens give more ground for hope than one could have expected as recently as in December 1959, when the terms of reference of the Monckton Commission were under discussion. Then it looked as if it were not Central African affairs that were being governed by British party politics (as Federal Europeans like to complain) but British policy that was being dictated by the Federal Prime Minister. The authority of Parliament over the northern Protectorates was being undermined by the Government's reluctance to take a firm line with Sir Roy Welensky. Since Mr. Macmillan's visit to Salisbury and Mr. Macleod's assumption of the Colonial Secretaryship, the British Government appears less disposed to believe in the indissolubility of Federation simply because the Federal Prime Minister does.

Unprejudiced enlightened opinion of all parties in Britain seems to be reaching the conclusion that political Federation in its present form has failed, and must either be changed in such a way that it can succeed, or else abandoned. But "what can we do?" it asks despairingly, "what can we urge on our Government and M.P.s? Has Britain not already surrendered so much power that she cannot affect the situation?" The Federal Government is quite glad to encourage this impression but there is nothing whatever in it. There is plenty Britain can do.

She must face the fact that the aspirations of the Europeans in the Federation are completely opposite to those of the Africans, and to Britain's obligations to the Protectorates. Federation can only survive if one side changes. The Africans will not. The Federal and Territorial Constitutions all derive from Parliament and the Crown, who are fully entitled to revoke or change them. Britain should, therefore:

(a) Test European willingness to abandon white supremacy by *negotiating with the Federal Government for a new Constitution giving political representation to Africans* in some relation to their numbers and leading quickly to general suffrage, even if this means Southern Rhodesia's secession.

(b) If these negotiations fail, *abrogate the Federal Constitution, revoke the Federal Order in Council and resume full responsibility for Northern Rhodesia and Nyasaland*, introducing genuinely liberal constitutions.

It is a policy which involves certain undeniable risks, but they are less than the dangers of the present situation; and it promises the realization of British aims in Central Africa, aims which can never be accomplished by means of a Federation patently hostile to them.

[1] So does the Southern Rhodesian. But we have consented to it for so long that it is not in the same category.

Britain is not, and should not appear as, the enemy of Federation. She is the protector of Northern Rhodesia and Nyasaland. These territories do not belong to the Federal Government, nor to Britain. Britain holds them in trust for their African inhabitants. The Federal Government is little more than a caretaker put in to look after them. Britain's duty is to ensure that the Federal Parliament and Government reflect African opinion and African wishes at least as much as European. (The necessary further developments would ensue from this in the course of time.) If they will not do this, Britain cannot countenance their continued existence. This aim can be achieved by making changes in the Constitution and the franchise which can quite easily be embodied in Bills and Acts. Indeed, much the happiest outcome of the coming Constitutional Review Conference would be for it simply to recommend negotiations between the British and Federal Governments with a view to agreeing on such changes and framing the requisite legislation (though unfortunately there is little chance that it will be content to do so).

If Europeans were willing to make the machinery of government more responsive to African opinion, considerable changes would take place in the policies of the Federal Parliament and Government. Co-operation between the sort of Europeans who would be elected by an enlarged franchise—Sir John Moffat, Dr. Alexander Scott, Mr. Harry Franklin, Mr. Garfield Todd, for instance—and the heads of the predominantly African parties and movements is in no way impossible. African leaders have continually emphasized their desire to work together with Europeans on a footing of freedom and equality. They cannot collaborate with the present Federal Government because it offers nothing but subordination and African under-representation.[1] The liberal Europeans have been brought to a much closer understanding of Africanism by their recognition that the official attitude to the 1959 emergencies led nowhere. Inter-racial government by members of these two groups would be an intensely fruitful and educative experience for all concerned and a new and viable Federation might result. It is sheer illusion to suppose that an extension of the franchise would bring barbaric and irresponsible black chauvinists to power. The suggestion which

[1] The Congress leaders, as Guy Clutton-Brock points out, are the moderates in Central Africa. They are asking for nothing more than a real partnership with Europeans and recognition of the existence of 7 million Africans. The Federal Party and the majority of settlers, with their claim for white supremacy and their refusal to co-operate with Congress, are the extremists.

Sir Roy Welensky is so fond of making[1] that to give political power to Africans would mean a return "to the dark tribal past" is both false and disingenuous. African leaders are most anxious to carry their people forward. It is Sir Roy who is preventing them.

If negotiations broke down and the differences between the British and Federal Governments proved irreconcilable, this would be clear proof that the Federation was incapable of achieving the purpose for which it was set up and should be dissolved. Dissolution would be politically and morally necessary as well as legally and constitutionally practicable. With the abrogation of the Federal Constitution and the revocation of the Federal Order in Council, responsibility for the government of Northern Rhodesia and Nyasaland would revert to the Colonial Office;[2] Southern Rhodesia would have to be left to choose her own course.

Nor is there, as is often asserted, anything economically, administratively or practically impossible about returning to the *status quo ante* Federation in 1953. The Northern Protectorates both possess effective machinery for their own government and administration, which, expanded and adapted under the protection of Britain and in the interests of all the inhabitants, could readily take over territorially the present functions of the Federal Government and see the Protectorate safely through a transitional period to a new situation. It is not

[1] He wrote of the Congress in the *Central African Examiner* on 25th April 1959: "There are some who find it hard to believe that men who pay so much lip-service to non-violence can have planned the violence they have in fact planned. There are people who have not realized that primitive Africans easily turn to violence to settle matters which elsewhere are more naturally dealt with in the framework of law and order. Until the coming of Europeans, the whole history of Africa was one of violence and pillage. Respect for law and order is still something of a veneer and the primitive African can be easily influenced—a fact which is of course well known to educated African leaders." The anthropology, history, and interpretation of contemporary politics in this statement are all at fault. And Africans argued patiently against Federation for six years before even demonstrating against it. Few Europeans would have put up for so long with a system that was odious to them. And, as the Devlin Commission reported, no violence was ever planned.

[2] It is sometimes argued that these measures are unnecessary; that all Britain need do is to develop African self-government in the northern territories by full use of her powers there and leave the Federal structure alone. It is true that she can introduce what constitutions she pleases without, theoretically, the consent of the Federal Government. She cannot however alter the competence of the various governments (the Exclusive and Concurrent Lists) nor the electoral basis of the Federal Assembly and Government without legislating over its head. A protracted controversy within the present Federation between predominantly African Protectorate governments and a European-dominated Federal one about their responsibilities and rights, or between Britain and the Federation about the Federal franchise, would be more deleterious to stability and advance than the one major operation advocated here, and would involve greater risks.

our task here to suggest details of their new constitutions. But they would need to provide for a reversion to full Protectorate status under the ultimate authority of Britain, to lay open a clear road to self-government within measurable time; to give effective representation and preponderant power to the African majorities; and to guarantee by the authority of Britain and her Parliament, the most binding and stringent safeguards for existing European and Asian minorities. The example set by Tanganyika of how much can be achieved, and how quickly, in this direction needs no underlining and there is no reason why the same progress should not be made in Northern Rhodesia and Nyasaland. The Protectorates would be free to form any kind of closer association with each other that they wished and it can be taken for granted that, without the compulsion and restraint of imposed Federation, a representative Northern Rhodesian Government would arrange to share the copperbelt revenues with Nyasaland. Africans in the two Protectorates are more aware of common Africanism than of European-drawn political frontiers and would desire to help each other. The two together should be encouraged to consider the creative and hopeful possibilities of federation with the newly independent Tanganyika if common consent of all three were forthcoming.

Many details beyond the scope of our present argument would remain to be settled. The best means of giving white minorities full security, and the most favourable inducements that can be offered to all races to achieve a co-operative relation would need to be worked out. The composition of the Legislative and Executive Councils, the position of British officials with regard to them, the powers and appointment of the Governor, and much else would have to be thought out in the closest consultation with African representatives. Any arrangements imposed without their consent would be unlikely to be effective. But all this could be done. The argument that it will take years more of paternal rule to lay the foundations of representative government in countries "so primitive and backward", that all African representatives will be wild men, that there will be too few Africans qualified to take the higher offices in government and administration, and that the whole thing will simply not work, is disproved by the extraordinary ease with which representative government has been introduced into Ghana or Nigeria. Without entering into the argument about Dr. Nkrumah's attitude to the opposition—or the opposition's attitude to Dr.

Nkrumah—one can state incontestably that Ghana works as an efficient modern state. Unlike Northern Rhodesia and Nyasaland it has no settler problem; but this difference would be compensated for by Britain's continuing responsibility for safeguarding minorities. The paternalist argument is the colonists' last line of defence. Where there are no settlers, African representation works perfectly well. Now Tanganyika is showing that it can work where there are settlers too and that reciprocal toleration and creative co-operation between the races can be attained on a basis of wide African representation, if the necessary goodwill is there.

The average educational standards of the population of, for instance, Ghana, Nigeria, Tanganyika, Northern Rhodesia and Nyasaland are very little different, though the meaninglessness of attempts to estimate educational standards is shown by Lord Hailey:[1] "On the strength of the 1931 census it was generally considered that Nyasaland, where over 50 per cent of Africans were shown as literate, had attained an outstanding measure of literacy. The census of 1945, however, which adopted a different test of literacy, reduced this figure to a mere 6½ per cent." John Gunther[2] gave Ghana between 15 and 25 per cent literacy in 1955. But events in contemporary Africa are showing with increasing speed and clarity that it is not the formal educational standard of the African population nor the number of highly educated men it contains, which makes it easy or difficult for an African country to run itself successfully, but the degree of real responsibility both enjoy, the confidence they can feel in the constitutional basis of their freedom, the degree of trust they can place in the intentions of Europeans working with them, and the absence of arbitrary European authority or other causes of inter-racial tension. If Britain can create these conditions in Northern Rhodesia and Nyasaland, within or without Federation, their futures will be assured and Britain's aims fulfilled.

This leaves the problem of Southern Rhodesia. This country would certainly secede from a Federation founded on a negotiated liberalization of the Constitution and franchise. If, on the other hand, the Constitution were abrogated, there would be no Federation left for it to remain in. So, either way, one must reckon with Southern Rhodesia's return to the position of an independent self-governing colony practising white supremacy. This is logical since the fatal

[1] Op. cit., p. 139.
[2] Op. cit., p. 804.

inconsistency of Federation has been shown to be the attempt to link the futures of the Northern Protectorates (which historically, politically and ethnically have the same opportunity and necessity as Tanganyika to develop as African countries) with that of Southern Rhodesia, which, through now irreversible past mistakes, cannot avoid white supremacy for a time. Britain created this necessity in 1923 and, though it damages 2½ million Africans, she must face with the same realism as they themselves do the fact that she can do nothing to help them except use to the full her powers in the Northern Protectorates. No one who knows them doubts that the majority of Southern Rhodesian Africans, and their leaders, would choose to continue in their own difficult situation alone rather than support a Federation which exposes another 5 million Africans to the same helotry; they would prefer freedom for some, even if not themselves, to subjection for all. They are realistic and can see that Federation holds no promise for any African advancement anywhere. They also see that the example of African advance in the northern territories will support their claim to similar treatment in the end.

Southern Rhodesia will in any event not be left in an economic impasse. Whether or no it could have extricated itself from the difficulties it faced alone before Federation—and there is little doubt that it could—the lion's share of the economic benefits of Federation has gone to Southern Rhodesia. (This is one of the reasons why Federation has failed.) Southern Rhodesia's position has been fundamentally improved. During the financial year 1958–59, the Southern Rhodesian payment of income-tax, including company profits tax, to the Federal Exchequer was greater than Northern Rhodesia's.[1] Kariba, an enormous source of income, would be Southern Rhodesian property whatever happened. Virtually all the new industry that public enterprise and private investment have set up as a consequence of Federation is situated in Southern Rhodesia. (Northern Rhodesia and Nyasaland, which badly needed new industry, were neglected in this respect.) The Southern Rhodesian Government would inherit enough investment and new sources of wealth from Federation to be able to do very well on its own. As Guy Clutton-Brock has lately argued in *The Times*, there is a strong case for believing "that Southern Rhodesia on its own, without the

[1] See A. Hazlewood and P. D. Henderson, *Nyasaland: The Economics of Federation* (Blackwell, 1960), pp. 45–7.

continuing obligation of having to 'boss up' 5 million Africans in vast territories beyond its border, might be better able to come to grips with its own local racial, political and economic problems".[1]

Federalists, to gain our pity or to make our flesh creep, tell us that Southern Rhodesia would join the Union, but this is most unlikely. The Southern Rhodesians do not want to; and the South African Government has no desire to admit a hundred thousand anti-Afrikaner English voters to weigh the balance in favour of the United Party. The reversion of Southern Rhodesia to the *status quo ante* presents no really serious problems. The copperbelt is not now necessary to its economy. Sir Edgar Whitehead admitted as much to a press conference on 29th January 1960 by saying that if Southern Rhodesia seceded from Federation "it would cause a severe recession for at least three or four years and would damage the economy". He did not claim that Federation was *indispensable* to a healthy Southern Rhodesian economy.

The real opposition to the dissolution of Federation will not come from Southern Rhodesia, where the majority party, the Dominion Party, believes that the country can stand on its own feet in white supremacy for many years to come, and where the Government Party under Whitehead is beginning to say that secession is inevitable unless Britain guarantees the rule of "civilized" men in the north. Southern Rhodesia would choose secession in preference to the necessary extension of African political rights. Nor will the real opposition to dissolution come from any band of generous Federal philanthropists who are too tender-hearted to allow Northern Rhodesia and Nyasaland to forgo the benefits of Federation with Southern Rhodesia, as Sir Roy Welensky and Lord Malvern like to suggest. It will come from three sources, closely allied and associated, which add up to a pretty formidable force.

First, the 80,000 white inhabitants of Northern Rhodesia who see in Federation the only chance of creating a second Southern Rhodesia, a white man's country, in the north. They would soon learn, if Federation were dissolved, that interracial government did not lead to their extinction, just as the settlers of Tanganyika have already discovered, and those of Kenya are in process of discovering, the same truth. But they will resist the discovery by every possible means.

Second, from the powerful but diminishing group of old-style

[1] Letter published on 19th December 1959 in *The Times*.

paternalists in all three territories who truly believe that it is both desirable and possible for a few white men to "boss up" millions of Africans for a long time to come and to force upon them a limited degree of economic advance in a society where money and power will remain by and large in white hands. These are the people who have no conception of the volcanic strength of the African awakening that is going on around them and cannot perceive that it makes their aim quite unattainable.

Third, from the increasing number of people in all three territories to whom the advance of the Federation to Dominion status means the realization of strong personal ambitions and the occupation of positions of power and importance such as they could never otherwise hope for. To hold office of any kind, after all, in a country of a standing similar to Canada's is quite a different matter from the future any European in Central Africa can have foreseen for himself fifteen years ago. Dominion status offers alluring mirages—opportunities of playing parts on a world stage, Embassies, delegations to the United Nations, high civil and military appointments of varied kinds, real power at home and prestige abroad on a scale hitherto undreamt of. Sir Roy Welensky is the prototype. He is not a paternalist; he is simply a Federalist. Federation provides him with a unique platform at home and in the world. Without it he would be nothing, and there would be nothing for him. He represents his own interests and those of his group in playing for the integrity of Federation as a White Dominion at any price and this accounts for the expediency and inconsistency of his attitudes and utterances. He is in quite a different position from Sir Edgar Whitehead who believes, with doctrinaire conviction, in an antediluvian order of society and will never budge from its principles. Welensky and his group of Federal politicians and officials would be likely to accept almost any compromise, to turn in any direction, so long as it preserved a Federation for them to lead. This is why the present governing group in Central Africa will not, cannot afford to, see the truth about the Federation today, cannot draw the obvious conclusions from the 1959 Emergencies and will produce endless rationalizations which take no account of real facts to prove that it is in the best interests of all concerned for millions of Africans to be subjected to a system they will not accept; or more frequently, that they really like it very much and the appearance that they do not is deceptive. They are like hunting men who must convince us that the fox enjoys the chase.

The one thing they would never willingly accept is the end of their own leadership of the Federation. This is a pity because, whether it comes by reform or dissolution, it is the only thing that makes sense in Central Africa.

This is not a large group—the politicians, civil servants, soldiers and security forces who run the Federation. It is a very important one because its aims are identical with those of the Northern Rhodesian settlers and the old-fashioned paternalists, and it receives their support; and because it would inevitably have to some extent itself to carry out, or at very least passively to acquiesce in, British demands for the reform or dismemberment of Federation. It would be required to preside over its own demise and to organize its own funeral. It would only do so under intense pressure; a situation of explosive tension would be unavoidable. Here lies the risk. It is no good being intimidated by threats of a "Boston tea party" and of "going it alone"; but it is no good writing them off as feeble bluff without looking at them very closely. Would the Federal Government resist firm action by Britain, challenge her authority, and force the British Government to choose between an unusually humiliating defeat, which it would not survive at home, and the use of armed force against its "own kith and kin" in Central Africa, which a British electorate inadequately informed about, and not unduly interested in, the real issues, would never back? Would the Federal Parliament legislate its own independence in defiance of British orders? Sir Roy Welensky's government is in a strong position tactically. It controls its own civil service, which might simply refuse to hand over Federal prerogatives to the relevant departments of the territorial governments when the time came. The loyalty of European Federal officials is very distinctly a loyalty to the Federation which promises them power, prestige and importance in a new Dominion, not to Britain, who in these circumstances would be offering them disbandment, compensation and a pension, with the opportunity of renewed service under relatively insignificant, largely "native" governments if they chose it.[1]

Still more important, as Lord Malvern and Sir Roy have reminded

[1] The disbanding of the Federal Civil Service would be a perfectly practicable operation. Such things have happened in India, the Sudan, Ghana and Nigeria. The cost of it, which would not be great, could be paid from local resources with perhaps British aid. A number of Federal officials would be absorbed by the increased needs of Southern Rhodesia and a few might elect to serve black Africa under the new dispensation.

us, the Federation controls its own armed forces (which profess to be "Britain's only all-weather allies in Africa"). They include a good many European regulars, as well as a European Air Force and some formidable European riot squads. They are fanatically pro-Federal. A Federal Dominion offers obscure majors or security police officials the chance of becoming Major-Generals, Chiefs of Staff, military attachés, and who is to blame them? In an acutely strained situation such as must be envisaged, their allegiance would belong wholly to the Federal Government. If Britain were resuming control of Northern Rhodesia, and the Federal Government decided to resist, the Federal Army would obey Federal orders. If these orders were to occupy government buildings, radio stations and other centres of power in Northern Rhodesia and Nyasaland, they would be efficiently carried out. The forces might even express their loyalty by arresting the Governors and Chief Secretaries who, by obeying the Colonial Office, would become traitors to the Federation. It would all be in the sturdy tradition of the American colonists and it might happen. What could Britain possibly do? Dare she take the risk?

This is precisely how the Federal Government wants Britain to think. But it *is* bluff; it *can* be disregarded. It will never happen. It is true that the Federal Government can gain a tactical advantage over Britain, but to do so would bring no long-term strategic gains at all. It would only bring a slower, more painful defeat. The Federation would not survive unilateral defiance in such a way as to bring the Federalists any of the advantages and benefits they hope for. They depend for these upon Britain's recognition and support; they cannot get them without it, and they know this. If Britain made it perfectly clear that she meant to be firm, and would be neither intimidated by threats nor charmed by fair words, there would be no question of civil or military resistance. They would have to accept whatever solution she imposed and cut their losses as best they could.

A unilateral declaration of independence would be a grossly illegal act and the majority of the Commonwealth would be opposed to it. It would find no resonance in Canada, India, Pakistan, Ceylon, Ghana, Nigeria, Malaya or the Caribbean Federation; little in Australia and much less in New Zealand; the support that came from South Africa would be sheer embarrassment. Membership of the Commonwealth would be closed to a community which likes to describe itself as Her Majesty's most loyal subjects.

The Federation would find it hard to stand alone before a

politically hostile and economically suspicious world opinion. It would not be well received by the United Nations—if it were received at all. America, despite its own experience of a Boston tea party, would not be sympathetic.[1] The overseas investment which, the Federal Government so often proclaims, is necessary to the future of the Federation, would not be encouraged by a Central African *coup d'état* and its implications. European and especially British immigration, which again the Government claim is necessary in ever increasing volume, would come sparsely if at all to a precarious, unattached, independent rebel state. For all its great size and wealth, the Federation must have a filial attachment to some greater Power to become any of the things Welensky and his supporters want it to become. It cannot do without a *point d'appui* in the great world. Less than half a million Europeans sitting in explosive isolation on top of 7 million resentful and discontented Africans in the middle of vast areas of empty African country could not form or run a Great Independent Country. The only available *point d'appui* would be South Africa; and this would not help them at all in a world which is at the moment hardening its attitude very quickly against South Africa. They would be regarded as renegades and traitors to liberal ideas if they sought the protection of the Union and would incur the political and economic disadvantages, as well as the contempt and obloquy of such treason. The Federal Europeans do not in the least want to be protected by Dr. Verwoerd and the Nationalists. It would be just as repugnant as being ruled by Britain or accepting equality with Africans. Joining up with South Africa is a good talking point but not a practicable way out.

Finally there are the 7 million Africans. They would not sit quiet and watch while the Federal Government declared its independence and forced it through by political and military defiance. A considerable confusion of authority and collapse of law and order would inevitably result; the Federal forces and administration would be strained to the limit by defying Britain and it would be very surprising if Africans did not take advantage of this. Federal independence would extinguish their last hope; they would not welcome it; they would be desperate people. Even sporadic outbreaks of passive resistance and civil disobedience at such a moment could

[1] The Africa Defence and Aid Fund, launched at the end of 1959, is sponsored, according to the *Guardian* of 30th December 1959, by "many leading figures in American public life" and is concerned especially to aid African victims of white government in Central Africa, Kenya, the Union and South West Africa.

seriously embarrass the Federal Government; and untrue though Sir Roy Welensky's statements were about "directing brains" co-ordinating Congress and Communist influence among Africans during the 1959 crisis, Africans are by now well enough organized to express themselves fairly vigorously. If independence were achieved, they would have nothing more to lose and would accordingly become more intractably irreconcilable to the White Federal Dominion. They could find varied and almost interminable means of making it impossible for 300,000 Europeans to run the country. To shock world opinion by violently repressive measures against them, by establishing an evident racial tyranny, would not help the young rebel state to find its footing among the nations nor to create the impression of liberalism it would wish to. The hostility of all free African countries would not make life any easier for it. There are disadvantages in being sent to Coventry by one's neighbours. Someone other than South Africa, an industrial competitor to a great extent, has got to buy Kariba current and Federal products. In Africa, or beyond it, there would be few markets. Britain could hardly, in the circumstances, import Rhodesian corned beef. Survival would be impossible. It is hard to be sure even how much support the senior partner, Southern Rhodesia, would give to the Federal Government. Opinion there is divided about Federation, as we have seen. Southern Rhodesians want a quiet life and can lead one with or without Federation. They are sentimentally very loyal to the Crown. If complete success could be guaranteed, white supremacy firmly imposed in the north and the Federation received in the Commonwealth and the world, they would back a Declaration of Independence. But association with troubled territories, where dissident African populations had perpetually to be kept down by force and order was always precarious, might not appeal to them. Faced with all the imponderable questions raised by a Boston tea party, they might well excuse themselves from attending it.

No, a Declaration of Independence would confront the Federal Government with a very ugly situation within its own frontiers, on the African continent and in the world. It would hardly survive it and will not enter into it. The risks the Federation would incur are so much greater than any Britain could run by a policy of firmness that she can perfectly safely go ahead on the lines suggested here. The imposition of white Federal rule by rebellion and force is so retrogressive a conception, so out of tune with the whole trend of history in the world and, outside the Union, in Africa, that it is grotesque to believe it could succeed or ever be attempted. Unilateral defiance would remove all the preconditions necessary for the success of the White Dominion as thoroughly and effectively as the liberalization or dissolution of Federation by Britain. It would end Federation violently, destructively, unpleasantly and protractedly, while to accede to all Britain's demands would leave the settlers free to enjoy a high standard of living, large material assets, and the fulfilment of all their justifiable claims in complete security; they would lose nothing of substance except the unjustifiable degree of political power they now possess. In their hearts they know this. Welensky's party followers are not blind Hitlerian fanatics who would rather throw themselves and their environment to destruction than forgo the aims they have set themselves. They are hard-headed and not over-scrupulous men of business out to drive as hard a bargain as they can.

Sir Roy must have calculated pretty accurately the possibilities and advantages of "going it alone". The balance sheet can only have worked out one way. He must be well aware that it cannot be done. It is part of his tactics to pretend that it easily can and until recently these tactics seemed to be serving him remarkably well. He went every inch as far as he could to see whether Britain would fall for his bluff. But he must always have known that in the last resort he was in the weaker position, that Britain is necessary to the Federation though the Federation is not necessary to Britain. He cannot compel our support as we can his withdrawal. If he cannot win it, whether by bluff and threats, by cajolery or charm, by any available form of political prestidigitation or constitutional *trompe l'oeil*, he has nothing left to lose. He has no alternative to playing daringly for the highest stakes. There is no reason why he should not pursue victory to the crumbling edge of defeat because if he cannot win he must fall. There is no second line of reserves for him to fall back on. The Declaration of Independence, like joining South Africa, is a good talking point, not a practicable course of action. Britain can demand no less than the liberalization or dissolution of Federation. She has power to obtain one or the other; either will fulfil her duties in Central Africa.

Sir Roy seems to have had less inkling of the wind of change that is blowing through Africa—and seems to be blowing through Britain's African policy—than might have been expected of so astute a politician. Mr. Macmillan is good at keeping secrets, and can change his mind with unusual urbanity. Even so it is interesting that Welensky could say, in Salisbury, on 30th December 1959, a bare few weeks before the British Prime Minister's carefully calculated speeches in Lagos, Salisbury and above all Cape Town, that the Federation must get complete independence in the fields for which it was responsible by 1961 at latest. (We have seen in our review of the Constitution that these are all the fields of real importance.) He said that Africans must be encouraged to look to the Federal Government rather than constantly "looking over their shoulders to Whitehall"[1] and called for "a steady transfer of power from London" to the authorities on the spot—though the Federal Government has done nothing to earn African gratitude and Britain is the legally constituted protector of over two-thirds of the population. He demanded the abolition of the African Affairs Board—one of the only two constitutional safeguards Africans possess against his government. He then went on to say: "We can hardly expect the support of certain ambitious African leaders while they still think there is some chance of their becoming Prime Minister of an independent Black State." (What, after all, does Sir Roy want to be but Prime Minister of an independent white state?) "How can our British critics think we are not worthy of independence and running our own affairs when they look at the bloodshed all over the rest of Africa? Is it really to the advantage of black people to give them self-government when they are not ready for it?" The point is not easy to take. Sir Roy cannot have been referring to the recent bloodshed in Nyasaland, which took place within the Federation. What other bloodshed "all over Africa" had he in mind? Ghana, Nigeria, Tanganyika and all the countries of what was French Black Africa (excepting only the Cameroons) have notably avoided it. He can only have had in mind Algeria or the Union.

Finally, and almost incredibly, he demanded the end of Britain's right to veto Federal legislation and the exemption of his Federation from the provision of the Colonial Laws Validity Act, which prevents the passing in dependent territories of legislation repugnant to the principles of British justice. This Act has been suspended in the case of sovereign countries in the Commonwealth, where Britain had

[1] We should remember here Sir John Moffat's point, previously quoted on p. 96: "The Africans do not distrust Federation because they look to Britain. They look to Britain because they mistrust Federation."

no further responsibility and where acute problems of social justice did not arise. But neither of these conditions is satisfied in Central Africa.

It is clear that Britain cannot accede to any of his demands. It is not too much to suggest that British support for European supremacy "for the foreseeable future" in the Federation could cause the disruption of the Commonwealth as well as the disintegration of Central Africa. It would be unacceptable to more than half its members and, as racial tension and injustice there became increasingly apparent, they might well feel unable to remain in association with a Britain who was responsible for them. The case of South Africa is different in that Britain has never assented to, let alone legislatively underwritten, what goes on there. It would be strange if a Conservative government preferred the risk of destroying the Commonwealth to that of affronting 300,000 Federal Europeans.

A Conservative government is in a uniquely favourable position to assert its authority. Labour is suspect to the Federal electorate. The emotional temptations to resistance would be at their strongest against a Labour government, even if the prudential objections were the same. The colonists regard themselves as an outpost of conservatism and feel that Conservative views on white supremacy and race relations are their own. Ghana, Nigeria or Tanganyika appear to them to be the anomalies of Conservative policy; support for the loyal white populations of Rhodesia its natural bent. The discovery that this was no longer true, that they themselves are, with Kenya, the only remaining anomaly in British Africa, and that they are so anomalous that conservatism could no longer feel confidence in the future they had planned for themselves, would emphasize the dangers that resistance would entail. Further, conservatism is fairly closely equated with loyalty to the Crown and the non-Afrikaner majority of Europeans in the Federation needs to believe in its loyalty to Queen and Commonwealth as a protection against a sense of isolation that would otherwise become intolerable. The demonstration that loyalty to Crown, Commonwealth and conservatism all demand either a revision of Federation in favour of the self-determination of the African populations or its dissolution, is perhaps the only means of persuading the Federal electorate that it is at present on the wrong tack. They will accept, with a good deal of initial complaint, but with ultimate resignation, whatever a Conservative British Government firmly requires. Such a government with the eyes to see and the intelligence to understand what must be done in Central Africa can still rescue progress from reaction and interracial harmony from incipient chaos.

In Britain there is a lot of evidence that Conservative Members of Parliament have begun to realize this. Wide areas of Conservative opinion in the country are certainly aware of it. The Liberal and Labour Parties in and out of Parliament have declared their opposition to the continuation of Federation in its present form and to the policies of the Federal Government. A majority of the House of Commons is ready to support the assertion of British authority to make far-reaching changes.

There is nothing in the first seven years of the Federation's history, nor in the origins or handling of the 1959 crisis, nor in the truculent, often incoherent and contradictory, and occasionally unintentionally revealing remarks of its Prime Ministers to encourage confidence in its future. The British Government can expect no desirable results from giving the United Federal Party and its leaders a free hand, and to do so would be to betray the futures of Africans who have trusted us, to connive in the slow disintegration and demoralization of British Central Africa and to discredit Britain in the eyes of Africa and the world. It is useless to place any further faith in the axiom that if you leave things in Africa to the superior wisdom and knowledge of the local Europeans, everything will work out all right in the end. They have shown themselves in 1959 to be more out of touch with the true facts of the situation than anyone else. By misjudging alike the "massacre plot" in Nyasaland, the bitterness and intensity of African discontent in the whole Federation, the true strength and representative nature of the Africanist movements and the possibilities of reducing them to quiescence by sharp harsh measures, they have shown the truth of Lord Palmerston's observation that "if you wish to be misinformed about a foreign country, you need to seek the advice of an Englishman of long residence there". Their information has proved to be faulty and their conclusions false. They are extending their field of error in believing that it is possible to go on with Federation as they envisage it, or that it can be rescued by the removal of "racial pinpricks". Nothing could be clearer than that a state whose Government is opposed by 7 million of the inhabitants and maintained only by the power and privilege of 300,000 is heading for trouble.

The aim of this book has been to show that the Federal Constitution as operated by the present Federal Government does nothing to meet the wishes of Africans or to offer them the kind of future they have been promised. The events of 1959 were the first active demonstration of protest against government without consent. They were mild enough by any standards and the governments did everything they could to exacerbate them. But it is absurd to imagine that they will be the last or that it is possible to ignore their decisive significance and enforce Federation as if nothing had happened. The Central African Federation is founded upon a volcano whose first rumblings have just been heard. Nothing that is built there can endure until means have been found to relieve its pressure, and only the most far-reaching political and constitutional changes can do this.

The final appeal for a reconsideration of Federation before it is too late does not need to be an ideal one. In the cool light of practical politics, it is evident that a state founded upon the discrepancies between Southern Rhodesia and the Northern Protectorates, upon the prevarications and half-truths behind the Federal Constitution and franchise, a state subject to the tensions and pressures between unequal groups and to their intensely conflicting ambitions can find no stability. Sir Roy Welensky's claim that he can handle 7 million Africans if left alone to do so, is an expression of blind ambition, and the present signs that the British Government does not propose to let him try are the first reasons for hope in Central Africa for seven years.

For the second half of 1959 it looked as if not only the Federal, Nyasaland and Northern Rhodesian Governments, but also the British, intended to disregard the one sound piece of advice given them officially on the subject of Federation—that of the Devlin Commission. Attempts were made in Parliament when the Devlin Report appeared—and are still made almost daily by the authorities and the Press in Central Africa—to dismiss the most penetrating study of colonial problems written in this century as the work of a single wayward lawyer, assisted by three ill-informed laymen. By 1960, both the findings and the implications of the Devlin Report seem to have been tacitly accepted in Westminster. Mr. Justice Devlin and his colleagues probably know well enough that "truth like a bastard comes into the world, never without ill-fame to him who gives her birth" to be more glad that truth has been received than desirous of the honour that should have been done them. But it is monstrous that it was ever suggested that the Devlin Report deals in legal niceties. No government publication can have been more in touch with realities; no official study of African affairs was ever so near the grass roots. It represents the unanimous opinion of four distinguished and independent minds experienced in the evaluation of evidence, the interpretation of intelligence, in colonial government and in administration. Irresponsibility and enthusiasm are not qualities one looks for in a High Court judge, a Governor of the Gambia, a Lord Provost of Perth or in Field-Marshal Montgomery's wartime Chief of Intelligence. It cannot be overlooked that all these men are Conservatives in British politics. If they had approached their task with even an unconscious *parti pris* it would have been in favour of the established order. Yet their report is an almost complete condemnation of the policies of the British and Nyasaland Governments and a deep questioning of the principle of Federation. A dispassionate study of the overwhelmingly persuasive facts of the case led them to views which the Federal or Nyasaland Government would consider subversive.

The suggestion that "people on the spot knew better" was fatuous. The Governments' attempts, whether in Westminster, Blantyre or Salisbury, to vindicate themselves by appealing to the statement, in a document they were otherwise trying to discredit, that the Nyasaland Government had either to "act or abdicate", that it had to declare an emergency, were ludicrous.[1] The remark conferred no approval on the Government's action; it was a neutral statement of fact, that the Government had either to do something or to lose power. The report went on to say that long before the Government faced this dilemma "the prospect of collision sooner or later was almost certain" and traced this unequivocally back to the imposition of Federation in 1953 upon an African population which did not want it. It confirmed that this rejection was general, almost universal, among chiefs, people, rich, poor, educated and illiterate, and that both the advantages and disadvantages of Federation were correctly interpreted and understood by most of them. It was the Governments' refusal to heed the protests of the Africans, or of any other critics of Federation, sustained as they were over a period of six years, that was responsible for the Emergency. It drove Congress, not into violent rebellion, but into a policy of deliberate defiance of

[1] The authorities also claimed a triumph in the Commission's statement that the Governor declared the Emergency on his own initiative, not under Federal pressure. But this only shifts responsibility from one part of the set-up to another.

an unpopular and unresponsive government, which clearly might lead to violence. Congress, no less than the Government, had to abdicate or act, and it could not have done less than it did. The Commission did not accept the Government's estimate of Congress as a small gang of unprincipled agitators intimidating their fellow Africans into opposing a paternal government which they would otherwise have accepted with gratitude and devotion. They considered it to be widely representative of African opinion as a whole.

The Devlin Report makes it clear that paternalist government, when it ceases to regard the wishes of the governed, becomes despotism. And despotism, even "the despotism of a kindly father", as the Commission described the Nyasaland Government, leads to the creation of "a police state", which as it truly remarked, Nyasaland now is; a state in which "it is not safe to express approval of the policies of the Congress Party . . . and unwise to express any but the most restrained criticism of government policy". It makes it clear that government without consent becomes tyranny, and leads to violence and disturbance which are harder to condemn than the tyranny which causes them.

The Commission was not concerned with Northern Rhodesia, but there can be little doubt that it would have reached the same conclusions there. They are conclusions which are fundamentally opposed to the conceptions on which Federation has been constructed—that a minority can govern without the consent of a majority and can still interpret and promote the interests of the majority in a way that will be acceptable to it.

It is hard to see how the Monckton Commission can add to, or improve upon, the advice given to the British Government by the Devlin Report. Considering its size, and varied composition, it is unlikely to achieve the same imposing unanimity. And it is no reflection upon Lord Monckton's own impartiality to say that a Commission containing so many representatives, both African and European, of the ruling minority in the Federation can hardly be expected to approach its subject so dispassionately. The Constitutional Review to be begun in 1960, for which it is supposed to pave the way, will be composed of delegations from the British, Federal and Territorial Governments, and as the unrepresentative nature of all the Central African Governments becomes clearer and clearer, and the division of opinion between the British and Federal Governments becomes more and more apparent, it is difficult to see what it can hope to achieve. If it is not prepared to discuss the radical revision of the Federal Constitution, or the dismemberment of Federation, there is very little it can talk about. Sooner or later the British Government too must either abdicate or act. There are signs that, after a period of not very creditable nor explicable torpor, it has recognized this.

Mr. Macmillan and Mr. Macleod are most favourably placed for action; the opportunity to remedy injustice and discontent, to keep faith with the Protectorates, to promote peace, stability and progress all over Africa, will not recur. Their task requires firmness and vision and the courage to accept certain risks. They are smaller than the dangers of drifting along in the wake of the Federal Government as it sails complacently towards self-destruction in rapids more precipitous and turbulent than the Victoria Falls.

Appendix and Postscript

APPENDIX

Southern Rhodesia

African National Congress

STATEMENT
OF
PRINCIPLES, POLICY
AND
PROGRAMME

September 1957

MOTTO:

Forward Ever — Backward Never

The African National Congress of Southern Rhodesia is a people's movement, dedicated to a political programme, economic and educational advancement, social service and personal standards.

Its aim is the NATIONAL UNITY of all inhabitants of the country in true partnership regardless of race, colour and creed. It stands for a completely integrated society, equality of opportunity in every sphere, and the social, economic and political advancement of all. It regards these objectives as the essential foundation of that partnership between people of all races without which there can be no peaceful progress in this country.

Congress affirms complete loyalty to the Crown as the symbol of national unity.

It is not a racial movement. It is equally opposed to tribalism and racialism.

It welcomes as members all of any race who are in sympathy with its aims and are prepared to fulfil the conditions of membership.

It recognizes the rights of all who are citizens of the country, whether African, European, Coloured or Asian, to retain permanently the fullest citizenship.

It believes that this country can only advance through non-racial thinking and acting, and that an integrated society provides the only alternative to tribalism and racialism.

Congress believes that individual initiative and free enterprise are necessary to the life of a young country and must be fully encouraged, but that a considerable measure of Government control is necessary in a modern state.

The immediate economic concern of Congress is to raise the standard of living of the under-privileged. The peaceful development of the country demands above all things that the gap between the lowest and highest in the social and economic order should be greatly reduced.

Congress believes that in the whole of Southern and Eastern Africa there are three outstanding needs which it is supremely important to meet:

(*a*) The standard of living of millions of people must be raised in a short space of time through their rapid social, economic and political advancement.

(*b*) This is only possible with the aid of skills, techniques and capital from overseas. These must be attracted to this country not only by the offer of material advantages but also by appeal to the altruism and sense of service prevalent in the world. This is a challenge to the more advanced and privileged people in the world whose help is required in the interests of world peace and the total development of mankind.

(*c*) In view of the inevitable uprising of national feeling among the peoples of Africa and the need to enlist the full co-operation of the mass of the people in this great enterprise, full participation of African people must be provided for in Government, and the legitimate political aspirations of the people be thus fulfilled.

Congress realizes that to meet these three needs is a task of gigantic proportions, but believes that nothing short of this can ensure the peaceful development of this country for the benefit of all its inhabitants. Congress is therefore dedicated to the fulfilment of these needs and regards it as a matter of the most urgent necessity.

APPENDIX

POLITICAL PROGRAMME

(1) *Land*

Congress believes that the land belongs to the people. Thus the use of land must be controlled and administered by Government. Government must ensure that the use of land is not limited by undue speculation in land values. Government must promote the fullest freedom for the economic use of land by competent people regardless of race, and must provide for this now largely through the system of freehold land tenure. It is, however, both uneconomic and also socially undesirable that land should be apportioned racially. Congress believes therefore that the Land Apportionment Act must be repealed and the land of this country freed from racial restrictions for economic development in both rural and urban areas. Unjust distribution of land is one of the fundamental causes of social discontent, and Congress regards measures of land reform as of the utmost importance.

(2) *Agriculture*

Congress believes that this country must become self-supporting in all agricultural produce and may well become an exporting country. It recognizes the need for large-scale agriculture, but does not believe that this should be confined by law to a particular racial group. A rural economy for the country must be founded primarily on the small farmer. Government must therefore support the peasant farmer strongly with land settlement schemes, research, and the provision of capital so that his farming may develop along modern lines. Agriculture will benefit greatly if racial restrictions are removed and the large and small farmer are permitted to farm side by side to their mutual advantage. Agriculture must become increasingly intensive and undeveloped land in any area must be freed for economic use. Farming must become as attractive an occupation as industry and a proper balance must be maintained between rural and urban development. Government efforts to open up overseas markets, arrange for orderly marketing schemes and regulate and maintain price levels and a price structure in the interests of both the producer and the consumer must be motivated by economic considerations alone. The change-over to modern intensive farming methods requires the utmost encouragement from Government for the benefit of both producer and consumer regardless of race.

(3) *Urban Areas*

Congress believes that urban areas must be freed from racial restrictions and that industry and housing must be planned according to the best modern considerations in the interests of the community as a whole. Every effort must be made to promote the development of industry, but also to decentralize it, and to avoid large agglomerations of population. Government must promote the development of housing estates on an economic, not a racial basis and, whether through ownership or tenancy, security of occupation must be provided for people of all races who elect to live and find employment in urban areas.

(4) *Local Government*

Congress believes that the same pattern of local government must prevail in all areas and for all races, and that separate communal administration must cease. The Ministry of Native Affairs must be abolished and government by "Native Commissioner" and the "Native Affairs Department" must give way in all areas to a system of local government authorities elected on a democratic franchise. Local government services must develop, and the fullest opportunity must be open to all people according to ability and regardless of race in the local government service.

(5) *Social Services*

Congress aims at the rapid development of modern social services, including social insurance, and their application to all people regardless of race. It regards community development and adult education services as of great importance in the task of enabling the adult population to develop rapidly in both urban and rural areas. It believes not only in government initiative in the provision of social services but also in voluntary effort. Voluntary Associations must be encouraged and given the fullest freedom in the religious, cultural and social spheres. The initiation and extension of social services is most necessary for those in the lower income groups, who are predominantly African, and Congress is primarily concerned to promote them there. The cheap labour of the African and Non-European is the major source of the wealth of the country, and it is from that accumulated wealth that provision must be made for full social security for all workers, for unemployment pay, for sickness allowances and for adequate pensions. Until such facilities are available, it is a dangerous step for any African to leave the Reserve and opt to become an urban worker, for he has thereby forfeited his right to return to and live in the Reserve, and in unemployment, sickness or old age no provision is made for him in the town.

Full social security must be the terms upon which the African worker contributes to the development of the country.

(6) *Education*

Congress wholly supports the principle of free compulsory universal primary education on a non-racial basis. No child must be deprived of educational opportunity from which he or she will benefit. Secondary education must be greatly expanded but with no lowering of standards. New secondary schools must be established on a non-racial basis and must accept pupils on grounds of academic ability alone. In this way the younger generation will be educated for an integrated society. Technical Colleges must be started on the same non-racial basis, offering equal opportunity to all with the ability to make use of it. Education at the University level must be unrestrictedly available to all who attain the required standards and if this involves a quicker growth of the University College than is at present planned, this growth must be facilitated. Opportunities for further education, study and training overseas must be opened up by the generous establishment of state bursaries and scholarships awarded to qualified ability without distinction of race. Government must provide equality of opportunity in education regardless of race and colour and a single educational system taking no account of race must be the objective.

Government should at the same time give the greatest encouragement to private schools maintained by voluntary bodies so that they may make their contribution to education in co-operation with the state.

Congress realizes that education is expensive and must be paid for. No state can make light of the difficulty of doing so. But it is the most important single need confronting the country and must have top priority in its claim on revenue and resources. This is not a poor country; it is prospering greatly, and the redistribution of resources required to finance the educational programme will prove the best possible investment for the prosperity of citizens of all races.

(7) *Health*

Congress believes that in order to provide adequate health services throughout the country for the whole population, provision must be made for greatly increased medical staff, for training doctors, nurses and medical orderlies. The selection, training and service conditions of these must be without discrimination as to race if enough competent candidates are to be received into the medical services.

The difficulties of financing increased health services are not to be underestimated, but the increase in production to which this would lead would rapidly offset the cost. Congress believes that a further way to meet this cost is by making all hospitals multi-racial, and the savings effected by ceasing to maintain separate institutions can be used in the provision of the additional services required.

(8) *Industry and Trades Unions*

Congress believes in the necessity of the rapid development of industry, yet under such conditions that rural economy and social life will not be destroyed but improved. In particular, secondary industries must be based on the products of the primary industries of the country. Conditions must be promoted under which the establishment of industry will be encouraged; these conditions include appropriate financial arrangements, provision of efficient transportation, of cheap power, of adequate housing for employees and of an efficient labour force. Capital, skills and techniques must be attracted from overseas, yet it is necessary to make the fullest use of the capital resources and potential of the population of the country. Education and training in crafts and trades must therefore be strenuously promoted by Government through training schemes and through the encouragement of apprenticeship. Opportunities to acquire skills must be open to all people equally regardless of race and according to ability. Trade Unions must be encouraged to participate in these schemes so that they may fulfil the role of maintaining and increasing the efficiency of industry as well as that of improving the working conditions of their members. Congress believes in collective bargaining and in the Trade Unions and Employers' Organizations which make this possible; these must be organized on an industrial and not a racial basis, and must not exist to maintain an artificially high standard of living for one class of persons at the expense of another.

(9) *Cost of Living*

Congress believes that the basic costs of living should be controlled and kept low. A reasonable basic standard of living must be assured for all people, and to this end capital must be applied to the increase of productive effort within the country and not to the import of luxuries from overseas. There must therefore be, in the present stage of development of the country, a strict control of imports. Congress believes in the full development of natural resources, both human and material, within the country so that the basic costs of living may be reduced for all people.

(10) *Taxation*

Congress realizes that more widespread social services mean a higher rate of taxation but regards such services as a necessary insurance for the future. It believes in indirect taxation falling most heavily upon luxuries, in the present situation of the country where necessities have yet to be spread widely throughout the population. It is against Poll Tax and Hut Tax and favours direct taxation according to means through income-tax, which must begin at a low income level in order to raise revenue from the majority of citizens of all races.

Taxation must not be levied nor its proceeds spent on a racial basis; both collection and spending of revenue must be administered to meet the needs of the people of the country as a whole.

(11) *Foreign Investment*

This country greatly needs capital investment from overseas. Congress recognizes that to obtain this, security must be provided for both public and private investment. Government must therefore

R

establish conditions under which capital may be invested and industry established with sufficient security to encourage investors. Congress believes that solving the racial problem by developing a fully integrated society on non-racial lines will give the greatest encouragement to investment from overseas.

(12) *Immigration*

Congress believes that any policy of immigration aimed at increasing the non-indigenous population of the country for political reasons or for relieving other parts of the world of their surplus population is economically, politically and socially unsound and dangerous to peaceful development. Yet Congress recognizes that people with capital, skills and techniques which are not available in this country in sufficient quantity are needed from overseas. Those who have such assets must be encouraged to bring them into this country as and when they are needed provided that these immigrants are people of good character, prepared to enter fully into the life of this country on a basis of equality with the existing population, and to become integrated into a society in which there will be no discrimination as to race or colour. Immigration must therefore be strictly regulated and immigrants be very carefully selected both for their character and their abilities. In this way the country will become populated as fast as it can be developed and the immigrant population will become absorbed gradually and integrated in a stable social order.

(13) *Freedom of Movement*

Congress believes that, while a system of registration of all citizens of all races is necessary, there must be freedom of movement for all people on their lawful business throughout the country, without regard to race and without special passes. To make this possible, the Pass Laws must be repealed and ordinary administrative measures used for controlling the population.

Visitors to this country from overseas and from other African territories must be encouraged, and inhabitants from this country must only be refused permission to travel out of it or their movements otherwise controlled on grounds which can be challenged by appeal to the highest judicial authority.

(14) *Police*

Congress believes in the necessity of a police force but considers that the growth of the modern state and the political conditions of the mid-twentieth century have given the police and security services an influence which too easily becomes a threat to individual freedom. No modern country is free from this danger. Congress therefore believes that an emerging modern democratic government must take the most careful precautions to control the activities of the police and security services and to make them subject in all things to the prompt scrutiny of an independent judiciary.

(15) *Political Representation*

Congress can see no justification for continuing any limitation of the franchise on grounds either of income, educational standard or race. The only form of government now acceptable to the vast majority of peoples in the British Commonwealth is parliamentary democracy, based on universal adult suffrage, since this alone can produce a government responsible to all inhabitants of the country and aware of the needs of all. Further, only by this system can the enthusiasm of the whole people for government enterprise and national development be evoked; and only by this system can we arrive at that fully representative government which, in the eyes of the United Kingdom and the world, is the condition of complete national independence. The real danger to future stability lies in keeping the majority of the people voteless, not in extending the franchise.

Congress believes that the present electoral arrangements are designed to keep political power in the hands of one small racial section of the population, and that the continuation of a racial alignment of political forces will be disastrous. The vote must be cast for the good of the whole country, not to promote the sectional interests of any one race. Racial politics will be disastrous for all. They can be avoided by universal suffrage *now*.

(16) *Citizenship*

Congress believes that full citizenship must be extended to all those of any race or colour who are lawful and permanent inhabitants of the country, and have demonstrated this through their satisfactory residence and integration in the life of the community over the course of five years' residence in the country.

(17) *Racial Discrimination*

Congress totally rejects the whole idea and practice of discrimination or segregation according to race or colour. It believes that this country can only develop peacefully as a society in which the different races become increasingly integrated in social, cultural, economic and political life, and in which there is no discrimination according to race, colour, creed or political opinion. Congress believes that such integration is both practicable and urgently necessary. It is in fact not an idealistic dream but the only practical way through existing racial problems. Present discriminations which exist, and which are a grave menace to society, must be strongly discouraged by government and government publicity services, and must be eliminated from all public institutions. All clauses in legislation which are directly discriminatory or are discriminatory in effect, must be repealed, and racial discrimination must be abolished entirely throughout the field of public administration. It must be made illegal by statute for racial discrimination to be practised in any institution holding a public licence. If such measures are taken, backed by a widespread government propaganda campaign, such racial discrimination as is of significance can be eliminated from society within a short space of time.

(18) *Federation*

Congress believes that the federation of Central African territories against the will of the vast majority of the inhabitants was both a moral and political error. It recognizes the need for consultation and closer association between neighbouring territories, but believes that a Federation can only endure in so far as it is acceptable to the majority of the population and is voluntarily entered into by governments representative of the people of the territories. Such governments can only be elected on a wide franchise through which the will of the people can be expressed. Congress is primarily concerned to promote the establishment of popular representative government in Southern Rhodesia. When this is achieved, questions involving Federation can be faced, and will then be found to take on a quite different aspect.

(19) *Independence within the Commonwealth*

Congress believes that at present any question of granting greater independence to Southern Rhodesia, either directly or through the Federation, is wholly premature. Until racial problems are completely solved and an integrated society is well advanced, the Government of the United Kingdom must be strongly discouraged from relinquishing any further control over the affairs of this country or any of the territories incorporated in the Federation. It should, in fact, be strongly encouraged to exert its influence to the utmost in favour of the creation of a non-racial integrated society with a government responsible to the people, as the first essential step towards the granting of greater independence.

(20) *Defence*

Congress believes that history has shown in modern times that the best form of defence against external aggression is internal strength. The settlement of the racial problem through the provision of equality of opportunity for people of all races in all spheres will produce an integrated society, which is the essential foundation to defence policy. In any form of conscription for necessary National Service for defence, recruitment and conditions of service must be according to ability and without regard to race or colour.

Defence forces must at no time be used either in this country or beyond it to silence the legitimate aspirations of the uprising peoples of Africa or elsewhere.

(21) *Foreign Affairs*

Congress believes that this country should remain within the British Commonwealth of Nations playing such part as is appropriate and practicable in the affairs of the Commonwealth and in the relationships of the United Kingdom Government with foreign powers and the United Nations Organization.

APPENDIX

SOCIAL PROGRAMME

Congress encourages hard voluntary work for the development of community life. It will attempt to promote the following social organizations and will co-operate in their formation with all other bodies interested and devoted to non-racial principles:

Community Associations, Neighbourhood Centres and Settlements, to develop improved facilities for education, recreation, housing, health, and social, moral and intellectual advance in co-operation with local authorities and voluntary organizations.

Adult Education facilities including literacy classes, evening classes, courses and discussion groups.

Public Libraries and Reading Rooms to make available good books, periodicals and general information to local communities.

Men's and Women's Clubs for educational, social and recreational purposes.

Youth Clubs and Youth Organizations for the provision of healthy leisure occupation for young people.

Children's Nursery Schools and Play Centres to aid parents in the upbringing of their children and to provide facilities for early education and play for children.

PERSONAL PROGRAMME

Congress encourages all members in their daily lives to offer to all people, regardless of race, colour, creed, class or political affiliation, a good example in habits of:

Friendship, Courtesy, Good Manners and Respect in all dealings with individual people.

Honesty in all dealings with other people and in all money transactions.

Hard Work with hand and brain in industry, agriculture and all services of benefit to the community.

Temperance, Economy and Simplicity in personal living.

Avoidance of Violence or provocation to violence in all relations with other people or organized bodies.

Vigorous Effort to promote the social, economic and political welfare of all men and service to the community as a whole.

Congress will take all possible action in the social, economic and political spheres to establish these principles, pursue these policies and carry out these programmes.

It will co-operate with all other bodies pursuing similar aims, in the belief that through co-operation advance will be made *towards that Society in which Peace, Security and Progress will be assured for the whole population, regardless of differences of Race, Colour or Tradition.*

POSTSCRIPT

Additional Notes

P. 22. Footnote 1. I have given the 1931 definition, of paramountcy because, being later, it might be held to have superseded the more forthright one of the Devonshire White Paper of 1923. This was that "the interests of the African natives must be paramount, and if and when those interests and the interests of the immigrant races conflict, the former should prevail." Hailey, p. 135, says that this definition "though made with special reference to Kenya, expresses a general philosophy."

The policy of "partnership" which we shall meet later has never been so explicitly defined, but it is held by Africans to be a reversal and betrayal of the doctrine of paramountcy. European Federal politicians seem to think that Africans must be junior partners for the foreseeable future.

P. 26. Footnote 1. The full history of this slogan is as follows: "Rhodes did not become an upholder of the Cape liberal tradition until after the Jameson Raid, when, as leader of the Progressives, he wished to make sure of the non-European vote. Shortly before the general election of 1898 in the Cape, Rhodes had declared himself in favour of 'equal rights for every white man south of the Zambezi'. On being challenged by some Coloured voters he replied: 'My motto is "Equal rights for every civilized man south of the Zambezi". What is a civilized man? A man, whether white or black, who has sufficient education to write his name, has some property or works, in fact is not a loafer.' "

J. S. Marais. *The Cape Coloured People*. 1652–1937. Longmans 1939. P. 277, Note 2.

P. 33. It is of course an over-simplification to assume that chiefs and people knew, any more than the colonial powers did, what they were entering into when they accepted the various treaties and protectorate agreements referred to. Neither side thought out the future in precise detail. Each took for granted a certain general kind of relationship, but unfortunately not the same kind. Africans needed Britain's support at the moment for some specific purpose—defence against stronger Africans or more feared gangs of white men. They probably thought the Europeans would go away again quite soon, when they had ceased to be useful. In times of turmoil few people think very far ahead. In most of the treaties and agreements the Africans gave everything away and the Europeans promised nothing, and it is not helpful now to quote them on either side. The real European failure lies in our lack of any clear purpose, and the short-sighted materialism of our intentions, rather than in the failure to carry out specific promises.

P. 71. See also A. Hazlewood and D. Henderson, *Nyasaland. The Economics of Federation*. Blackwell 1960, for an expert survey.

P. 89. Footnote

Mr. Leys' figures are for Southern Rhodesia only and refer to several years ago. Average earnings *per capita* in the three territories in 1958 were as follows:

Southern Rhodesia	European £995	African £80
Northern Rhodesia	European £1,273	African £99
Nyasaland	European £889	African £46

(quoted by S. Williams on page 12 of *Central Africa: The Economics of Inequality*, Fabian Commonwealth Bureau, 1960, from the *Central African Examiner* of 13th February 1960).

The average African income for the whole population would be very much lower as a large number of Africans earn virtually nothing and live by subsistence agriculture.

P. 179. The first paragraph of Chapter XVIII still applied after the 1959 emergency until Whitehead's attack on the N.D.P. and arrest of its leaders in July 1960 led to African demonstrations. Now the courtesy has vanished from interracial relations and there is only forcible restraint by the white government. The remarkable lack of bitterness shown by Africans and their leaders has been quite destroyed, their determination and solidarity vastly increased. Mr. Todd joined with African leaders in condemning the government and resigned leadership of the C.A.P., which will probably cause its demise.

P. 213. Dr. Scott has since died.

P. 215. l. 7. It is sometimes argued that no safeguards ever work. The answer is that reasonable ones for enfranchised minorities can. It is safeguards for disenfranchised majorities, whose *raison d'être* is inherently unreasonable, like those in the Federal Constitution, that do not.

INDEX

INDEX

INDEX